Questions & Answers

Health Law

Carolina Academic Press
Questions & Answers Series

Questions & Answers: Administrative Law, Fourth Edition
Linda D. Jellum, Karen A. Jordan

Questions & Answers: Antitrust
Shubha Ghosh

Questions & Answers: Bankruptcy, Second Edition
Mary Jo Wiggins

Questions & Answers: Business Associations, Third Edition
Douglas M. Branson, Seth C. Oranburg, John Towers Rice

Questions & Answers: Civil Procedure, Fifth Edition
William V. Dorsaneo, III, Elizabeth G. Thornburg, Brooke D. Coleman

Questions & Answers: Constitutional Law, Fourth Edition
Paul E. McGreal, Charles W. Rhodes

Questions & Answers: Contracts, Third Edition
Scott J. Burnham

Questions & Answers: Copyright Law, Second Edition
Dave Fagundes, Robert C. Lind

Questions & Answers: Criminal Law, Fifth Edition
Paul Marcus

Questions & Answers: Criminal Procedure — Police Investigation, Fourth Edition
Wayne A. Logan

Questions & Answers: Criminal Procedure — Prosecution and Adjudication, Fourth Edition
Wayne A. Logan

Questions & Answers: Employment Discrimination
Marcia L. McCormick

Questions & Answers: Environmental Law
Dru Stevenson

Questions & Answers: Evidence, Fifth Edition
Paul C. Giannelli

Questions & Answers: Family Law, Fourth Edition
Mark Strasser

Questions & Answers: Federal Estate & Gift Taxation, Third Edition
James M. Delaney, Elaine H. Gagliardi

Questions & Answers: Federal Income Tax, Second Edition
James M. Delaney

Questions & Answers: Health Law
Melissa B. Alexander, Deborah R. Farringer

Questions & Answers: Intellectual Property, Third Edition
Gary Myers, Lee Ann Wheelis Lockridge

Questions & Answers: International Law
Rebecca Bratspies

Questions & Answers: Patent Law
Cynthia M. Ho

Questions & Answers: Payment Systems, Second Edition
Timothy R. Zinnecker

Questions & Answers: Professional Responsibility, Fifth Edition
Patrick Emery Longan

Questions & Answers: Property, Third Edition
John Copeland Nagle, Donald J. Kochan

Questions & Answers: Remedies, Second Edition
Rachel M. Janutis, Thomas O. Main

Questions & Answers: Secured Transactions, Fourth Edition
Bruce A. Markell, Timothy R. Zinnecker

Questions & Answers: The First Amendment, Fourth Edition
Russell L. Weaver, William D. Araiza

Questions & Answers: Torts, Fifth Edition
Anita Bernstein

Questions & Answers: Trademark and Unfair Competition
Vince F. Chiappetta

Questions & Answers: Wills, Trusts, and Estates, Fourth Edition
Thomas M. Featherston, Jr., Victoria J. Haneman

Questions & Answers

Health Law

Melissa B. Alexander
Carl M. Williams Professor of Law and Ethics
University of Wyoming College of Law

Deborah R. Farringer
Associate Dean for Academic Affairs
Associate Professor of Law
Director of Health Law Studies
Belmont University College of Law

CAROLINA ACADEMIC PRESS
Durham, North Carolina

Library of Congress Cataloging-in-Publication Data.

Names: Alexander, Melissa B., author. | Farringer, Deborah R., author.
Title: Questions & answers: health law / Melissa B. Alexander and Deborah R. Farringer.
Other titles: Health law
Description: Durham, North Carolina : Carolina Academic Press, 2024. | Series: Questions & answers series | Includes bibliographical references and index.
Identifiers: LCCN 2023046497 | ISBN 9781531024192 (paperback) | ISBN 9781531024208 (ebook)
Subjects: LCSH: Public health laws—United States—Miscellanea. | United States. Patient Protection and Affordable Care Act—Miscellanea. | Medical policy—United States—Miscellanea.
Classification: LCC KF3775 .A94 2024 | DDC 344.7304—dc23/eng/20231010
LC record available at https://lccn.loc.gov/2023046497

Carolina Academic Press
700 Kent Street
Durham, NC 27701
(919) 489-7486
www.cap-press.com

Printed in the United States of America

To my mom, Nancy Ballengee, R.N.
who inspired my interest in health law.—MBA

To John, my constant support.—DRF

Contents

Preface

This supplement is designed to aid your learning and exam preparation in health law, bioethics, and more specialized health law courses. It offers hundreds of multiple-choice questions to provide quick and easy self-assessment, as well as some short-answer questions. The text includes detailed answers to each of the questions, highlighting not only the correct answer but also the reasoning as to why the other responses are not correct, enabling you to develop a more complete understanding. This book is not intended as a substitute for the reading assigned by your professor. Its purpose is to test your knowledge and ability to apply health law principles. If you use the supplement after each reading or unit, you should be better prepared to excel in class participation and more formal assessment. To maximize the desired benefit, we recommend that you try to answer each question in a section before consulting the answer, as this will alert you to any areas where you may need further study. Please pick the best answer. Some questions should be pretty easy, whereas others are intended to challenge you. Even when you select the correct answer, it is helpful to read the answer explanation provided carefully, as the explanation often contains more information than the question alone. This study guide can also be used as an effective tool at the end of a course to review in preparation for exam success.

As the table of contents and index demonstrate, this book provides a comprehensive health law study aid, addressing a wide range of topics. Subjects covered range from fraud and abuse to public health, Employee Retirement Income Security Act (ERISA) to medical aid in dying, antitrust to human subject research, and beyond. While questions are organized by topic, different textbooks group subjects differently. If you are looking for questions on a particular issue, you may find the more detailed index in the back of the book helpful in locating appropriate questions.

Health law stems from a patchwork of federal, state, and local laws. When possible, this book focuses on answers that are accepted nationwide. Of necessity, however, it also tests majority rules that may differ in your state. Please be aware of this, and be sure to check applicable laws before providing legal advice. This is especially important in health law, which tends to change rapidly and vary, sometimes materially, by jurisdiction.

Finally, we wrote this book in response to years of requests from students for a health law questions and answers supplement. We hope that it will give you comfort and deepen your understanding of health law. To help us improve future editions, we welcome constructive feedback. Please don't hesitate to email us with requests for additional coverage, concerns about neutrality, or perceived mistakes. Learning is a cooperative venture. Special thanks to Tess Anderson, Torin Shanahan, and James Bell for their thoughtful and detailed work on editing these questions. Thanks as well to Stacey Tovino for her feedback and encouragement and helping us ensure we were on the right track! We appreciate you utilizing our resource and wish you the best with your studies and beyond.

Melissa B. Alexander, melissa.alexander@uwyo.edu
Debbie R. Farringer, deborah.farringer@belmont.edu

November 2023

About the Author

Melissa Ballengee Alexander serves as Carl M. Williams Professor of Law & Ethics at the University of Wyoming College of Law. She received her undergraduate degree *with distinction* from Yale University and her law degree from the University of Virginia School of Law. Upon graduation, Professor Alexander clerked for the Honorable John G. Heyburn II of the U.S. District Court for the Western District of Kentucky. She then practiced law with Bradley Arant Boult Cummings LLP for more than a decade, earning partnership and an AV-Preeminent Martindale Hubbell rating. Professor Alexander joined the law faculty at the University of Wyoming College of Law in 2015 after several years on the faculty of Belmont University College of Law. She has more than a decade of experience teaching courses on Health Law, Bioethics, Public Health, Global Health and Human Rights, Intellectual Property, and Civil Procedure. Professor Alexander is the recipient of a law-school wide teaching award and has published extensively on health law and policy, often focusing on health equity, health economics, and realizing autonomy.

Deborah R. Farringer is the Associate Dean for Academic Affairs, Associate Professor of Law, and Director of Health Law Studies at Belmont University College of Law. She received her undergraduate degree *summa cum laude* from University of San Diego and her law degree from Vanderbilt University Law School, where she was named to the Order of the Coif. After graduation, Professor Farringer clerked for the Honorable H. Emory Widener Jr. of the U.S. Fourth Circuit Court of Appeals. After clerking, Professor Farringer practiced law in the health care regulatory group at Bass, Berry & Sims, PLC. Following that, she served as Senior Associate General Counsel for Vanderbilt University Medical Center. Professor Farringer joined Belmont University College of Law in 2013 and teaches a variety of subjects, including Health Law, Health Care Business and Finance, Health Care Fraud and Abuse, Biomedical Ethics, Business Associations, and Contracts. Professor Farringer's scholarship focuses on the operation and impact of health laws and health policy on providers and suppliers.

Questions

Introduction: The U.S. Health Care System & Its Challenges

1. How does U.S. access to health care and per capita spending compare to other affluent nations?

   (A) The U.S. spends LESS per person and provides LESS access to care.
   (B) The U.S. spends LESS per person and provides MORE access to care.
   (C) The U.S. spends MORE per person and provides LESS access to care.
   (D) The U.S. spends MORE per person and provides MORE access to care.

2. Health care can be expensive, but failing to provide care is costly, too. What are some costs of inadequate access to health care? Consider monetary and non-monetary losses to the individual and to society.

   ANSWER:

3. Which of the following has the LEAST impact on health outcomes?
   (A) Health care
   (B) Genetics
   (C) Behavior
   (D) Social determinants of health

4. Unlike most nations, the U.S. adheres largely to a market-based approach for the distribution of health care. Unfortunately, the health care market is imperfect and often experiences market failure. Which of the following is *not* considered a main cause of health care market failure?

   (A) Lack of competition

   (B) Poor information regarding quality and price

   (C) Health inequity

   (D) Central role of third-party payers and tax subsidies

5. What is the "triple aim" of health care policy, and what additional reform goals might be important?

   ANSWER:

6. What is the primary purpose of insurance? How do insurance companies set premiums?

   ANSWER:

7. What percentage of the American public consumes half of all health care expenditures?

   (A) 1%

   (B) 5%

   (C) 11%

   (D) 25%

8. The following individuals plan to purchase marketplace benchmark health insurance: (1) James, who is 27 years old, lives in Wyoming, has no known health conditions, runs every day, and otherwise has a healthy lifestyle; (2) Mary, who is 51 years old, lives in Wyoming, has no known health conditions, and has a healthy lifestyle; (3) John, who is 27 years old, lives in New Hampshire, is morbidly obese, does not exercise, and regularly overconsumes alcohol; and (4) Robert, who is 27 years old, lives in New Hampshire, is a cancer survivor, and has multiple sclerosis. Wyoming is a sparsely populated, rural state with only two insurance companies

participating in the exchange. Whose premium would likely be highest? Assume no wellness plans, and list in order from MOST expensive to LEAST expensive insurance premiums, noting any likely to be the same.

(A) All the same

(B) Robert, John, Mary, James

(C) Mary, then James, John, and Robert as the same

(D) Mary, James, then John and Robert as the same

9. Millions of Americans lack health insurance. What percentage of uninsured, non-elderly adults are part of a household with a full-time worker?

(A) 7%

(B) 25%

(C) 55%

(D) 70%

10. Illness is often defined as much by social construct as by biological facts. Which of the following is *not* influenced by how we define illness?

(A) Insurance coverage

(B) Functional impairment

(C) Individual responsibility

(D) Appropriateness of medical attention

11. Which of the following is covered care under most health insurance policies?

(A) Non-emergency transportation to reach a specialist an hour away

(B) A clean, safe, temperature-controlled apartment

(C) An annual check up at the doctor's office

(D) Wilderness therapy to treat post-traumatic stress disorder

Provider Licensing & Discipline

12. Dr. Wendy Carr is an anesthesiologist who recently opened a pain specialty clinic. One of Dr. Carr's patients, Bill Tench, was recently hospitalized after a suicide attempt, which his hospital physician believed was due to side effects of antidepressants that Dr. Carr had prescribed to treat Mr. Tench's lower back pain. Dr. Carr received a letter from the state Board of Medical Examiners notifying her that she is in violation of state law because of her failure to conform to minimal standards of medical practice for her treatment of Bill Tench. Dr. Carr is very worried about losing her license and her livelihood. Assume that Dr. Carr had the opportunity to raise all applicable defenses to the hearing officer. If the Board of Medical Examiners nevertheless suspends her license and she appeals the action of the Board in court, what would be her best argument?

    (A) Bill Tench's wife left him for another man two days before his attempted suicide.

    (B) The dosage Dr. Carr prescribed Bill Tench was appropriate for his weight and size.

    (C) The Board of Medical Examiners improperly excluded testimony from Dr. Carr's proposed expert that antidepressants can be a medication option for back pain if the pain is neuropathic (shoots down the leg).

    (D) The Board of Medical Examiners does not have any physicians who specialize in pain management on the Board.

13. Sally Allgood is a licensed nurse practitioner within her state of residence and practices at a retail clinic located inside a national pharmacy chain. Nurse Allgood provides standard primary care services, including treatment of sinus infections, strep throat, UTIs, flu, colds, sports physicals and check-ups/well-visits. The Board of Medical Examiners recently sent Nurse Allgood a cease-and-desist letter alleging that she is providing diagnostic services and ordering prescriptions in a manner that is beyond her scope of practice and constitutes the practice of medicine. If you agree to seek a declaratory judgment that Nurse Allgood is practicing within her scope of practice, what facts, if true, would represent her best argument?

    (A) Nurse Allgood is an employee of the retail clinic and is actively supervised by a physician who is also employed by the clinic.

    (B) Nurse Allgood has been practicing this way for thirty years without complaint or previous notification from the Board of Medical Examiners.

(C) Nurse Allgood does not prescribe any controlled substances under federal law.

(D) Nurse Allgood, as a nurse, is not subject to the control and jurisdiction of the Board of Medical Examiners.

14. You represent Sansa Stark, a certified nurse midwife who is licensed to provide midwifery services in her state. Ms. Stark received a letter from the local Board of Nursing (the "Board") notifying Ms. Stark that her license was going to be suspended because of Ms. Stark's practice of administering homeopathic remedies for the treatment of preeclampsia. Preeclampsia is a pregnancy complication characterized by high blood pressure and signs of damage to another organ system, often the kidneys. Preeclampsia, if left untreated, can be fatal for both baby and mother. The Board stated that administering any type of homeopathic substance for this condition is against prevailing practice and thus considered "unprofessional, dishonorable, or unethical conduct" and "ignorance, negligence, or incompetence in the course of nursing practice." Ms. Stark says the treatment is available without a prescription in most natural food stores and has been used by midwives for centuries as a natural remedy when symptoms of preeclampsia first appear. Ms. Stark only administers the homeopathic substance while closely monitoring the patient's blood pressure and refers patients to a physician if symptoms persist. None of Ms. Stark's patients have ever been harmed by use of the treatments. The hearing officer found that (1) Ms. Stark's homeopathic administration practices are done in a controlled manner with appropriate protocols for transferring the patient if her condition worsens and (2) there is no law prohibiting the administration of the treatment. The hearing officer recommended that no action be taken against Ms. Stark or her license. The Board reviewed the hearing officer's report and reversed, noting that preeclampsia is a serious condition and Ms. Stark's practices depart from acceptable and prevailing nursing practices. The Board suspended Ms. Stark's license to practice for five years. Will Ms. Stark prevail in an action in state court alleging that the action of the Board was not based on substantial evidence?

(A) Probably not. Ms. Stark was given the opportunity to have an attorney represent her at the hearing.

(B) Probably not. Even if Ms. Stark's practices caused no harm to patients, the Board of Nursing nevertheless has authority to determine what constitutes unprofessional or unethical conduct under the applicable regulations.

(C) Probably yes. Ms. Stark's practices have not been shown to cause harm to patients.

(D) Probably yes. The hearing officer determined that Ms. Stark's actions were within acceptable standards of practice.

15. Jackie Smith owns and operates her own teeth whitening kiosk at the mall in which she provides teeth whitening services to individuals. Jackie recently received a letter from the Board of Dental Examiners stating that her teeth whitening services constitute the unauthorized practice of dentistry and she should cease and desist immediately. The statute states that one is deemed to be engaging in the practice of dentistry if one "[d]iagnoses, prescribes for or treats any disease, pain, deformity, deficiency, injury, disorder, and condition of the oral cavity,

maxillofacial area, and the adjacent and associated structures and their impact on the human body." The Board of Dental Examiners claims that teeth whitening is treating a condition of the oral cavity. What is the best advice to Jackie as to whether teeth whitening services constitute the unauthorized practice of dentistry and how she should proceed?

(A) Jackie should continue to practice until the Board issues an injunction against her activities; only then can she be heard in court.

(B) The cease-and-desist letter serves as notice that Jackie will have a hearing before the Board to determine whether she will be allowed to continue to practice. She should wait for the hearing.

(C) Jackie does not have to worry about the letter as the Board has no authority over her because she is not a licensed dentist.

(D) Jackie may file an action seeking a declaratory judgment from a court that teeth whitening services do not constitute the practice of dentistry under the statute.

16. Same facts as in Question 15 above, but instead of the teeth whitening kiosk being owned and operated by Jackie, it is owned and operated by White Teeth, Inc., a company with over 100 kiosks set up in malls throughout the state. After receiving the cease-and-desist letter, White Teeth, Inc., files a complaint with the Federal Trade Commission, which then files an antitrust action against the Board of Dental Examiners claiming that the cease-and-desist letters are anticompetitive and that the Board is engaging in unfair competition in violation of the Federal Trade Commission Act. What statement, if true, will enable the Board of Dental Examiners to defend itself from this claim?

(A) The Board of Dental Examiners was established in 1900 as a member-run organization and is self-governed. All Board members are elected by the state's dental association (a private-member, dues-paying organization).

(B) The Board of Dental Examiners has previously been successful in filing injunctions against other teeth whitening service providers.

(C) The Board of Dental Examiners was established pursuant to state charter, all members are appointed by the governor of the state, and the state's administrative agency liaison attends all meetings and has oversight of the Board's actions.

(D) The Board of Dental Examiners is made up of 10 licensed dentists, only two of whom offer in-office teeth whitening services.

17. Christina Juarez is a practicing physician in a town that sits within ten miles of the border of a neighboring state. Dr. Juarez treats patients from both states. Recently, Dr. Juarez invested in an electronic medical records system that has the capability for telehealth visits. She has begun to see some of her patients via telehealth, as she finds this convenient and efficient for both her and her patients. She recently received a letter from the state Board of Medical Examiners in the neighboring state, in which she is not licensed, accusing her of the unauthorized practice of medicine. Dr. Juarez states that all her patients established care by visiting her office located

in the state in which she is licensed to practice and that she is providing all care in or from her office. What can Dr. Juarez expect in terms of the process for fighting this issue?

(A) She should expect the Board of Medical Examiners in the neighboring state to issue a statement denying her licensure to practice in the state.

(B) She should expect the Board of Medical Examiners in the neighboring state to either issue an injunction against her for her actions in providing telehealth services across state lines or conduct a hearing to determine whether she is engaging in the unauthorized practice of medicine.

(C) She should expect an action taken by the Board of Medical Examiners in the state in which she is licensed to restrict or limit her license to practice in some manner.

(D) She should expect no further communication because she is not violating the law so long as the patients were established patients.

18. Mitchell Pritchett is a licensed physician practicing in primary care. Dr. Pritchett has recently begun prescribing Botox for weight loss. Dr. Pritchett injects the substance into the jaw of his patient, which freezes the jaw for a time, making it difficult to eat. The Board of Medical Examiners is concerned about the use of Botox for this purpose and is in the process of promulgating a rule that will put some parameters around Botox use. In the meantime, the Board sends notice to Dr. Pritchett ordering him to cease and desist his use of Botox for weight loss and stating his use thus far constitutes unprofessional conduct under his license. He goes before the hearing officer who examines the evidence and finds that, while unconventional, there is evidence that Dr. Pritchett is appropriately monitoring his patients and this process is practiced by a minority of physicians. The hearing officer recommends no action be taken. The Board reverses and suspends his license. What is Dr. Pritchett's next step in fighting the suspension of his license?

(A) Dr. Pritchett will be unable to do anything at this point because the decision of the Board is final.

(B) Dr. Pritchett will be able to file a claim in state court, which the court will review *de novo*.

(C) Dr. Pritchett will be able to file a claim in state court, which the court will review to determine whether the Board's decision was based on substantial evidence.

(D) Dr. Pritchett will be able to file a claim in state court, which the court will review for whether the Board's decision was based on a preponderance of evidence.

Topic 3 Questions

Regulation of Health Care Institutions

19. Your client is interested in opening a nursing home in the area and has come to you seeking advice on how to proceed properly. Which of the following best describes the regulatory scheme for nursing homes in the United States?

    (A) Nursing homes are governed by federal regulations only, and the applicable state department of health is responsible for ensuring compliance with such federal regulations.

    (B) Nursing homes are licensed under state licensure laws only and are governed by the state department of health for purposes of compliance with applicable laws.

    (C) Nursing homes are licensed under state licensure laws and, if enrolled in the Medicare and/or Medicaid programs, are governed by federal regulations, which are monitored by third-party accreditation agencies.

    (D) Nursing homes are licensed under state licensure laws and, if enrolled in the Medicare and/or Medicare programs, are governed by federal regulations, which are monitored by state licensing agencies.

20. Your client, a nursing home, was sanctioned for its failure to maintain adequate staffing ratios and for its 5% infection rate. A Health and Human Services Administrative Law Judge (ALJ) determined that the nursing home was not in substantial compliance and ordered the imposition of civil monetary penalties. This decision was affirmed by the Departmental Appeals Board. You have filed a Petition for Review of Agency Decision in district court on behalf of your client. What argument below would provide the best proof for prevailing in the Petition for Review?

    (A) The ALJ prevented the nursing home from providing any evidence regarding its staffing plan or the condition of the residents prior to their admission to the nursing home.

    (B) The ALJ improperly weighed the testimony of residents over that of nursing home administrators.

    (C) The nursing home timely submitted a plan of correction.

    (D) The surveyors had a history of bias against your client, which was presented to the ALJ.

21. Same facts as in Question 20 above, but assume that the nursing home discovers these deficiencies before a report is made to the state Department of Health and before the Department of Health conducts a planned or spontaneous survey. What would be the nursing home's best option to avoid or mitigate the imposition of sanctions?
    (A) The nursing home likely has limited options because it cannot reduce applicable statutory sanctions even if the non-compliance is self-reported.
    (B) The nursing home can self-report these violations prior to discovery by the Department of Health or the Centers for Medicare and Medicare Services (CMS), and any reduction in applicable penalties is in the discretion of CMS.
    (C) The nursing home can self-report these violations, but it must be within 10 days of the date of discovery and the nursing home must have taken prompt action to correct the deficiencies to receive up to a 50% reduction in applicable penalties.
    (D) The nursing home is unlikely to be able to self-report these violations as they are too serious.

22. Shady Acres Nursing Home's Chief Executive Officer has received notification that a resident has filed a complaint about care that she received while living at Shady Acres. Specifically, the resident has claimed that she was constantly sedated while at the nursing home because she liked to get up and wander the halls, and the care aids did not like for her to be wandering. Assuming the appropriate agencies received the complaint, what agency will be responsible for conducting a site visit and/or doing a survey of Shady Acres to investigate the complaint in connection with violations of federal regulations?
    (A) Representatives from Shady Acres's accreditation organization (e.g., the Joint Commission)
    (B) Representatives from the Centers for Medicare and Medicaid Services (CMS)
    (C) Representatives from the applicable state Department of Health
    (D) Representatives from the Medicare Administrative Contractor

23. Upon surveying Shady Acres, the surveyors identified several deficiencies that they determined posed a great risk to the health and safety of the residents. Although Shady Acres submitted a plan of correction, it was rejected by the surveyors as inadequate. Under federal law, what is the most drastic penalty that could be imposed on Shady Acres in connection with these deficiencies?
    (A) A fine in excess of the total asset value of the nursing home
    (B) Revocation of the facility's state-issued license
    (C) Mandatory transfer of all residents until the deficiencies can be addressed
    (D) Termination of the provider agreement between Medicare and Medicaid and the facility

24. Scranton General Hospital had an incident a month ago involving a medication error with a patient. As a result of the error, the patient was in the intensive care unit for eight days and had a total extended hospital stay of sixteen days. Assuming that the appropriate agencies received the complaint, what agency will be responsible for conducting a site visit and/or doing a survey of Scranton General Hospital to investigate the complaint in connection with possible violations of federal regulations?

    (A) Representatives from Scranton General Hospital's accreditation organization (e.g., the Joint Commission)

    (B) Representatives from the Centers for Medicare and Medicaid Services

    (C) Representatives from the applicable state Department of Health

    (D) Representatives from the Medicare Administrative Contractor

25. What is generally considered the biggest advantage to hospitals in being accredited by the Joint Commission?

    (A) The ability to market itself to patients/customers as being of a certain quality because it is accredited by a third-party agency

    (B) Being "deemed" to have complied with the Medicare Conditions of Participation without further inspection from the Centers for Medicare and Medicaid Services (CMS)

    (C) Not having to comply with applicable federal regulations so long as the hospital complies with the standards of the Joint Commission

    (D) There are no additional advantages; this is a requirement under federal law

Physician-Patient Relationship: Formation, Duties, & Termination

Facts for Questions 26–32:

Pat Smith has a rare and life-threatening cancer. Pat wants to see the world-renowned expert who specializes in Pat's condition, Dr. Mo Money. Dr. Money is currently accepting new patients at their private practice, but the doctor refuses to take Pat as a patient because Pat's only health insurance is Medicaid. Medicaid has low physician reimbursement rates. Dr. Money is the only provider in the state with expertise in treating Pat's condition, and Pat is expected to die within the year without treatment. Pat goes to Dr. Money's office in hopes of seeing the physician.

26. Which of the following is correct regarding Dr. Money's legal obligation to Pat?
    (A) Dr. Money is obligated to treat Pat because Pat is likely to die without such treatment and Dr. Money is the only physician reasonably available that could meet Pat's needs.
    (B) Dr. Money is obligated to treat Pat because a physician may not refuse to accept Medicaid patients.
    (C) Dr. Money is obligated to treat Pat at least until he is stable because Pat has an emergency medical condition.
    (D) Dr. Money is not obligated to treat Pat under the circumstances.

27. If Dr. Money never expressly agreed to undertake Pat's care but physically examined Pat and provided Pat with a diagnosis, was a physician-patient relationship formed?
    (A) No, because formation of a physician-patient relationship requires express consent.
    (B) No, because formation of a physician-patient relationship requires written agreement.
    (C) Yes, because a physician-patient relationship is formed if a physician manifests consent by affirmative acts such as providing services that meet the patient's medical needs.
    (D) Yes, because a physician-patient relationship is formed whenever a patient presents at the physician's office seeking medically necessary treatment.

28. If Dr. Money had instead declined to treat Pat because Pat is deaf, which of the following would be correct regarding Dr. Money's legal obligation to Pat?
   (A) Dr. Money may refuse to treat Pat for any reason.
   (B) Dr. Money may generally refuse to treat Pat for any reason, but Dr. Money may not refuse based on Pat's disability if reasonable accommodation is possible.
   (C) Dr. Money may refuse to treat Pat because physician's offices are not considered places of public accommodation.
   (D) Dr. Money is obligated to treat Pat.

29. Once a physician-patient relationship is formed, the duties accompanying that relationship are generally set by which of the following?
   (A) Express agreement
   (B) Standard of care
   (C) Fiduciary or quasi-fiduciary obligations
   (D) B and C

30. Once a physician-patient relationship is formed, which of the following is *not* a duty owed by the physician to the patient?
   (A) Reasonable charges
   (B) Reasonable care
   (C) Continuing attention
   (D) Confidentiality of health information

31. Which of the following limits on the physician-patient relationship is most likely to be void as against public policy, even if mutually agreed?
   (A) Limited duration (i.e., relationship limited to only 1 visit)
   (B) Limited scope (i.e., relationship limited to diagnosis)
   (C) Exculpatory clauses (i.e., no malpractice liability)
   (D) Forum selection clauses (i.e., limiting where any litigation can be brought)

32. Assuming that Pat and Dr. Money did in fact form a physician-patient relationship, which of the following is *not* an appropriate basis for Dr. Money to terminate the relationship?
   (A) Pat's cancer is cured.
   (B) Pat terminates the relationship.
   (C) Dr. Money terminates the relationship upon learning of patient complaints with services.
   (D) Dr. Money terminates the relationship, but only after notice and a reasonable opportunity for Pat to find another provider.

HIPAA & Confidentiality

33. What type of person/entity is *not* considered a "covered entity" for purposes of the Health Insurance Portability and Accountability Act of 1996 (HIPAA)?
    (A) Dr. Smith
    (B) Blue Cross Blue Shield of Tennessee
    (C) WebMD
    (D) Shady Pines Psychiatric Hospital

34. Seattle Grace Hospital contracts with Billing Associates, Inc., to conduct billing and collection on behalf of Seattle Grace Hospital. Billing Associates, Inc., is not a provider and does not itself render health care services. Seattle Grace Hospital is just one of many clients with which Billing Associates, Inc., contracts for services. Last week, an employee of Billing Associates, Inc., disclosed information about five hundred Seattle Grace Hospital patients by negligently sending bills for services rendered at Seattle Grace Hospital to the wrong recipients. What is Billing Associates, Inc.'s liability under HIPAA for the disclosure?
    (A) None. Billing Associates, Inc., can only be liable under a breach of contract claim from Seattle Grace Hospital because Billing Associates, Inc., is not liable under HIPAA as a "business associate."
    (B) None. Only Seattle Grace Hospital will be liable under HIPAA since the employee responsible will be considered a member of Seattle Grace Hospital's workforce.
    (C) Billing Associates, Inc., will be liable under HIPAA because as a "covered entity" it is subject to all of the requirements of the HIPAA Privacy and Security Rules.
    (D) Billing Associates, Inc., will be directly liable under HIPAA because as a "business associate" it is subject to all of the requirements of the HIPAA Privacy and Security Rules.

35. Same facts as in Question 34 above. Jane Smallwood recently visited the emergency room at Seattle Grace Hospital when she was not feeling well but left without being seen because the wait was too long and she was starting to feel better. She heard about the breach in the news. She is very concerned that she is one of the 500 people involved in the breach, but she is not certain of how much information she disclosed when she was meeting with the triage nurse. If Jane only gave one "identifier" to the triage nurse, which information would *not* be considered "protected health information" under HIPAA?

(A) Jane's Internet Protocol (IP) address

(B) Jane's state

(C) The fax number for Jane's personal business

(D) The VIN (vehicle identification number) from Jane's car

36. A surgery center receives a call from an attorney stating that he is thinking about filing a lawsuit against a physician who practices at the surgery center. The attorney states that he needs access to the medical records of three patients of the physician in question. The attorney assures the surgery center that the surgery center is not a party to the suit and that they are only going after the physician personally. Can the surgery center disclose the records?

(A) Yes. Because this relates to treatment of a patient of the surgery center and the surgery center's actions, the surgery center can defend itself by disclosing this information.

(B) No, because the attorney does not appear to have a valid subpoena for the information, and under these facts, disclosure cannot be made without a valid subpoena.

(C) Yes, because the attorney is representing those patients and it is in their interest to have these records disclosed to the attorney.

(D) No, because there is no indication that this would be the minimum necessary amount of information.

37. Ms. Harris has been involved in a contentious divorce and custody battle with her estranged husband. To deal with some of the stresses of her marriage, Ms. Harris has been seeing a psychiatrist for the last 12 months. Last month, Ms. Harris was hospitalized on the recommendation of her psychiatrist for a 72-hour stay. Her children were on a trip with her estranged husband at the time, so no one other than Ms. Harris and her psychiatrist were aware of her stay. Yesterday, Ms. Harris received a new filing from her husband seeking full custody of their children on the basis that Ms. Harris's psychiatric condition, as evidenced by her recent hospital stay, makes her an unfit parent. The filing indicates that the estranged husband became aware of the hospital stay when he called the psychiatrist's office to confirm an appointment and the receptionist stated that Ms. Harris would now be having appointments three days a week, as recommended by her physician following her discharge from the hospital. Livid, Ms. Harris called her psychiatrist's office about the disclosure, but they were unaware of it and were unable to determine who on their staff may have shared this information. She has reported the action to the Office for Civil Rights, but she wants to sue the psychiatrist. What would Ms. Harris's best option be if she wants to file a lawsuit?

(A) Because there is no private right of action under HIPAA and HIPAA preempts state law, Ms. Harris cannot file a lawsuit. She has done all she can do by reporting.

(B) Ms. Harris has no legal remedy under state or federal law because she cannot prove that there was a disclosure, since the office has no knowledge of it and Ms. Harris cannot identify who was responsible.

(C) Ms. Harris can attempt to file an invasion of privacy claim for the disclosure of her protected health information by showing HIPAA was breached as to the standard of care.

(D) Ms. Harris can attempt to file a breach of confidentiality claim for the disclosure of her protected health information by showing HIPAA was breached as to the standard of care.

38. An internal medicine physician has been struggling financially with her practice. She recently received a few negative reviews on her Yelp page stating that she (the physician) pushed patients to have surgery when physical therapy was an available option. The physician has always performed surgery to address the medical issue cited by each of these patients, and several of the patients who have complained have been prescribed physical therapy for other issues in the past and have not followed through with the treatment plan. The physician would like to respond to the Yelp review publicly to protect her good name and defend herself against these accusations. Can the physician respond to the negative reviews on Yelp under the law by explaining why she chose surgery for these patients?

(A) Yes, the physician can now respond because the patients have shared their protected health information publicly.

(B) Yes, because the physician has a right to defend herself against disparaging or defamatory comments.

(C) No, because HIPAA prevents the physician from disclosing protected health information even if the patient has self-disclosed.

(D) No, because responding to the Yelp review with that information would not be the minimum necessary protected health information.

39. Nurse Jackie travels to a conference approximately 500 miles from her home. At the conference, Jackie accidentally leaves her computer in one of the conference rooms. When she goes back to get it, the computer is not there. No one turned it in, and Jackie was not able to recover the computer. On the computer, Jackie had medical records and other protected health information from approximately 150 patients, including names, social security numbers, and medical diagnoses. The computer is password-protected to access files on the hard drive. Jackie is not certain if the protected health information was accessed by a third party. Jackie reports the lost computer to her hospital employer's privacy officer. Will the hospital have to notify patients that this was a HIPAA breach?

(A) Yes, under HIPAA this is likely a breach and requires notification because the protected health information is of a sensitive nature, the person with access is unknown, the hospital cannot determine that the information has not been accessed, and the computer was never recovered.

(B) Yes, under HIPAA this is likely a breach because the disclosure of the information from the laptop poses a significant risk of financial and reputational harm to the affected patients.

(C) No, under HIPAA this is likely not a breach because there are fewer than 500 patients affected, and thus no notification is necessary.

(D) No, under HIPAA this is likely not a breach because it cannot be proven whether the protected health information on the laptop was actually accessed by whoever has the laptop.

40. Juanita Stevens is a single mother of three who lives with her mother. Recently, Juanita's mother threatened to call Child Protection Services to report Juanita as a neglectful mother unless Juanita gives her mother primary custody of the children. Juanita's mother said that this was all prompted by an incident last week in which Juanita was admitted to the hospital due to a drug overdose. Juanita was in fact admitted for a short stay in the hospital last week for a medical complication that she experienced with buprenorphine prescribed as part of a treatment program. Juanita is not certain, however, how her mother would have access to this information. Her mother was not in town while Juanita was in the hospital, and the kids were with Juanita's ex-spouse. Juanita requested her medical record from the hospital and there is no indication in the record that the information was disclosed to Juanita's mother. However, Juanita's daughter told her that the hospital called and left a message on the answering machine at home that Juanita and her children share with Juanita's mother stating that the hospital was following up after Juanita's hospital visit last week in connection with her buprenorphine incident. Juanita is livid and would like to take action against the hospital. What recourse does Juanita have, and what is her likelihood of success in court?

ANSWER:

41. County Community Hospital is a victim of a ransomware attack that causes a complete loss of access to the electronic records system for about five days. The hospital was not able to conclude definitively whether protected health information was accessed. Six months after the attack, a patient discovers her medical records are available on the dark web. She is convinced that the ransomware attack at the hospital is the reason why her records are on the dark web. She would like to file a claim in state court alleging breach of confidentiality against the hospital. If she does this, what standard will the court most likely apply to determine whether the hospital breached its duty to the patient?

(A) The typical privacy obligations for other hospitals in the same community as County Community Hospital, as established by an expert, which are less restrictive than HIPAA

(B) Standards set forth under HIPAA for protection of protected health information

(C) The hospital's own policies and procedures, even if they are less restrictive than HIPAA

(D) Standards set forth by the Federal Bureau of Investigation for reporting of ransomware attacks

Informed Consent

42. What is the process of communication between patient and provider to obtain the patient's authorization to undergo a specific medical intervention known as?
    (A) Advance directive
    (B) Informed consent
    (C) Autonomous decision-making
    (D) None of the above

43. Which bioethics principle provides the primary foundation for modern informed consent?
    (A) Beneficence
    (B) Non-maleficence
    (C) Autonomy
    (D) Justice

44. The common law tort basis for informed consent claims is best described as
    (A) Battery
    (B) Negligence
    (C) Battery when the provider breaches his or her disclosure duty, proximately causing harm to the patient, and negligence when the patient did not provide any consent to the specific medical intervention
    (D) Battery when the patient did not provide any consent to the specific medical intervention, and negligence when the provider breaches his or her disclosure duty, proximately causing harm to the patient

Facts for Questions 45–47:

Quinn visits Doctor because Quinn has been experiencing lower back pain. Doctor diagnoses Quinn with degenerative disk disease. There are three treatment alternatives: spinal fusion surgery, physical therapy, and non-treatment. Spinal fusion surgery has six known risks: 1, 2, 3, 4, 5, and 6. Physical therapy has 3 known risks: 7–9. The potential benefit of surgery and physical therapy is that each may decrease Quinn's back pain. Surgery is most likely to provide the longest lasting relief. None of the treatments is guaranteed to be effective. Non-treatment risks that Quinn's back pain may continue or even become worse, but back pain sometimes resolves on its own over time.

Most physicians consider risks 1, 2, and 3 of surgery to be material under the circumstances and would disclose them. Most patients would also want to know about risk 4 in deciding whether or not to undergo surgery, although few physicians disclose this potential risk since it is rare. Quinn really cares about bruising, which implicates risk 5, although most patients would not consider this risk relevant and such is arguably not a reasonable concern.

Doctor was in the bottom 10% of Doctor's medical school class and initially failed the medical licensing exam. Quinn would not authorize spinal surgery performed by a physician who struggled in medical school and on the licensing exam, but Quinn is unaware of these facts. Quinn does not ask, and Doctor does not volunteer them.

45. In a physician-based disclosure state, which of the following best describes the scope of required disclosures under the facts provided?

(A) Diagnosis and prognosis, nature of each treatment alternative (including non-treatment), anticipated benefits of each, and material risks of each (including 1, 2, and 3)

(B) Diagnosis and prognosis, nature of each treatment alternative (including non-treatment), anticipated benefits of each, and material risks of each (including 1, 2, 3, and 4)

(C) Diagnosis and prognosis, nature of each treatment alternative (including non-treatment), anticipated benefits of each, and material risks of each (including 1, 2, 3, 4, and 5)

(D) Diagnosis and prognosis, nature of each treatment alternative (including non-treatment), anticipated benefits of each, material risks of each (including 1, 2, 3, and 4), and Doctor's medical school and licensing exam performance

46. In a patient-based disclosure state, which of the following best describes the scope of required disclosures?

(A) Diagnosis, nature of each treatment alternative (including non-treatment), anticipated benefits of each, and material risks of each (including 1, 2, and 3)

(B) Diagnosis, nature of each treatment alternative (including non-treatment), anticipated benefits of each, and material risks of each (including 1, 2, 3, and 4)

(C) Diagnosis, nature of each treatment alternative (including non-treatment), anticipated benefits of each, and material risks of each (including 1, 2, 3, 4, and 5)

(D) Diagnosis, nature of each treatment alternative (including non-treatment), anticipated benefits of each, and material risks of each (including 1, 2, 3, and 4), and Doctor's medical school and licensing exam performance

47. Assume Doctor only discloses risks 1 and 4 prior to Quinn's surgery. Which of the following describes a possible result if Quinn brings an informed consent case against Doctor?

(A) Liability if Quinn is harmed by risk 1

(B) Liability if Quinn is harmed by risk 6

(C) Liability for non-disclosure of risk 3, regardless of harm

(D) Liability if Quinn is harmed by risk 3

48. What is the difference between the evidence required to establish decision-causation in subjective decision states as compared to objective decision states?

ANSWER:

49. What two types of causation are required to prevail in informed consent cases?

ANSWER:

50. Which element of an informed consent claim is more likely to require expert proof in a physician-centered state than in a patient-centered state?

(A) The scope of the physician's duty of disclosure

(B) The breach of the physician's duty of disclosure

(C) The physician's non-disclosure proximately caused the patient to select surgery instead of another treatment approach.

(D) The physician's non-disclosure proximately caused the patient to select surgery instead of another treatment approach and a non-disclosed, material risk injured the patient, resulting in damages.

51. **True or false**: Under some circumstances, a patient who is harmed by a side effect from a medical intervention may be able to recover for breach of the duty of informed consent, even though the physician correctly diagnosed the disease and properly performed the medical intervention itself. State the basis for your answer.

    ANSWER:

52. Identify potential disadvantages of disclosing more risks than required for informed consent.

    ANSWER:

53. Which of the following provides a legally valid excuse for a physician's failing to obtain informed consent from a patient?

    (A) A nurse obtained the patient's informed consent.

    (B) An emergency where the patient cannot consent and delay to obtain consent would increase risk to the patient

    (C) The patient is of limited means and cannot afford to pay for the additional time associated with informed consent.

    (D) There is never a legally valid excuse for a doctor to forego informed consent.

54. While courts have generally been reluctant to require disclosure of individual physician risk information as part of informed consent, CMS sponsors a Physician Compare website containing certain physician performance data. In order for this and the similar Hospital Compare site to influence care, what must be true of patients and the health care market?

    ANSWER:

55. For what type of care are decision aids most useful? Why?

    ANSWER:

56. The Physician Payment Sunshine Act (also known as the Open Payment Program), enacted as part of the ACA, requires disclosure(s) of which physician financial interests?

    (A) Manufacturers of items covered by Medicare or Medicaid must disclose payments over $10 made to physicians.

    (B) Physicians referring patients for certain radiology tests must disclose any ownership interest the physician has in the radiology provider.

    (C) A and B

    (D) None of the above

Health Care Decision-Making for Others

57. Not all patients are able to make health care decisions for themselves. Under the Uniform Healthcare Decisions Act (UHCDA) (1993) and (2023), what does decisional capacity require?
    (A) That the patient can make and communicate a choice
    (B) That the patient's choice accords with the provider's recommendation, or at a minimum, is a choice the provider deems reasonable
    (C) That the patient has the ability to understand the risks and benefits of proposed care
    (D) A and C

58. Pursuant to the UHCDA, an advance health care directive includes which of the following?
    (A) Individual instructions regarding health care
    (B) Designation of an agent to make health care decisions for the individual
    (C) Power of attorney to allow an agent to make most financial and medical decisions
    (D) A and/or B

59. Pursuant to the UHCDA, what is the ideal standard to use when making health care decisions for another?
    (A) Individual instructions and other expressed wishes
    (B) Patient's best interest, according to an objective standard of what a reasonable patient would want under similar circumstances
    (C) Patient's best interest, according to the patient's values to the extent known
    (D) None of the above

60. An accident leaves a person in a persistent vegetative state. After several years and three physicians opining that the patient is unlikely to improve, the patient's spouse seeks to have the patient's feeding tube removed. The spouse reports that, before the accident, the patient expressed a preference not to have life artificially prolonged once there was no material hope of recovery. The spouse provides no other evidence of the patient's wishes, and the patient did

not have an advance directive. Will health care providers follow the surrogate's request to remove the feeding tube?

(A) No, because health care providers should not withdraw life-sustaining care from an incompetent patient.

(B) It depends on state law regarding the authority of surrogate health care decision-makers and related evidentiary standards, which vary by state.

(C) Yes, because the surrogate has shown that the patient more likely than not would have preferred withdrawal of the life-sustaining care.

(D) None of the above

61. An authorized guardian, agent, or default surrogate can make most health care decisions for a patient who lacks capacity, but there are limits. Which of the following is *not* one of the common limits on surrogate health care decision-making?

(A) A provider should not render care that fails to maximize the likelihood of medical benefit.

(B) A provider should not render care that is contrary to generally accepted medical standards.

(C) A provider has no obligation to render care that is unavailable to the provider.

(D) A provider should not sterilize an incompetent person, at least without a court order.

62. There is a presumption that parents may make health care decisions for their minor children. However, a state, as *parens patriae*, also has a special duty to protect minors. Which of the following is *not* a factor courts consider in determining when to override parental decision-making?

(A) Whether the minor's condition is potentially life-threatening

(B) The anticipated benefits and risks of the treatment opposed by the parents

(C) The minor's expressed wishes, values, and interests

(D) Whether the parent's beliefs are consistent with an established religion

63. What type of state statutes are typically cited when a state seeks to override parental decision-making for a particular minor?

ANSWER:

64. A five-year old child presents at the emergency room, and physicians determine that the child needs a blood transfusion to survive. With the transfusion, the child's chance of survival is 99%; without the transfusion, it is 10–15%. Risks associated with transfusions are rare and typically short-term. The parents, who are Jehovah's Witness, refuse to consent to the blood transfusion. If the hospital seeks to override the parents' choice, how is a court likely to rule?

(A) Defer to the parents' decision; parents have the right to make health care decisions for their child

(B) Defer to the parents' decision; the state may not interfere with the parents' religious freedom

(C) Order the blood transfusion; the state has an interest in the life of the child

(D) Order the blood transfusion; given the best interests of the child, the state's interest in the life of the child outweighs the parents' interest in making health care decisions for the child under the circumstances

Medical Malpractice

65. In a medical malpractice case, the duty owed by the physician to the patient is generally established through which of the following?
    (A) Lay testimony of what constitutes reasonable care
    (B) Expert testimony on the standard of care
    (C) Expert testimony on clinical practice guidelines
    (D) Expert testimony on empirical evidence of efficacy

66. In order to prevail in a medical malpractice case in most jurisdictions, a plaintiff must establish that the physician did which of the following?
    (A) Treated the patient with less knowledge and skill than the average physician in the same field would treat a similar patient under similar circumstances
    (B) Treated the patient with less knowledge and skill than the average physician in the same field would treat a similar patient under similar circumstances, given the facilities, resources, and options available
    (C) Treated the patient with less knowledge and skill than a minimally competent physician in the same field would treat a similar patient under similar circumstances
    (D) Treated the patient with less knowledge and skill than a minimally competent physician in the same field would treat a similar patient under similar circumstances, given the facilities, resources, and options available

67. Some jurisdictions base the standard of care primarily on custom and practice. Jurisdictions that treat custom and practice as dispositive generally recognize which of the following defenses, if any?
    (A) Two schools of thought defense (also known as minority practice)
    (B) Clinical innovation defense
    (C) A and B
    (D) None of the above

68. In January 2020, Ezra, a 30-year-old male with a high body mass index (BMI), began to experience severe pain in his lower right abdomen. He went to the emergency room where he had an emergency appendectomy. Before surgery began, a nurse counted 30 surgical sponges. After the procedure, the nurse counted 29 sponges, but neither an x-ray nor search of Ezra revealed the missing sponge. The surgical team assumed that the initial count had been a miscount, as sometimes happens, and did not mention the issue to Ezra. Ezra recovered well from the appendectomy and returned to normal life. However, in June 2022, Ezra began experiencing abdominal pain. After many tests, in September 2022, doctors determined that a retained surgical sponge from his appendectomy had migrated to his intestine, causing permanent digestive issues and requiring another surgery to remove it. If Ezra files a medical malpractice suit in October 2023 in a state that follows the discovery rule and has a two-year statute of limitations and a four-year statute of repose, is his suit timely?

(A) No, because the alleged malpractice that injured Ezra occurred more than two years prior to the filing of suit.

(B) No, because Ezra should have discovered his injury and filed suit sooner.

(C) Yes, because Ezra filed suit within four years of when he discovered or reasonably should have discovered his injury.

(D) Yes, because Ezra filed suit within four years of his appendectomy and within 2 years of when he discovered or reasonably should have discovered his injury.

69. In August 2021, Sebastian visited his doctor complaining of fatigue, abdominal pain, and diarrhea. Based on Sebastian's medical history and a physical exam, his physician diagnosed him with irritable bowel syndrome and recommended a high fiber diet, regular exercise, and meditation. Sebastian followed the physician's advice, but a year later, his symptoms remained and he also suffered from rectal bleeding, so Sebastian sought a second opinion. The second doctor performed a colonoscopy, biopsied abnormal tissue, and diagnosed advanced stage colorectal cancer. Sebastian was told he had only an 11% chance of five-year survival. Sadly, Sebastian died in late 2023. Sebastian's estate hired an expert who opines that Sebastian's first diagnosis was a misdiagnosis and that if his cancer had been properly detected in 2021, Sebastian would have had a 40% chance of five-year survival. If the first physician negligently misdiagnosed Sebastian, would his estate be able to state a claim for a survival action for his death in the majority of jurisdictions?

(A) No, because a medical malpractice claim does not survive the death of the patient.

(B) No, Sebastian's estate may not recover because, even in August 2021, it was more likely than not that colon cancer would cause Sebastian's death.

(C) Yes, Sebastian's estate likely may recover under the loss of chance doctrine.

(D) Yes, Sebastian's estate likely may recover under the loss of chance doctrine, although the damages will likely be reduced because, even in August 2021, it was more likely than not that cancer would cause Sebastian's death.

70. A physician operated on the wrong site of Terrance's body, causing an unnecessary operation and delaying a needed procedure. After the incorrect surgery, Terrance never felt well enough to return to his job. It is unclear, however, to what extent his post-surgery ill health stemmed from the physician's negligence versus Terrence's ongoing drug and alcohol abuse. Both likely contributed. Which of the following correctly reflects the law in most jurisdictions?

(A) Terrance cannot recover if he is even partially at fault for his post-surgery ill health.

(B) Terrance can likely recover for his post-surgery ill health and any contribution his behavior made is irrelevant, given the physician's negligence.

(C) Terrance can likely recover for his post-surgery ill health, but fault will be apportioned and damages reduced proportionally.

(D) None of the above

71. Studies indicate that medical malpractice suits do not effectively motivate physicians to provide higher quality care. List two reasons that medical malpractice suits fail to incentivize quality care.

ANSWER:

Liability of Health Care Institutions

72. In a negligence action, what two theories of liability are commonly asserted against a hospital?
    (A) Direct liability and successor liability
    (B) Direct liability and vicarious liability
    (C) Direct liability and corporate negligence
    (D) Direct liability only because hospitals are not responsible for the acts of individual physicians

73. David Jones was in a car accident and was rushed to a nearby hospital. While at the hospital, David was seen by Dr. Nick Parker. Dr. Parker is an employee of Emergency Physicians, PLLC ("EP"), which contracts with the hospital to provide 24-7 coverage of the hospital's emergency room through EP's employed and contracted physicians. Under the contract, EP is required to ensure "sufficient staffing to meet all emergency medical needs." Under the contract, all physicians must be members of the hospital medical staff, must be able to be credentialed with all payors with which the hospital contracts, and must be insured at insurance levels set forth by the hospital. Further, the hospital can request termination of any physician working in the hospital's emergency room (although such a right does not require that the individual be terminated by EP). Dr. Parker has worked in the hospital's emergency room under this arrangement for over ten years. While Dr. Parker was treating David, Dr. Parker negligently sliced David's liver, causing bile to pour into David's body cavity. While Dr. Parker eventually discovered the issue and was able to correct the leak, David experienced prolonged complications requiring another month in the hospital and he now has some chronic medical issues. David would like to sue the hospital for what happened to him. Is there sufficient evidence to show that the hospital can be held liable for Dr. Parker's actions?
    (A) No, because it was Dr. Parker who was negligent and Dr. Parker is merely a member of the medical staff and not the hospital's employee, which does not establish sufficient evidence to show the hospital's liability.
    (B) No. Because Dr. Parker is an employee of EP, he cannot be found to be an agent of any other organization, including the hospital.

(C) Yes, because the arrangement between the hospital and EP provided the hospital with substantial control over Dr. Parker such that Dr. Parker may be considered by a jury to be the hospital's actual agent.

(D) Yes. Because Dr. Parker can be terminated by the hospital, the hospital becomes Dr. Parker's employer-in-fact.

74. Same facts as in Question 73 above. Because Dr. Parker works in the emergency room, what state law doctrine would be of benefit to David if applicable in that state?

(A) The hospital is liable for the acts of Dr. Parker in states that deem all members of the medical staff to be actual agents of the hospital.

(B) The hospital is liable for the acts of Dr. Parker in states that apply the "nondelegable duty doctrine."

(C) The hospital is liable for the acts of Dr. Parker in states that require all physicians in an emergency room to be employees.

(D) There are no state laws applicable here; David will have to prove that Dr. Parker was an actual or apparent agent of the hospital.

75. University Hospital is a 250-bed hospital in a suburb of Chicago. All physicians who render services at the hospital are members of the medical staff, but none are employees of the hospital. Patient Jane Smith had heart surgery at the hospital last month. She chose the hospital because of its solid reputation for cardiology. There are billboards all around town promoting its cardiology services as the "#1 Heart Program in the Region" and "Best Heart Doctors Around." Jane specifically sought out Dr. James Brown because he was featured prominently in the hospital's advertisements and she heard from several friends that he is one of the best cardiologists in town. Jane's hospital registration paperwork did not discuss physician agency. During surgery, Dr. Brown accidentally nicked an artery, causing severe blood loss, anemia, additional surgery, and a lengthier hospital stay. Not only was this emotionally traumatic for Jane, but she also had to pay $100,000 in additional medical bills and be off work for an additional six weeks. To ensure payment, her lawyer wants to sue the hospital and not Dr. Brown. Will they be successful in suing the hospital based on the information above?

(A) Yes, the hospital is potentially liable because it is obligated to provide oversight of the physicians on its medical staff.

(B) Yes, the hospital is potentially liable because the nursing staff should have been monitoring complications, and failure to not do so was negligent.

(C) Yes, the hospital is potentially liable because a jury could find Dr. Brown to be an apparent agent of the hospital.

(D) No, liability is unlikely to attach to the hospital under the above facts.

76. Brooklyn Brown was injured while playing in a high school lacrosse game. She was rushed to the nearby hospital, requiring immediate surgery. The on-call physician came to the hospital and performed the necessary surgery. Post-surgery, the physician waited at the hospital for 30 minutes to confirm Brooklyn was stable and then left. The physician told the nurse that she (the physician) was leaving that day for vacation. The physician stated, "I did my part. You and the other nurses should be able to take it from here. Call only in an emergency." Brooklyn was doing well at first, but her condition deteriorated after a few hours. She first started complaining about a headache and nausea. The nurse told Brooklyn it should resolve itself. When the nurse checked on Brooklyn an hour later, Brooklyn had spiked a fever and appeared worse. The nurse called the physician stating that Brooklyn appeared to have an infection and needed to be seen. The physician told the nurse to give Brooklyn something for the fever and monitor her for another hour. The nurse did as she was told, but 30 minutes later Brooklyn went into septic shock. A physician from the emergency room performed surgery and discovered a sponge that had been left in the wound cavity during the previous surgery. It was removed, but Brooklyn has suffered severe damage from having been in septic shock. Brooklyn would like to sue the hospital for what happened to her. Is there a legal basis to sue the hospital based on the facts above?

(A) No, there is likely no liability for the hospital because the issues were really caused by the negligence and neglect of the on-call physician.

(B) No. The nurses were always acting pursuant to the physician's order, and thus the hospital and its nurses cannot be held liable.

(C) Yes, but *only* if you can prove that the nurses at the hospital were responsible for counting the sponges post-surgery and failed to do so.

(D) Yes. Although the physician was negligent in leaving the sponge in Brooklyn, the nurses and administrators at the hospital have an obligation to monitor the physicians who are performing services within their walls.

77. Chief Executive Officer (CEO) of Spring Hill Community Hospital, a 50-bed hospital about 45 minutes outside of a major metropolis, has contacted your law firm to assist with some strategic planning. The hospital is looking to expand some of its services and capabilities to encourage residents of the county to come to Spring Hill Community Hospital instead of bypassing it and going to the larger hospitals in the metropolis 45 minutes away. The CEO has come up with a couple of strategies: (a) recruit new cardiologists and orthopedic physicians to expand specialty offerings, and employ these physicians at the hospital; or (b) engage with a local multi-specialty group to recruit new cardiologists and orthopedic physicians to their group, with the promise by the hospital of increased facilities, operating room access, new state-of-the-art robotic/surgical tools, and a heavy marketing campaign for these services in the area (which can potentially include photos of the newly recruited physicians). Assume

that both options are legal under state law and meet all applicable fraud and abuse considerations. Please explain to the CEO what the potential liability risk to the hospital is for each of these options.

ANSWER:

78. A woman about to give birth presented at a hospital emergency room. At check-in, the pregnant woman made it clear that she did not have a private physician and had not sought any prenatal care; therefore, she needed to see whoever was serving as the on-call obstetrician-gynecologist. One of the forms that the pregnant woman was required to sign as part of the check-in process was labeled "Waiver of Liability." The form stated that the hospital is a non-profit and engages in human-subjects research to advance medical care for the good of the general public. It further stated that anyone who signs the form is agreeing to release the hospital from any and all liability that may arise out of the negligent, reckless, or willful acts or omission of the hospital's physicians, including the obstetrician-gynecologists. The woman signed the form, in part, because the baby's birth was imminent. Complications arose during the birth when the umbilical cord became wrapped around the baby's neck, which deprived the baby of oxygen and caused cerebral palsy. When the woman sues the hospital, the hospital cites its "Waiver of Liability" as an absolute defense. Is this defense likely to be successful?

(A) No, because it is never permissible for hospitals to have patients sign any forms that would release the hospital from liability because it is unconscionable.

(B) No, because if the waiver attempts to be a blanket release from all liability it is likely unenforceable as void against public policy.

(C) Yes, the waiver will be sufficient reasonable notice to the patient and will be enforceable.

(D) Yes, the waiver is enforceable because the patient signed the form and it was for the services set forth on the form.

Hospital Privileges & Other Labor & Employment Issues

79. Dr. Jones has just moved into Big City and has received an offer from a company called Orthopaedix, a national company that contracts with physicians and physician practices to manage their practice and, often, contracts for exclusive arrangements with the local hospital. Under the offer, Dr. Jones would become an employee of a physician group that is managed by Orthopaedix. The physicians who are part of the group are bound by a covenant not to compete, and the practice cannot be sold to anyone without approval of Orthopaedix. Dr. Jones would prefer not to be part of a group or a management company, but the hospital CEO told Dr. Jones that it is illegal for the hospital to employ Dr. Jones directly. Further, the hospital contracts with Orthopaedix to provide orthopedic services at the hospital on an exclusive basis, which it provides through the physician group from which Dr. Jones received the offer. So Dr. Jones cannot have privileges to provide services at the hospital unless Dr. Jones works with the group that is managed by Orthopaedix. Dr. Jones tells you he just wants to be an employee of the hospital and asks why that won't work. He was a hospital employee in his previous state. What is the best explanation for why Dr. Jones's options are more limited in this jurisdiction?
    - (A) The state in which Dr. Jones now lives likely has a common law or statutory prohibition on the corporate practice of medicine.
    - (B) The hospital has absolute authority over management of its medical staff and can decide to exclusively deal with one provider/physician group.
    - (C) The hospital is prohibited from employing physicians under the Physician Self-Referral Statute otherwise known as the Stark Law.
    - (D) Dr. Jones's previous place of residence was likely a right-to-work state and thus has different rules.

80. Michael Scott is a radiologist at Scranton General Hospital. He is one of 10 radiologists, and they divide up their on-call shifts (required under the medical staff bylaws) based on seniority. This has led to quality concerns. Within the last six months, several of Dr. Scott's patients have sought a second opinion after his diagnosis seemed off. Many of the second opinions were contrary to Dr. Scott's initial diagnosis. The hospital would like to remove Dr. Scott from

its medical staff. The hospital provided notice to Dr. Scott that, due to concerns regarding his ability to practice effectively, it was revoking his privileges. The notice regarding revocation referenced several of the cases in which a patient had sought a second opinion. The hospital followed the process set forth in the medical staff bylaws and ultimately revoked Dr. Scott's privileges. If Dr. Scott sues in state court, what is the standard of review that will be applied by courts in the majority of states?

(A) Whether the decision of the hospital's medical staff was arbitrary and capricious

(B) Whether the decision of the hospital's medical staff was supported by substantial evidence

(C) Whether the decision of the hospital's medical staff was consistent with the requirements set forth in the medical staff bylaws

(D) Whether taking this adverse action against Dr. Scott would be void as against public policy

81. Same facts as in Question 80 above. After Dr. Scott's privileges are revoked, the problems in radiology are not solved. The rest of the radiologists who have privileges at the hospital — nine in all — divide on-call shifts required under the medical staff bylaws based on seniority. This means that newer and less experienced physicians often end up working late at night and on weekends and holidays. Recently, one newer radiologist was the on-call overnight radiologist and did not feel comfortable reading any high-risk pregnancy ultrasounds due to lack of experience. Patients had to be turned away. Concerned about quality, the hospital decided to close the radiology department and enter into an exclusive contract with Vance Radiology, Inc., a radiology company owned and operated by a large private equity firm. The hospital revoked the clinical privileges of all nine radiologists. The medical staff bylaws permit removal of privileges in this manner if privileges are revoked for purposes of closing a department. One of the nine radiologists sues the hospital for revocation of privileges. Which of the following is the hospital's best defense?

(A) The hospital has immunity under the Health Care Quality Improvement Act of 1986.

(B) Retaining the radiologist under the current structure would be corporate negligence.

(C) Hospitals can remove physicians at any time based on quality concerns.

(D) Closing the radiology department is an absolute defense.

82. City Hospital has a policy prohibiting all members of its medical staff from having privileges at certain hospitals that City Hospital identifies as competitor hospitals. Dr. Smith has privileges at all area hospitals and refuses to relinquish his privileges at other hospitals despite the policy. If Dr. Smith's medical staff membership is suspended or revoked, this is an example of what?

(A) "Clean sweep" provisions

(B) Economic credentialing

(C) Due process violations

(D) Restrictive covenants

83. County Hospital fires a physician who has been working at the hospital as an at-will employee with no contract. Physician alleges that she was fired because she reported a fraudulent billing scheme to the chair of her department. The hospital responds that she was fired for being "disruptive" and "non-cooperative." What exception to the at-will employment doctrine is the physician's best state law claim?

    (A) A workplace discrimination claim

    (B) A wrongful termination claim

    (C) A constructive termination claim

    (D) A retaliatory discharge claim

84. The medical staff of a hospital are all employees of the hospital and have also organized themselves as an association that qualifies as a labor organization. The hospital has imposed a new requirement that all physicians work in the hospital a minimum of 45 hours per week. The physicians held several meetings and issued a collective statement to the administrators of the hospital objecting to the change to work hours and demanding a meeting. Hospital administrators responded by telling the physicians that anyone not willing to work the 45 hours per week would be fired and replaced by physicians who are. The labor organization has filed an action against the hospital alleging violations of the National Labor Relations Act (NLRA). Can this labor organization state a claim pursuant to the NLRA?

    (A) No, because the NLRA only provides protection for groups formally organized as unions.

    (B) No, because hospitals have authority to remove members of their medical staff if they have quality or other concerns.

    (C) Yes, because the labor organization will have the same protections as a union under the NLRA.

    (D) Yes, because physicians cannot be required to work more than 45 hours per week as employees.

85. Which of the following individuals is most likely to be excluded from the National Labor Relations Act's definition of an employee?

    (A) A nurse practitioner who works as a floater, providing services in whatever department needs the most help at the time

    (B) A permanent charge nurse who is responsible for assigning other nurses to shifts based on the charge nurse's independent judgment as to which nurse might have the best skills for each area

    (C) The front desk person who is responsible for assigning patients to individual rooms as the rooms become available

    (D) The physician whose primary role is to screen patients in the emergency room and to decide whether they should be admitted and to which floor

86. A hospital discovered that a surgical assistant had narcolepsy that was occasionally difficult to control with medication. Given the severity of the condition and concern that the employee would fall asleep on the job, the hospital told the surgical assistant that he was being moved to the position of scheduler. If the surgical assistant sues the hospital pursuant to the Americans with Disabilities Act for this job change, alleging it is a demotion and an adverse action against him on the basis of his disability, what is the hospital's best defense?

(A) The surgical assistant was not, in fact, fired but rather was offered another job.

(B) The surgical assistant with narcolepsy poses a direct threat to the health or safety of others.

(C) The job of scheduler is a reasonable accommodation.

(D) The surgical assistant is an at-will employee.

Discrimination: EMTALA, Title VI, ADA, GINA, & ACA

87. Brooklyn Davis was experiencing severe stomach pains. She went to the emergency room at the hospital closest to her house and was sent directly to the triage nurse. The nurse took down Brooklyn's demographic information and then asked Brooklyn for her insurance information. Brooklyn handed the nurse her insurance card for insurance that she had purchased online several months earlier when she lost her job. The nurse told Brooklyn that she would need to call the insurance company first because under her insurance plan all services in an emergency room require pre-authorization. Brooklyn was forced to wait on her insurance company's approval for an additional four hours, and by the time it was approved, Brooklyn's appendix had burst. Brooklyn would like to file suit against the hospital for its refusal to treat her condition appropriately. Under what legal theory is Brooklyn most likely to achieve success?
    (A) The Emergency Medical Treatment and Active Labor Act (EMTALA) for delay in screening
    (B) Common law claim for breach of duty of care
    (C) Common law claim for breach of contract for improper action under her insurance contract
    (D) Common law claim for corporate negligence for its failure to follow the proper standard of care

88. Same facts as in Question 87 above, but assume that the nurse did not question Brooklyn's insurance and instead sent Brooklyn immediately to an examination room for an emergency medical screening. A physician came into the room and manually examined Brooklyn's stomach. The physician told Brooklyn that her stomach pains were likely just gas and would dissipate over the next few days and to call if there were further issues. Brooklyn went home, and a few hours later, her appendix burst. By the time she arrived back at the hospital, she had developed a severe infection and had to spend several days in the hospital. She has been experiencing long-term effects from the infection. Does Brooklyn have a claim under EMTALA under the above facts?
    (A) Likely yes, as the physician was negligent in rendering the screening.
    (B) Likely yes, because the physician should have conducted an x-ray to see if the appendix was inflamed.

(C) Likely no, assuming the physician followed consistent screening practices for all similar patients.

(D) Likely no, because there is no private right of action under EMTALA.

89. Noah Green has type two diabetes. Noah came to Dr. Hudson's office complaining of numbness in his feet, which Dr. Hudson thought was due to high blood-sugar levels. Dr. Hudson ordered Noah to follow a special diet and stop smoking to get Noah's blood sugar levels under control. Dr. Hudson followed up with Noah several times, but each time Noah was still smoking and his blood-sugar levels remained dangerously high. When Noah arrived for his next appointment, he showed clear signs of gangrene in both feet. A frustrated Dr. Hudson told Noah that Noah was warned about this all along and that it was clear that Noah had no intention of following Dr. Hudson's advice. Dr. Hudson stated that he could not work with Noah anymore because of Noah's lack of compliance and asked Noah to leave. Dr. Hudson did not explain to Noah that the gangrene was serious and could result in amputation of his legs. Noah found another physician within 30 days, but the gangrene was too advanced at that point, and so Noah's feet had to be amputated at the shin. Noah would now like to sue Dr. Hudson. What is Noah's best claim?

(A) Breach of duty of care based on patient abandonment

(B) Breach of contract based on Dr. Hudson's refusal to treat

(C) EMTALA for failure to screen for gangrene as an emergency medical condition

(D) Breach of standard of care based on Dr. Hudson's negligence in his treatment of Noah

90. Same facts as in Question 89 above. Which fact, if true, is Dr. Hudson's best defense against a complaint from Noah?

(A) Noah's pre-treatment smoking and poor eating choices were the proximate cause of any injury and not Dr. Hudson's lack of notice.

(B) Although gangrene is a known complication of type two diabetes, Dr. Hudson did not owe a duty of care because the gangrene was a new condition and Dr. Hudson could refuse to treat a new condition.

(C) Dr. Hudson was under no duty to discover the gangrene.

(D) Dr. Hudson had previously sent three letters to Noah informing him that because of Noah's non-compliance, Noah needed to seek the care of another provider, and Dr. Hudson's office had transferred Noah's medical records upon Noah's request to another provider three months earlier.

91. A patient with sickle cell anemia, a genetic disease found most commonly in individuals of African or Middle Eastern descent, presented in the emergency room of the hospital with swelling hands and feet and complaining of extreme pain, common symptoms of a sickle cell anemia crisis. The physician on call who examined the patient had seen this patient before.

The patient did not control his sickle cell anemia well and he was always in and out of the hospital seeking treatment. The physician was tired of dealing with the patient because the physician thought that he was just using the emergency room as his primary care provider. After examining the patient, the physician concluded that the patient was likely exaggerating about the pain. The physician said to the nurse, "Get him out of here. I am tired of seeing people from the south side of town who don't have a doctor and decide to come here for pain meds." The south side of town is a predominantly low-income, African American neighborhood. The patient was discharged but collapsed on the sidewalk outside the hospital and died. The estate is suing the physician. Can the estate sue the physician under Title VI of the Civil Rights Act?

(A) Yes, because the physician's words and actions were evidence of bias against the patient due to his disease.

(B) Yes, because the physician's words and actions were evidence of bias against the patient due to his race.

(C) No, because it is not clear from the physician's words what precisely his motive was for discharging the patient.

(D) No, because it is unlikely that the physician's actions were the proximate cause of the patient's death.

92. Same facts as in Question 91 above, but the estate also plans to sue under the Americans with Disabilities Act (ADA) and the Rehabilitation Act of 1973 (Rehabilitation Act). Is the estate likely to succeed under either of these claims?

(A) Likely not on either claim, because the reason the patient was turned away was most likely because of his race.

(B) Likely not on either claim, because the patient was given a proper screening.

(C) Likely yes for both claims, because the evidence supports that the sole reason for turning the patient away was his sickle cell anemia diagnosis.

(D) Likely yes for the ADA but not for the Rehabilitation Act because of the mixed motive.

93. If a plaintiff would like to bring a disparate impact claim against a health care company for discrimination, under what federal law, if any, may such a claim be possible?

(A) It is not possible, as the Supreme Court prohibited disparate impact claims in *Alexander v. Sandoval*, 532 U.S. 275 (2001).

(B) A plaintiff can only bring a disparate impact claim for racial discrimination under Title VI of the Civil Rights Act, not for discrimination on the basis of disability.

(C) A plaintiff can bring a disparate impact claim under Section 1557 of the Affordable Care Act.

(D) A plaintiff can bring a disparate impact claim for discrimination on the basis of sex but not disability.

94. Latonya Jackson is four months pregnant. She experiences abdominal pain and, based on her doctor's recommendation that she go to the hospital immediately, she calls 911. Four employees from the Washington County Emergency Medical Services respond to the call. Ms. Jackson requests that she be taken to St. David's Medical Center, but the emergency personnel take her to Washington County Hospital against her wishes. They do this because the county has a practice of requiring their emergency personnel to go only to county hospitals. Ms. Jackson goes into premature labor, and her child does not survive. Ms. Jackson files a lawsuit alleging that the actions of the county through their emergency personnel violated her constitutional rights under the 14th Amendment. Is Ms. Jackson's claim likely to be successful?

(A) Yes. Ms. Jackson has a right to receive health care services from the county or state under the U.S. Constitution and the county's actions violated that right.

(B) Yes. Ms. Jackson has a right to emergency services under the U.S. Constitution and such services must comply with the patient's service needs.

(C) No. There is never a general right to the provision of medical care and services by the state under the U.S. Constitution.

(D) No. Absent a "special custodial relationship," Ms. Jackson does not have a general right to the provision of medical care and services by the state.

95. A state Medicaid program expands income eligibility to individuals who earn up to three times the previous poverty level. To make this expansion economically feasible, the state excludes individuals who are categorically eligible because they are disabled, due to the higher costs of insuring that population. A disabled individual who would otherwise qualify for Medicaid under the new poverty threshold plans to sue the state, alleging that the new eligibility requirements violate the Americans with Disabilities Act (ADA) and Section 1557 of the ACA. Is the individual likely to be successful?

(A) No. As long as the state sets its Medicaid income threshold within the federal maximum and minimum for individuals who are categorically eligible based on disability, the state can determine its own income eligibility threshold.

(B) No. The state has no obligation to provide Medicaid at all, and thus, because it is an optional program, there are no eligibility obligations.

(C) Yes. Once a state opts to provide a Medicaid program, the state discriminates in violation of the ADA and Section 1557 of the ACA if that program fails to provide the same eligibility threshold for similarly situated disabled individuals as non-disabled individuals.

(D) Yes. Federal law requires Medicaid income eligibility threshold limits to be uniform across all individuals and states.

96. Ella carries the genetic mutation for Huntington's disease but has not yet manifested any symptoms. Which of the following is correct regarding the use of Ella's genetic information pursuant to the Genetic Information Nondiscrimination Act of 2008 (GINA)?

(A) Ella may be charged a higher premium for health, life, disability, and long-term care insurance based on her genetic information.

(B) Ella may *not* be charged a higher premium for health, life, disability, or long-term care insurance based on her genetic information.

(C) Ella may be charged a higher premium for life, disability, and long-term care insurance based on her genetic information but not for health insurance.

(D) Ella may be charged a higher premium for life insurance based on her genetic information but not for health, disability, or long-term care insurance.

Topic 12 **Questions**

Regulation of Private Health Insurance

97. Which was *not* a key initiative of the Affordable Care Act?
    (A) Improving how patients receive and experience health care
    (B) Reducing overall health care costs for families and individuals by decreasing the uninsured rate
    (C) Encouraging states to reduce overall costs through tort reform
    (D) Improving the health of populations across the United States through basic benefits

98. Dante Young is a 35-year-old male who lives in the state of Kentucky. Dante works construction during the summer months and often bartends or waits tables in the winter when construction is slow. Dante does not have insurance through any of his various employers, primarily because he does not work consistently enough to be eligible for benefits. Dante is a U.S. citizen and has no dependents and no spouse. Please tell Dante about his various insurance options.

    ANSWER:

99. The Governor of the state of Tennessee is interested in forming a health insurance exchange for Tennessee residents that will operate outside the federal exchange and the requirements of the ACA. The exchange will be funded through state dollars. The Governor is reviewing two proposals: The first is a proposal to create minimum standards with which all insurers wishing to offer insurance on the new state insurance exchange will be required to comply. Only insurers who agree to these minimum obligations will be eligible to offer insurance on the exchange. The second proposal is to create a competitive bidding process whereby any insurers wishing to offer insurance on the exchange will be required to submit a request for proposal to the state, and only certain of the insurers will be selected to offer their products

on the exchange. What are the advantages and disadvantages of each of these approaches, and which model does the ACA adopt with healthcare.gov?

ANSWER:

100. With some exceptions for religious objections, employers are required to provide birth control under which of the 10 essential benefits?

(A) Preventative and wellness services

(B) Pediatric services

(C) Prescription drugs

(D) Maternity and newborn care

101. What metal tiered plan is an individual required to purchase on a health insurance exchange (either healthcare.gov or a state exchange) if the individual would like to be eligible for premium assistance subsidies and cost-sharing reduction payments?

(A) Gold plan

(B) Platinum plan

(C) Silver plan

(D) Bronze plan

102. Under *King v. Burwell*, 576 U.S. 473 (2015), the Supreme Court was asked to consider what key issue?

(A) Whether Congress had properly appropriated payment of the cost-sharing reduction payments to insurers

(B) Whether Congress had the authority to require states to expand their Medicaid population to individuals who met financial eligibility criteria only

(C) Whether premium tax credits are available to purchasers on both the federal health insurance exchange (healthcare.gov) and state health insurance exchanges

(D) Whether Congress had the authority to impose the individual mandate

103. Frank Taylor's large employer offers health insurance. This year, Frank received notice that his premiums had increased by 7% year over year. This increase means that in 2023 12% of Frank's salary would go towards payment of Frank's premium. Will this result in an employer fine under the Affordable Care Act?

(A) No, because the annual increase was still under the 10% threshold.

(B) No, because employers cannot be responsible for increased costs established by an insurance company.

(C) Yes, because Frank cannot be required to purchase insurance that is this expensive.

(D) Yes, because an employer cannot charge premiums in excess of 9.12% of an employee's household income.

104. Both Chloe and Oliver have private health insurance. Chloe is injured in a serious accident and taken by ambulance to an out-of-network hospital selected by the first responder for emergency treatment. Oliver has scheduled knee replacement surgery at an in-network hospital. While hospitalized, unbeknownst to Oliver, his x-ray is read by an out-of-network radiologist. The providers would like to maximize reimbursement by charging the patients the highest amount allowable, consistent with the law. Which of the following is correct regarding legally authorized medical bills?

(A) Both Chloe and Oliver may be balance billed (billed for the difference between the amount charged by the provider and the amount paid by insurance) for out-of-network charges.

(B) Neither Chloe nor Oliver may be balance billed for out-of-network charges.

(C) Chloe may be balance billed for out-of-network charges, but Oliver may not.

(D) Oliver may be balance billed for out-of-network charges, but Chloe may not.

Topic 13 Questions

Health Care Markets & Reform

105. Better Health is an insurance company that provides insurance products primarily to large employers. It has been exploring the idea of selling short-term health plans to individuals, but it wants to ensure that it does not risk losing money by selling individual policies to high-risk individuals. Assuming it is not planning to sell on the federal health insurance exchange (healthcare.gov) or a state exchange, what tactic could it use to guard against risks in the individual market?

    (A) Community rating

    (B) Experience rating

    (C) Moral hazard

    (D) Adverse selection

106. Assume that Better Health (referenced in Question 105 above) has expanded into the individual market. Based on market data, Better Health knows that individuals who live in the area in which Better Health is marketing its products tend to overutilize services. That is, insured individuals in this geographic region tend to visit the doctor more on average than others and tend to have higher claims than similarly situated individuals in other geographic regions. Which of the following will *not* assist Better Health in preventing overutilization?

    (A) Co-pays

    (B) Co-insurance

    (C) Stop-loss insurance

    (D) Deductibles

107. A health insurance policy is considered a "managed care" plan because of the management of what two attributes?

    (A) The payment of care and the delivery of care

    (B) The payment of care and the limitation on services

    (C) Control of choice of provider and the total amount paid to the provider

    (D) Capitated payments and narrow networks

108. A patient is admitted to the hospital for elective surgery and develops an infection. The patient's physician orders the patient to stay for an additional five days. A month later, the patient receives notice from his insurance company that the five-day stay was not deemed to be medically necessary and would not be reimbursed. What is the name for this type of control by the insurance company?

   (A) Capitation

   (B) Utilization review

   (C) Primary care physician management

   (D) Reference pricing

109. What common practice utilized by health insurance companies to control costs was significantly curbed in the group commercial market with the enactment of HIPAA in 1996 and then in the individual commercial market with the enactment of the Affordable Care Act in 2010?

   (A) Adverse selection

   (B) Community rating

   (C) Denial for pre-existing conditions

   (D) Moral hazard

110. The Affordable Care Act generally prohibits insurers from charging beneficiaries higher premiums due to being part of a group with higher-than-average usage of services (e.g., charging women higher premiums than men because women's claims are historically higher than men's). What statement below best describes this change?

   (A) From actuarial fairness to distributive justice

   (B) From adverse selection to favorable selection

   (C) From experience rating to community rating

   (D) From moral hazard to equitable distribution

Employee Retirement Income Security Act (ERISA)

111. There is a state law that prohibits hospitals from charging insurers more than such hospitals pay to the Medicare program. Under which section(s) in the Employee Retirement and Income Security Act of 1974 (ERISA) would a court review this state law to determine express preemption?
   (A) Section 514(a), 29 U.S.C. § 1144(a)
   (B) Section 502, 29 U.S.C. § 1132
   (C) A and B
   (D) None of the above

112. Sally Smith works part time at a large manufacturing facility. She has insurance through an HMO that she has purchased on healthcare.gov. Sally developed an ulcer that required surgery. Sally experienced some complications because of the surgery, and her physician would have liked to keep her in the hospital for three additional days. Her HMO refused coverage and insisted a one-day stay was sufficient. Sally was discharged, had a stroke, and is now permanently paralyzed. Sally would like to sue the HMO for its refusal to approve the extra stay in the hospital. Independent of the case on the merits, will Sally be able to bring a negligence claim against the HMO in state court?
   (A) No. Sally's claim will be preempted by Section 502 of ERISA and will be required to be heard as an ERISA claim in federal court.
   (B) No. Sally's claim will be preempted by Section 514 of ERISA and will be required to be heard as an ERISA claim in federal court.
   (C) Yes. Sally will be able to show that the applicable state law is "saved" under Section 514 and can be heard.
   (D) Yes. ERISA is not applicable to this claim.

113. Juan Gonzales works at a large university and has health plan benefits for himself and his family through his university, which it purchases through a third-party insurance company. Recently, a claim for Juan's hospital services was denied. Under Juan's policy, he had only 10 days to appeal that denial, and failure to timely appeal extinguished any appeal rights.

The policy is in violation of a state law requiring that all beneficiaries of all health insurance policies operating in the state have at least 30 days for an appeal and the opportunity for an independent review when a claim is denied. If Juan brings a claim against his health plan in state court to enforce the state law, what is the best argument that this should be removed to federal court?

(A) None. Juan will likely be successful on his state law claim because his insurer is clearly in violation of state law.

(B) Juan's case will likely be removed to federal court because of the "deemer" clause under ERISA.

(C) Juan's case will likely be removed to federal court under Section 502 complete preemption.

(D) Juan's case will likely be removed to federal court under Section 514 express preemption.

114. Same facts as in Question 113 above, but assume that the university Juan works for has a self-insured health plan instead of purchasing a plan from a third-party insurance company. If Juan brings a claim against his health plan in state court to enforce the state law, what is the easiest, legally accurate result?

(A) Juan will likely be successful on his state law claim because his insurer is clearly in violation of state law.

(B) Juan's case will likely be removed to federal court because of the "deemer" clause under ERISA.

(C) Juan's case will likely be removed to federal court under Section 502 complete preemption.

(D) Juan's case will likely be removed to federal court under Section 514 express preemption.

115. Tennessee has decided to implement a program that would help to curb exponential health care expenses. The Health Care Cost Reduction Act requires all hospitals and physician services to be capped at no greater than ten percent of the average charge for a particular service (based on the all-payor DRG or the Medicare physician fee schedule) for the immediately preceding calendar year. Hospital Company of America has filed suit (in its capacity as an employer that provides health benefits to its employees) in federal district court in Tennessee alleging that the new Tennessee law is preempted by ERISA. What is the test a court will use to determine whether the state law relates to an ERISA plan?

(A) Whether the law bears an impermissible connection with an ERISA plan

(B) Whether the law is specifically designed for insurance

(C) Whether the law interferes with the uniform plan

(D) Whether the law targets insurers as the primary focus

Medicare & Medicaid

116. Medicare is best described as which of the following?
    (A) A joint federal-state program that aids certain Americans of advanced age and/or who have a disability
    (B) A joint federal-state program that aids certain Americans of limited economic means and/or who have a disability
    (C) A federal program that aids certain Americans of advanced age and/or who have a disability
    (D) A federal program that aids certain Americans of limited economic means

117. If medically necessary, Medicare may cover which of the following for eligible beneficiaries?
    (A) Some prescription pharmaceuticals
    (B) Hearing aids
    (C) Long-term nursing home care
    (D) Eye exams

118. In *National Federation of Independent Business v. Sebelius (NFIB)*, 567 U.S. 519 (2012), the U.S. Supreme Court considered the ACA in connection with arguments regarding the federal government's limited and enumerated powers and held that:
    (A) the ACA is unconstitutional.
    (B) the individual mandate is in essence a tax and therefore a constitutional exercise of congressional authority.
    (C) conditioning all future federal Medicaid funds on state expansion of Medicaid is coercive and therefore exceeds congressional authority.
    (D) B and C

119. Medicaid eligibility varies by state. Assume that all individuals are 28 years old, work 40 hours a week earning $10 per hour at a non-benefited job ($400 per week), and have no disability and no children. Abdul is a foreign national, lawfully in the U.S. on a student visa, who lives in an expansion state. Brett is a U.S. citizen and lives in an expansion state. Cai is a U.S. citizen,

lives in an expansion state, and has assets worth more than $100,000. Don is a U.S. citizen who lives in a non-expansion state. If 138% of the federal poverty level (FPL) for single-individual households is $1,563 per month, who is eligible for Medicaid?

(A) All are eligible.

(B) None are eligible.

(C) Brett, Cai, and Don are eligible.

(D) Brett is eligible.

120. Using the same facts, who, if anyone, is eligible for a premium subsidy to purchase heavily subsidized health insurance at low or no cost through the marketplace?

(A) All are eligible.

(B) None are eligible.

(C) Brett, Cai, and Don are eligible.

(D) Brett is eligible.

121. Assume the same facts, except that the gentlemen now are only able to work 20 hours per week. Who, if anyone, is eligible for Medicaid?

(A) All are eligible.

(B) Brett, Cai, and Don are eligible.

(C) Brett and Cai are eligible.

(D) Brett is eligible.

122. Using the lower income in Question 121 above, who, if anyone, is eligible for a premium subsidy to purchase heavily subsidized health insurance at low or no cost through the marketplace?

(A) All are eligible.

(B) Abdul is eligible.

(C) Don is eligible.

(D) None are eligible.

123. Assume the original facts in Question 119 above, except that the gentlemen are now caretaker parents of a minor child, with a household of two. Assume 138% of the FPL for a household of two is $25,268 per year and that 100% is $18,310. Who, if anyone, is eligible for Medicaid?

(A) All are eligible.

(B) All children are eligible.

(C) Brett, Cai, and Don and their children are eligible.

(D) Brett and Cai and their children are eligible, as well as Don's child.

124. Assume the original facts in Question 119 above, except that the gentlemen are now 67 years old. Who, if anyone, is eligible for Medicare?

   (A) All are eligible.

   (B) None are eligible.

   (C) Brett, Cai, and Don are eligible.

   (D) Brett is eligible.

125. States can receive permission to deviate from otherwise mandatory federal Medicaid eligibility requirements by obtaining a Section 1115 waiver for a particular state project. What, if anything, must states establish to qualify for a Section 1115 waiver?

   (A) The state project must be effective and it must promote the objectives of the Social Security Act.

   (B) The state project must be effective and it must promote the objectives of the Medicaid Act.

   (C) The state project must be experimental and it must promote the objectives of the Medicaid Act.

   (D) None of the above are required, although they may be relevant to agency approval.

126. Federal law requires states participating in Medicaid to cover certain benefits for eligible beneficiaries. Which of the following are *not* mandatory Medicaid benefits?

   (A) Inpatient hospital services

   (B) Smoking cessation services for pregnant women

   (C) Nurse-midwife services

   (D) Dentures

127. While federal law imposes certain requirements on state Medicaid plans, not all of these requirements are privately enforceable against state officials by Medicaid recipients or providers. Which of the following is *not* one of the requirements for a particular provision of the Medicaid Act to confer a private right of action pursuant to 42 U.S.C. § 1983?

   (A) There is unambiguous congressional intent to create an "individual entitlement" by the use of "rights-creating language."

   (B) The right "is not so vague and amorphous that its enforcement would strain judicial competence."

   (C) Congress intended the particular provision to "impose a binding obligation on the States."

   (D) Plaintiff has a "likelihood of success on the merits" regarding the right.

128. The majority of courts do *not* recognize a private right of action to enforce which of the following Medicaid provisions?

(A) Reimbursement rates sufficient to enlist enough providers, 42 U.S.C. § 1396a(30)(A)

(B) Free choice of any qualified provider, 42 U.S.C. § 1396a(a)(23)

(C) Assistance provided with reasonable promptness, 42 U.S.C. § 1396a(a)(8)

(D) Provision of all mandatory categories of benefits, 42 U.S.C. § 1396a(a)(10)(A)

Structure & Governance of Health Care Entities

129. County Hospital is a non-profit corporation that was formed in 1905 for the purpose of providing health services to the residents of Hamilton County. The Board of Directors is made up of various members of the community, most of whom have no background knowledge or experience with hospital systems but who are large donors to the hospital. For the past 10 years, all major decisions for the hospital have been made by an executive committee of three members. These three members have become so powerful that the other members basically cede all decisions to them and rely on their recommendations often without review or questions asked. It has been discovered that the Board approved a deal to sell the hospital, based entirely on the recommendation from the executive committee and without any supporting documentation or materials. If there is a lawsuit filed against the directors for mismanagement, on what basis will the court determine liability?

    (A) Liability for negligence

    (B) Liability for gross negligence

    (C) Liability for willful neglect

    (D) Liability for intentional misconduct

130. Same facts as in Question 129 above; however, now assume that the Board did not merely defer to the executive committee but instead conducted robust due diligence prior to approving the sale. Nonetheless, the three members of the executive committee all had undisclosed ownership positions in the entity that was the proposed purchaser in the sale of County Hospital. What, if any, breach of fiduciary duty has occurred?

    (A) Breach of duty of care

    (B) Breach of duty of obedience

    (C) Breach of duty of loyalty

    (D) No fiduciary duty has been breached

131. Same facts as in Question 129 above. Which of the following is consistent with the directors' duty of obedience?

    (A) The Board of Directors of County Hospital decides to shut down its geriatric practice despite a strong need in the community (which has a population of over 50% of individuals who are 65+) due to disappointing financial returns under the program.

    (B) The Board of Directors of County Hospital accepts an unsolicited offer from a potential purchaser offering to buy the County Hospital building and adjacent land for an above-market price to put in a shopping mall.

    (C) The Board of Directors of County Hospital decides to start purchasing real estate in the area surrounding the hospital and around the county because of the market boom — it intends to hold the property with the goal of selling to developers for a large profit.

    (D) The Board of Directors of County Hospital decides to close a critical access hospital about 50 miles away in Washington County because the critical access hospital is losing money and compromising the financial stability of County Hospital as a whole.

132. Which of the following is *not* an attribute of an accountable care organization (ACO) under the Medicare Shared Savings Program set forth in the Affordable Care Act?

    (A) Must be organized as a legal entity

    (B) Must comply with quality metrics to be able to share in any savings generated

    (C) Must have beneficiaries assigned by CMS to it specifically

    (D) Must have a minimum of 5,000 Medicare beneficiaries to participate in the program

133. Hospital Company of America is a for-profit, publicly traded corporation owning and operating hospitals throughout the country. The company recently settled a False Claims Act case that had been filed by a whistleblower alleging billing and coding errors for emergency room patients. A shareholder has now filed a shareholder derivative suit alleging a breach of fiduciary duties for failure to monitor against members of the Board of Directors. What facts, if true, are most likely to result in the directors' successfully defending this lawsuit?

    (A) Hospital Company of America did not admit any fault in connection with the settlement and is maintaining that it was not in violation of the False Claims Act.

    (B) Hospital Company of America Board of Directors had not been aware of the alleged fraud and implemented its compliance plan once being notified of the fraud.

    (C) Hospital Company of America Board of Directors had previously adopted and implemented a compliance plan when it was hit with another False Claims Act lawsuit several years ago.

    (D) Hospital Company of America Board of Directors ordered its CEO to fire its head of billing and coding upon hearing about the allegations and feels comfortable about compliance under the current management team.

134. Before a non-profit hospital can sell all or substantially all of its assets, whose approval is likely required?

(A) The Board of Directors and the state Attorney General

(B) The Board of Directors and the shareholders

(C) The Board of Directors and the officers of the corporation

(D) The Board of Directors only

135. What is another name that courts use to describe the duty of obedience for directors of non-profit corporations?

(A) Mission creep

(B) Mission primacy

(C) Fiduciary obligations

(D) Obedience to the mission

Tax-Exempt Health Care Organizations

136. Sisters of the Divine Mission Hospital was first formed in 1896 as a non-profit corporation in Mississippi and has been providing health care services to the "poor and downtrodden" of the city of Wallace since that time. The hospital is exempt from federal income taxes. The hospital has been the only hospital in the city within a 50-mile radius for a long time. Recently, a for-profit hospital chain received a Certificate of Need from a state agency to build a new hospital in Wallace. The new hospital will be state of the art and will almost certainly impact the Sisters of the Divine Mission Hospital's market share. You have received a call from a local board member for Sisters of the Divine Mission Hospital who is concerned about the new hospital. The board member would like you to describe the key distinctions between a for-profit hospital and a non-profit hospital, including the ways in which Sisters of the Divine Mission Hospital might be at a competitive disadvantage when the for-profit hospital begins operations.

ANSWER:

137. Sisters of the Divine Mission Hospital is interested in expanding its operations to compete with a for-profit hospital that recently moved into its community. It would like to open an outpatient ambulatory surgery center (ASC) for the convenience of its patients and medical staff. The hospital has been approached by ASC Services, Inc., an ambulatory surgery center company that owns and operates ASCs across the country. The hospital has proposed a joint venture with ASC Services, Inc., in which the hospital will own 51% of the entity and ASC Services, Inc., will own 49%. Sisters of the Divine Mission Hospital's biggest concern is the ability to control the joint venture to ensure that all proceeds from the joint venture are tax-exempt for the hospital and do not jeopardize the tax-exempt status of the hospital. Please advise the

CEO on how to set up the joint venture in a way that will ensure the hospital will be able to maintain its tax-exempt status.

ANSWER:

138. Clark County Community Hospital is a non-profit hospital in the state of Kentucky. The hospital has a financial assistance policy that provides discounts on a sliding scale for people paying out-of-pocket and earning up to 300% of the federal poverty line. The financial assistance policy applies only if a patient is a self-pay patient and specifically asks about financial assistance. As a result of the policy, the average annual financial assistance/charity care amount that is provided by the hospital to all patients is approximately $1,000,000, which is equivalent to less than 1% of the hospital's total revenue. Under what standard will the Internal Revenue Service (IRS) determine compliance with applicable laws and regulations regarding federal tax exemption?

    (A) The primary purpose test
    (B) Mission primacy
    (C) The charitable trust doctrine
    (D) Community benefit standard

139. Same facts as in Question 138 above. If the IRS were to conduct an audit, is it likely that the IRS would conclude that it should revoke the hospital's tax-exempt status?

    (A) Likely yes, because the hospital should be providing financial assistance to those in need in an amount that meets or exceeds 5% of the hospital's total revenues.
    (B) Likely yes, because the hospital is not permitted to have a policy in which it does not affirmatively ask everyone if they need financial assistance.
    (C) Likely no, so long as the hospital can show that it is promoting health for the general benefit of the community.
    (D) Likely no, if the hospital can show that its bad debt when combined with the amount it provides in financial assistance exceeds 5% of its total revenues.

140. Same facts as in Question 138 above. The state Department of Revenue has noted that it has been providing property tax exemption for the property on which the hospital sits since the hospital's doors first opened 80 years ago. This year, the value of the property tax exemption was $1,500,000 (meaning, if a tax-paying entity owned the land, then the state would collect

$1,500,000 per year in property taxes). Which of the following facts would make state property tax exemption less likely for the hospital?

(A) The hospital has no stock and no shareholders.

(B) The hospital gives financial assistance to anyone with income up to 300% of the FPL but only if the patient asks for financial assistance prior to service.

(C) The hospital does not provide any gain or profit that the hospital derives to private individuals.

(D) The hospitals' payor mix is approximately 50% Medicaid patients.

141. A hospital owns and operates a medical office building that is adjacent to the hospital. To incentivize physicians from around the community to rent space in the building, the hospital has offered a discount for any and all physicians who rent space in the building. The discount is only available to physicians and not to other individuals seeking to rent space. The offer is good regardless of whether a physician currently has privileges at the hospital. The IRS has been looking into this and is investigating whether this is an example of what prohibited activity?

(A) Excess Benefit Transaction

(B) Private Inurement

(C) Tax Fraud

(D) Private Benefit

142. Same facts as in Question 141 above, but assume instead that the discount is only being offered to specific physicians. To be eligible for the discount, the physicians have to have privileges at the hospital, provide either cardiology or neurology services, and be one of the top referring physicians to the hospital. The hospital is not advertising this publicly but has spread the word verbally to the medical staff. The IRS has been looking at this and is investigating whether this is an example of what prohibited activity that could result in loss of non-profit status even if *de minimis*?

(A) Private Benefit

(B) Private Inurement

(C) Tax Fraud

(D) Tax-Exempt Bond Financing

143. The hospital Board of Directors has just approved a contract between the hospital and a local car dealership to provide company cars to all executives of the hospital, along with all clinical department chairs. The Chair of the Board of Directors owns a 50% stake in the car dealership with which the hospital is contracting. The Chair did not participate in the vote by the Board of Directors to approve the contract. The Board of Directors reviewed three other proposals and selected this dealership based on its superior pricing. An IRS agent is asking some ques-

tions about this transaction and has stated that this looks like an excess benefit transaction. What is the Chair's best defense that this is *not* an excess benefit transaction?

(A) The Chair is not a "disqualified person" under the law.

(B) The Chair is willing to pay any excess benefit back.

(C) This qualifies for the rebuttable presumption of reasonableness.

(D) This was approved by the "organizational managers."

144. A hospital sets up as a non-profit corporation in the state of Indiana. The mission of the hospital under its state charter is to "provide tertiary and quaternary care to the residents of Franklin, Indiana, including residents who may not have the ability to pay." The hospital would also like to apply for tax-exempt status with the federal government through the IRS. What steps does the entity need to take in order to receive tax-exempt status through the IRS?

(A) The hospital needs to establish a charity care policy that must be reviewed and approved by the IRS in advance.

(B) The hospital can apply for tax-exempt status and attest to compliance with requirements of Section 501(c)(3).

(C) The hospital must conduct a community health needs assessment under Section 501(r)(3) before it can apply for tax-exempt status with the IRS.

(D) No additional steps are required because a hospital that is organized as a non-profit organization in a state is automatically granted federal tax exemption.

145. To qualify as a federally tax-exempt entity under Section 501(c)(3) of the Internal Revenue Code, an entity must fulfill an "exempt purpose." Which of the following is *not* considered an "exempt purpose" under federal law?

(A) Religious

(B) Scientific

(C) Educational

(D) Ensuring health and safety

Fraud & Abuse

146. A hospital is interested in leasing office space to a large physician practice in a medical office building owned by the hospital. All of the physicians in the practice have admitting privileges at the hospital and provide services there. To entice the physicians to rent space in the new building and to keep them close by, the hospital CEO would like to offer a discount off the standard market rental rate for the first three years. Will this violate the Anti-Kickback Statute?

(A) Likely no, so long as the discount is not excessive.

(B) Likely no, if the CEO's primary motivation is rental income.

(C) Likely yes, because of the referral relationship between the parties.

(D) Likely yes, but only if the primary purpose is to entice the physicians to refer more patients to the hospital.

147. The Physician Self-Referral Law (Stark Law), was enacted due to what concern of federal regulators in connection with referrals from physician practices?

(A) Physicians are more likely to refer patients for items or services if the physician stands to benefit financially from the referral.

(B) Physicians who refer patients to themselves provide duplicative services.

(C) Physicians should only refer to other physicians to ensure patient safety and quality.

(D) Physicians should not have an ownership position in lab companies.

148. Assume that the lease referenced above in Question 146 has been in place for two years and the hospital is now interested in purchasing the physician practice and employing the physicians. What exception(s) will the hospital need to look to in order to put together a physician purchase under the Stark Law?

(A) The isolated transactions exception

(B) The employment exception

(C) The personal services exception

(D) A and B only

149. A physician clinic provides routine physicals for all its patients and always orders and bills for a full blood screen test, even when a more limited blood screen is all that is necessary. Is this permissible under applicable billing regulations?

(A) Yes, because billing for the full blood screen test is permissible if the physician uses some of the results for purposes of making a diagnosis.

(B) Yes, because there are no prohibitions regarding how tests are ordered.

(C) No, because federal regulations require that physicians only bill for those services that are medically necessary.

(D) No, because federal regulations do not allow blood work to be billed separately from physician services.

150. Community Hospital buys a new electronic medical records and billing system that enables the hospital to "maximize its revenues." Using the new system, the hospital is now classifying 50% of its inpatient cardiology patients with a code that implies that the patient's condition is more complex. What type of fraud might the Office of Inspector General investigate for this type of action?

(A) Medicare Secondary Payor Rule

(B) Diagnosis-Related Group Creep

(C) Upcoding

(D) Medically unnecessary services

151. Dr. Smith starts advertising in the local paper about her new discount program to attract a greater volume of patients. Under the program, all patients will receive a discount that is the greater of 10% off the total cost of services or a co-pay waiver. This discount applies to all patients regardless of payor. Is this discount permissible under applicable law?

(A) Yes, because this is applied regardless of payor.

(B) Yes, because it is capped at either the discount or co-pay.

(C) No, because discounts can only be given for charity care.

(D) No, because this is a violation of the Civil Monetary Penalties law.

152. Dr. Brown has an X-ray machine in her office for use as needed to diagnose broken bones. She recently discovered that the X-ray machine has developed a warp on its side that makes X-rays entirely unreadable on the left side of the produced image. Dr. Brown cannot afford to fix the machine right now, but she also cannot afford to forego the revenue. So, she continues to order X-rays and to bill Medicare for the services. However, she is largely unable to diagnose the patients based on the image and typically refers them for a follow-up X-ray or MRI at a local outpatient diagnostic center. Is Dr. Brown violating any applicable federal regulations?

(A) Yes. Dr. Brown is billing for worthless services.

(B) Yes. Dr. Brown is upcoding.

(C) No. Dr. Brown is still diagnosing and treating the patient appropriately, even though based on a second image.

(D) No. Dr. Brown's use of the machine still works for certain purposes.

153. A physician's wife is a nurse practitioner who has ownership in a staffing company. The staffing company employs nurses and contracts to provide its services to various physician practices and other provider entities, including a radiology practice that owns and operates its own imaging center. The contract between the staffing company and the radiology group is paid based on an established salary for staff nurses, set at fair market value. The physician is in a position to refer patients to the radiology practice. Is this arrangement prohibited under the Stark Law?

(A) Yes, the Stark Law is violated unless an exception applies. This is a financial relationship because the physician's wife's ownership is imputed to the physician.

(B) Yes, the Stark Law is violated. The nurse's company may benefit because the radiology group might need more staffing if the physician refers patients to the radiology practice.

(C) No, the Stark Law is not violated. Radiologists do not have private patients.

(D) No, the Stark Law is not violated. This arrangement does not constitute a financial relationship because compensation between the staffing company and radiology practice does not vary with the volume or value of referrals.

154. Physician neurologist Dr. Jones has part ownership in a medical equipment leasing company. The leasing company owns a one-third interest in a physician practice management company, which in turn has an ownership position in a physician practice in which one of the physician owners is also part owner of a sleep lab to which Dr. Jones makes referrals. The sleep lab is unaware of the connection between its owners and Dr. Jones. If the lease arrangement varies with the volume or value of referrals, does this arrangement violate the Stark Law?

(A) Likely yes, because Dr. Jones is in a position to generate referrals for an entity with which he has a financial relationship under the Stark Law.

(B) Likely yes, because Dr. Jones's referrals to the sleep lab constitute physician self-referrals under the law.

(C) Likely no, because the sleep lab does not appear to have actual knowledge of, or be acting in reckless disregard or deliberate ignorance of, the fact that Dr. Jones has an indirect ownership or investment interest in the sleep lab.

(D) Likely no, because Dr. Jones's ownership interest is too indirect to implicate the Stark Law.

155. Metro Hospital is considering offering a continuing medical education program for the physicians on its medical staff and any physicians in the community. The CEO hopes that it will help to bring other physicians from the community to apply for privileges and remind its current staff what great services it has at the hospital. The program will provide monthly "lunch and learns" that will be available to all physicians in the community. Metro will advertise via mass email, social media, its website, and physician newsletters. Each month, there will be a

physician on staff at Metro who will present information about a new medical treatment. To ensure that people come, the CEO has agreed to provide a modest lunch for all participants valued at around $15 per person. What exception under the Stark Law is most likely to allow this arrangement?

(A) The "medical staff incidental benefits" exception

(B) The "professional courtesy" exception

(C) The "nonmonetary compensation" exception

(D) There is no applicable exception that would apply

156. Surgical Associates, a company that owns and operates ambulatory surgery centers (ASCs), is interested in opening a new center in Nashville that specializes in gastroenterology (the bulk of procedures will be colonoscopies). They would like to contract with Dr. Hernandez to serve as a consultant for the next six months while they identify space and establish the new center and then also contract with Dr. Hernandez under a longer-term contract (in excess of one year) where Dr. Jones will serve as medical director once the center is operational. Does the Stark Law apply?

(A) Yes, because the contract will be in excess of a year while Dr. Hernandez refers patients to the ASC.

(B) Yes, because the consulting relationship creates a financial relationship under the Stark Law.

(C) No, because there is no confirmation based on the facts above that Dr. Hernandez is making referrals.

(D) No, because the Stark Law does not apply based on the facts above.

157. Community Hospital is interested in opening a new ambulatory surgical center in Nashville that focuses strictly on plastic surgery. The hospital would like to contract with Dr. Smith, who is on staff at the hospital, to serve as a consultant for the next six months while the hospital identifies space and establishes the new center and then also contract with Dr. Smith under a longer-term contract (in excess of one year) where Dr. Smith will serve as medical director once the center is operational. Does the Stark Law apply?

(A) Yes, because the contract will be in excess of a year while Dr. Smith refers patients to the hospital.

(B) Yes, because his role as medical director of the ASC necessitates referrals.

(C) No, because plastic surgery likely does not involve the billing of federal health care programs.

(D) No, because Dr. Smith's services will not involve designated health services.

158. Dr. Yang is a primary care physician with his own practice. Dr. Yang is also part owner of a medical waste disposal company that contracts with physician offices. Dr. Yang's co-owner in the medical waste disposal company is an entity known as Medi-Waste, Inc. Medi-Waste purchases a durable medical equipment (DME) business that it also markets to physician practices. Dr. Yang refers patients to Medi-Waste's DME company. Is it illegal under any federal health care laws for Dr. Yang to refer patients to the DME company?

(A) Yes, because this is a financial relationship under the Stark Law and would be illegal without an exception.

(B) Yes, because this would be illegal under both the Anti-Kickback Statute and the Stark Law unless a safe harbor or exception applies.

(C) No, because the financial relationship does not implicate any federal health care law.

(D) No, because referrals for DME do not constitute designated health services.

159. City Hospital operates a birthing center, which provides normal newborn birth services (including c-sections) but also midwifery services and water births. City Hospital has decided to contract with a local ob-gyn group to provide 24/7 staffing of the birthing center. The CEO proposes the following terms: (1) hospital will pay the group a flat fee of $1,000,000 annually (based on fair market value data for similar practices), and (2) each member of the group will be eligible for an additional productivity bonus based on the number of relative value units (RVUs) performed by such physician from a bonus pool based on 5% of the net collections for the birthing center. Is this arrangement permissible under applicable federal law?

(A) This arrangement likely violates the Stark Law and Anti-Kickback Statute because of its compensation structure.

(B) This arrangement likely violates the Stark Law, but there is a safe harbor that is applicable under the Anti-Kickback Statute.

(C) This arrangement likely complies with the Stark Law and Anti-Kickback Statute because the compensation is set at fair market value.

(D) This arrangement likely complies with the Stark Law and Anti-Kickback Statute because birthing centers are unlikely to involve Medicare patients.

160. Since 2019, Physician Group, P.C., has leased space from Community Hospital under a written contract that complied with the Stark Law at the time the lease was entered. On April 15, 2022, Community Hospital was doing a review of its leases and realized that the lease with Physician Group, P.C., expired on December 31, 2021. Is this arrangement now in violation of the Stark Law?

(A) Likely yes. The agreement is expired and the Stark Law is a strict liability statute.

(B) Likely yes. The agreement involves a payment relationship between the hospital and the group.

(C) Likely no. So long as the parties amend the agreement to extend its term or enter into a new contract, this is not in violation of the Stark Law.

(D) No. The agreement does not constitute a "financial relationship."

161. Your client owns and operates several imaging companies across the country. You have been representing the company in defense of an action under the False Claims Act. One of the company's former employees has alleged that the company was engaged in a fraudulent billing scheme from 2020–2022 due to a practice adopted in 2019 where it billed separately (or unbundled) for certain codes that were intended to be bundled. The lawsuit was filed in August 2022. In July 2022, there were congressional hearings before a committee of the U.S. Congress about billing irregularities generally in the imaging industry. The relator did not report her findings to the government prior to the filing of her lawsuit. Is there any way that you can get the case dismissed?

(A) Probably yes, because the details were publicly disclosed at the congressional hearing.

(B) Probably yes, because the relator was not the original source of the information.

(C) Probably no, because the information discussed at the congressional hearing was not sufficiently detailed.

(D) Probably no, because the information was only discussed before a committee of Congress and not all of Congress.

162. Same facts as in Question 161 above, except instead of congressional hearings, there was an article in the local newspaper where the company is headquartered that discussed the problem of unbundling and provided a detailed account of two patients of your client whose bills reflected procedures that were billed separately. Is there any way that you can get the case dismissed?

(A) The court will likely dismiss the case because the details of the false claim were publicly disclosed by others in the article.

(B) The court will likely dismiss the case, but only if the relator is the original source.

(C) The court is unlikely to dismiss the case because the information in the article is not sufficiently detailed.

(D) The court is unlikely to dismiss the case because the relator did not inform the government prior to filing the lawsuit.

163. The Office of Inspector General (OIG) has issued multiple advisory opinions, guidance documents, and other bulletins and commentary on the practice of gainsharing. Which of the following best describes the practice of gainsharing?

(A) An arrangement in which a hospital pays a physician a share of any of the savings that the hospital realizes for patient care services through, at least in part, efforts of the physician

(B) An arrangement in which hospitals and physicians organize a legal entity for the purpose of negotiating contracts with third-party payors on a collective basis

(C) The practice of hospitals paying physicians to reduce and limit services to patients in an effort to maximize hospital profits

(D) An arrangement whereby physicians form independent practice associations for the purpose of increasing amounts paid for services, which are then divided equally among the physicians

Antitrust

164. Which of the following is *not* considered to be a *per se* violation of Section 1 of the Sherman Act (15 U.S.C. § 1)?
   (A) Exclusive dealing
   (B) Price fixing
   (C) Monopolization
   (D) Group boycotts

165. A large non-profit hospital company owns and operates four hospitals within a three-county radius of a major metropolitan area and is contemplating purchasing three more hospitals in the same area from a struggling for-profit hospital chain. The non-profit hospital company has a current market share of 68%. With the purchase of the additional hospitals, it will have a market share of close to 78% in the three-county radius. The in-house counsel for the non-profit hospital company has called you to ask what antitrust laws may be implicated by the potential purchase. Without knowing any additional facts, into what laws would you advise the in-house counsel to look?
   (A) Sherman Act Section 1 and the Clayton Act
   (B) Sherman Act Section 2 and the Clayton Act
   (C) Sherman Act Sections 1 and 2
   (D) Clayton Act

166. Same facts as in Question 165 above, but instead of a call from in-house counsel for the non-profit hospital company, you get a call from the non-profit hospital's competitor, a large academic medical center that owns and operates two hospitals in the area. The CEO of the academic medical center says that she has heard that the non-profit hospital company has threatened to pull out of its contracts with insurance companies in the market if the insurers do not agree (1) to increase the rate paid by the insurers to the three new hospitals to the same rate that the non-profit hospital company is receiving at its existing facilities and (2) that all

rates must be higher than the rates paid to the academic medical center. If what the CEO is saying is true, is this likely to be actionable under Sherman Section 2?

(A) Likely no, because while these discussions seem for the purpose of controlling pricing, the non-profit hospital company does not seem to possess sufficient market power.

(B) Likely no, because this is only actionable if the insurance companies agree to this through a meeting of the minds.

(C) Likely yes, because based on all of the facts, it would appear that the competitor is likely to be able to prove the elements of a Sherman Section 2 claim.

(D) Likely yes, because this is *per se* price fixing and thus illegal.

167. The Tennessee State Medical Association is a private association of physicians licensed and practicing in the state of Tennessee. Due to challenges that individual physicians are having with getting insurance companies/payors in the state to pay physicians sufficient wages for services, the leadership of the association suggests to the members that they collectively refuse to sign contracts with the insurance companies, forcing the companies to agree to higher wages. The leadership stressed that it was important for everyone to participate; otherwise, the insurance companies will have no incentive to change their rates. Even if this move is ultimately unsuccessful, what kind of activity might this be considered under Sherman Act Section 1?

(A) Price fixing

(B) Exclusive dealing

(C) Tying arrangement

(D) Group boycott

168. Same facts as in Question 167 above, but assume that instead of suggesting to members that they refuse to contract with the insurers, the leadership wrote a letter to all insurers in the area demanding an increase in rates, explaining how low the rates are relative to other areas of the country and how the low rates impact a physician's ability to practice. If a lawsuit were filed against the association under Sherman Act Section 1, under what test will a court analyze this claim?

(A) Rule of Reason

(B) Noerr-Pennington Doctrine

(C) Coordinated effects test

(D) Unilateral effects test

169. A large rehabilitation hospital company has decided to merge with a nursing home company that has several facilities in the Houston metropolitan area. With the purchase of the nursing home system, the rehabilitation hospital company will own and operate 60% of the market for

inpatient rehabilitation services. In analyzing whether this merger violates the Clayton Act, what two pieces of information will be key for the Federal Trade Commission?

(A) (1) whether the services are inpatient rehabilitation services or hospital and skilled nursing services and (2) how many facilities will be owned in total in the Houston area

(B) (1) whether the services are inpatient rehabilitation services or hospital and skilled nursing services and (2) what is the market for patients and residents of the merged entity

(C) (1) whether the hospital and nursing homes have a previous referral relationship and (2) what is the market for patients and residents of the merged entity

(D) (1) did the hospital have market power in the Houston area prior to the merger and (2) was the purchase of the nursing homes organic growth

Controlling Reproduction: Contraception, Sterilization, & Abortion

170. Taylor is 19 and pregnant with her third child. She dropped out of school after having her first child at 15. With little formal education and no access to affordable childcare, Taylor has struggled to earn enough money to care for her family. Because of her pregnancy, she is currently eligible for Medicaid. When she arrives at the hospital to deliver her baby, she tells her physician that she would like to have a tubal ligation while she has government health insurance. Taylor feels strongly that her family is complete and that additional children will hinder her ability to care for her existing children. Will Medicaid cover her sterilization?

    (A) Yes, Taylor is a competent adult with decisional capacity free to make her own reproductive choices.

    (B) Yes, when voluntary, it is cost effective for the state to pay for sterilization instead of future childbirth and other costs.

    (C) No, federal funds may not be used for voluntary sterilization because it is not medically necessary.

    (D) No, federal funds may not be used for sterilization when the patient is under the age of 21.

171. At 24 years old, Anna is editor-in-chief of law review and a top law student. She wants to lead the development of blockchain and cryptocurrency laws and sees childbearing as a hinderance to her life plan. She would like to be sterilized while she is still on her parent's health insurance so that she does not ever have to worry about becoming pregnant. What is likely to be the most significant barrier to Anna's being sterilized?

    (A) Most private health insurance does not cover voluntary sterilization.

    (B) Her parents may object to her sterilization and can veto the procedure as the insurance policy's primary beneficiary.

    (C) Her provider may decline to sterilize her.

    (D) Her fiancé wants children, and Anna cannot be sterilized without his consent given the impact her sterilization will have on his procreative choices.

172. Isa works two jobs to keep a roof over her head and to care for her four young children. She is 31 years old and suffers from heart disease. She has wanted to be sterilized for years, but her part-time jobs do not provide health insurance, and even if they did, it is difficult for her to find childcare and transportation to see a doctor. When she unexpectedly becomes pregnant and then suffers a miscarriage, she asks her doctor to sterilize her while she qualifies for Medicaid and is already at the hospital. Will Medicaid pay for her sterilization during this hospital visit?

(A) Yes, Isa is a competent adult with decisional capacity free to make her own reproductive choices.

(B) Yes, when voluntary, it is cost effective for the state to pay for sterilization instead of future childbirth and other costs.

(C) No, Isa is no longer eligible for Medicaid as a result of her miscarriage.

(D) No, Medicaid will not pay for sterilization until after a 30-day waiting period.

173. The guardian for a 27-year-old woman, Helen, with an IQ of 40, petitions the court for a sterilization order. Helen is unable to consent to the procedure personally, but her guardian argues that the procedure is in her best interest since she cannot comply with daily birth control pills, fought the placement of an IUD, and would not be capable of caring for any future offspring. What should the court do?

(A) Grant the order only if sterilization is in Helen's best interest, as shown more likely than not by the evidence.

(B) Grant the order only if sterilization is in Helen's best interest, as shown by clear and convincing evidence.

(C) Deny the order. No one should be sterilized without personally consenting, except to address a serious physical health problem.

(D) It is not clear. Helen's rights vary by state law and this issue is still an undecided question of U.S. constitutional law.

174. In *Griswold v. Connecticut*, 381 U.S. 479 (1965), the U.S. Supreme Court held that the Constitution protects the liberty of married couples to buy and use contraceptives without government interference. What was the constitutional basis for this holding?

(A) Right to marital privacy within penumbras from the First, Third, Fourth, and Fifth Amendments, as well as the Ninth Amendment

(B) Right to marital privacy based on the Ninth Amendment

(C) Liberty based on 14th Amendment substantive due process

(D) Equal protection under the 14th Amendment

175. Sam and Stacey are in a sexual relationship but not yet ready to become parents or to marry. If their state passes a law prohibiting the sale of contraceptives to unmarried couples, what is their best constitutional challenge to the law?

(A) Right to privacy in the bedroom of your home based on the Ninth Amendment

(B) Liberty based on 14th Amendment substantive due process

(C) Equal protection under the 14th Amendment

(D) Procreative justice under the 14th Amendment

176. Before being overturned, *Roe v. Wade*, 410 U.S. 113 (1973), recognized a constitutional right to abortion primarily pursuant to what provision of the Constitution?

(A) First Amendment

(B) Fourth Amendment

(C) Ninth Amendment

(D) 14th Amendment

177. Legally, what characteristic determines who or what is a "person" in the sense of being a rights bearer?

(A) Species and stage of development

(B) Capacity for consciousness

(C) Ability to communicate

(D) Ability to reason

178. Emma has an intrauterine device (IUD) that works primarily by preventing sperm from reaching her eggs but can also make implantation less likely. Zara uses birth control pills with hormones that prevent her ovaries from releasing eggs, prevent sperm from reaching the uterus, and make implantation of any fertilized egg less likely. Anya took emergency contraception to delay ovulation, i.e., release of her eggs, after her primary birth control method failed. Gabi always relies on condoms, which prevents sperm from reaching the egg but has no impact on implantation. All of the women wish to avoid pregnancy. Riley has been trying for years to become pregnant. Riley provided eggs for in vitro fertilization (IVF) with donated sperm, creating 12 embryos. Riley had two embryos implanted and eventually delivered two healthy babies. Ecstatic, Riley believes their family is now complete. Storage fees for the remaining 10 embryos are costly, and Riley has limited means. Riley would like to dispose of the remaining embryos. Under current constitutional law, which of the following is most accurate?

(A) Gabi has a constitutional right to utilize condoms because there is no "person" before a sperm fertilizes an egg. All other women's decisions may be prohibited by state law.

(B) None of the women's decisions impact an embryo that has been implanted. Prior to implantation, a woman is not "pregnant" and cannot "abort." Therefore, all of the women have a constitutional right to make the decisions they seek without governmental interference.

(C) Emma, Zara, Anya, and Gabi only intend to prevent a sperm and egg from joining, although Emma and Zara are aware that they may also make implantation of a fertilized egg less likely. Only Riley intends to destroy an embryo. Given the difference in intent and causation recognized in *Washington v. Glucksberg*, 521 U.S. 702 (1997), only Riley's actions may be prohibited by state law.

(D) Any of the above conclusions are possible post-*Dobbs*.

179. The ACA requires most group health plans and health insurance issuers to cover all FDA-approved contraceptive methods for women, as prescribed, without cost-sharing. Dan is an evangelical Christian who opposes IUDs and emergency contraceptives, which he regards as abortion. He owns a closely held corporation that employs more than one hundred workers. Dan contends that offering IUDs in the health insurance plan his company provides to workers would violate his religious beliefs. One of those workers, Rae, wants access to an IUD without cost. Will Dan's company be subject to fines if its plan fails to cover IUDs?

(A) Yes. There is no religious exemption to the ACA contraceptive mandate.

(B) Yes. Only an individual, not a corporation, is entitled to religious accommodation.

(C) No. A closely held corporation whose owners have a religious objection to the provision of IUDs is exempt, as there is a less restrictive means of furthering the government's interest in providing access to contraceptives.

(D) No. The health insurance company will directly provide birth control at no cost to covered women, regardless of plan terms.

180. A 38-weeks-pregnant woman, who is currently homeless and under the influence of cocaine, with a history of depression, presents at the hospital. The hospital informs the woman that she needs a caesarean section to protect the life of her child. The woman initially consents but leaves against medical advice when the hospital declines to feed her in preparation for surgery. The hospital now asks the Court for an order allowing the hospital to perform the caesarean section if the woman returns to the hospital, regardless of her express consent. The court must decide how to rule on the requested order. Which of the following tests does *not* reflect reasoning endorsed by a judge in a contested caesarean section case?

(A) Yes. A pregnant woman's right to refuse medical treatment can be overridden by the state's compelling interest in the life of a viable fetus. Because a caesarean section poses relatively little additional risk to the woman and the physician has testified it is necessary to save the life of the viable baby, a balancing of respective interests favors issuing the order.

(B) Yes. The woman appears to lack decisional capacity and has been equivocal on this decision in the past. She owes a special duty to her viable fetus, and a caesarean section does not significantly increase risk to her. Accordingly, her possible wishes should not be weighed as heavily as the life of the baby.

(C) No. If the woman has decisional capacity when she returns to the hospital, she is entitled to make this decision. Courts should never compel the violation of one person's bodily integrity for the benefit of another person.

(D) No. Absent clear and convincing evidence of consent, a surrogate may only authorize the caesarean section if it is in the best interest of the mother alone.

Assisting Reproduction

181. Noah and Ashanti have struggled to conceive for more than a year and hope to grow their family through in vitro fertilization (IVF). They live in a state with a personhood statute that recognizes rights beginning at conception and with an abortion ban that does not expressly exempt IVF. The abortion ban does exempt procedures involving a fatal fetal anomaly. They would like to retrieve and fertilize 15 eggs and then test all 15 blastocyst embryos with pre-implantation genetic diagnosis for Huntington's disease. They plan to implant the most active female embryo without the genetic mutation. Because storing embryos is expensive, they would like to dispose of any embryos with the mutation immediately and the remaining embryos after two live births. Which of the following is the most likely result under the state law described?

    (A) The abortion ban will not prohibit the proposed embryo destruction, as abortion requires termination of a pregnancy, and pregnancy requires having a fertilized egg within the body.

    (B) The abortion ban will not prohibit the proposed embryo destruction, but the personhood statute may mean that the planned embryo disposal raises other potential legal jeopardy.

    (C) The abortion ban will prohibit the proposed embryo destruction.

    (D) The abortion ban will prohibit the proposed embryo destruction only for the embryos without the genetic mutation for Huntington's disease.

182. Which of the following forms a presumptive basis for parentage under the Uniform Parentage Act (2017)? Note that there are five answer choices.

    (A) Birthing the baby

    (B) Marriage to the person who births the baby (at the time of birth or within 300 days before birth)

    (C) Residing in a household with the child for the child's first two years of life and holding the child out as the individual's own

    (D) A and B only

    (E) All of the above

183. Wyo. Stat. Ann. § 14-2-903 provides that "[a] man who provides sperm for, or consents to, assisted reproduction by a woman . . . with the intent to be the parent of her child, is the parent of the resulting child." Rewrite the statutory language of Section 903 to provide equal rights to women, non-binary individuals, transgender individuals, and those in same sex relationships.

ANSWER:

184. Sara and Chris, a married couple, have been trying to have a child for years without success. They enter into a surrogacy contract with Susan, which provides that Susan will receive health insurance and be paid $20,000 in exchange for carrying an embryo formed by gametes from Sara and Chris to term. During the pregnancy, Susan learns that Chris is sometimes violent toward Sara. Susan loves the soon-to-be-born baby she has carried inside of her for months and is not comfortable relinquishing the baby to a home with domestic violence. Susan would like to raise the baby in her small, low-income home with her spouse and two other children. Will Susan be able to do so in a state that has adopted the Uniform Parentage Act (2017)?

(A) Yes, because the best interests of the child determine parentage when the birth mother and the genetic mother are different.

(B) Yes, because a surrogate has 72 hours after birth to withdraw consent to the surrogacy agreement.

(C) No, because a gestational surrogate has no claim to parentage to a child conceived by assisted reproduction under a surrogacy agreement.

(D) No, because the intent of the parties at the time of the agreement governs.

185. Gabbi and Rafael wanted to become parents. After having difficulty conceiving by traditional means, they created and preserved a dozen pre-embryos for use in in vitro fertilization. Shortly after banking the pre-embryos, the couple split up. Gabbi would still like to have some of the pre-embryos implanted so that she can realize her dream of carrying a child. Rafael is in a new relationship and no longer wants to become a parent. Under *Davis v. Davis*, 842 S.W.2d 588 (Tenn. 1992), should the fertility clinic implant the embryos?

(A) Yes. Gabbi has decisional autonomy and should be able to consent to a medical procedure involving her body.

(B) Yes. A pre-embryo is a person, and, therefore, Rafael agreed to become a parent when he agreed to the creation of the pre-embryo.

(C) No. Absent a prior agreement regarding use of the pre-embryos in the event of the demise of the couple's relationship, the interests of the party wishing to avoid procreation will ordinarily prevail.

(D) No. Either person who provides gametes should be able to avoid procreation at any time and no prior agreement to the contrary will be enforceable.

Organ Transplantation

186. Who is primarily responsible for setting standards for and managing the procurement and distribution of organs in the United States?
   (A) State governments
   (B) United Network for Organ Sharing
   (C) Medicare and Medicaid
   (D) Hospitals

187. Which of the following is *not* a factor in rationing organs?
   (A) Anticipated compliance with aftercare
   (B) Risk of graft failure
   (C) Support system
   (D) Social worth criteria

188. Which of the following is *not* included in the National Organ Transplant Act of 1984?
   (A) It is unlawful to knowingly receive or transfer any human organ for valuable consideration for purposes of transplantation.
   (B) The definition of an organ includes cornea, bone marrow, and skin.
   (C) Living donors shall receive paid leave from work.
   (D) The definition of an organ applies to fetal parts as well as to parts of a human who was born.

189. When Sammah renewed her driver's license, she agreed to donate her organs. Unfortunately, she was later involved in a deadly car accident. She never discussed organ donation with her husband, and at the hospital, he refuses to agree to the donation of her organs. Sammah did not have a more formal advance directive. Can Sammah's husband lawfully revoke her donation?
   (A) Yes, because her husband is her health care surrogate.
   (B) Yes, because the driver's license is not clear and convincing evidence of Sammah's intent.

(C) No, because Sammah may not revoke her anatomical gift once made.

(D) No, because another person cannot revoke Sammah's anatomical gift unless expressly authorized to do so.

190. The demand for organ transplants greatly exceeds the supply of available organs. As a result, ethicists regularly debate the advantages and disadvantages of switching to a presumed consent system. What is presumed consent?

(A) An opt-out system for organ donation

(B) An opt-in system for organ donation

(C) A type of form for registering as an organ donor

(D) A requirement that all donate their organs regardless of personal preference

191. Austin is a competent 42-year-old male with two healthy kidneys. Most people can live normal, healthy lives with only one kidney. Austin's son Rhett has end stage renal disease and needs a kidney transplant. While Rhett is on the transplant waiting list, there is not currently a matching kidney available. Austin has a matching kidney and could become a living donor but has not consented to surgery. Rhett's physician opines that Rhett is likely to die without a transplant. Can a court legally order Austin to donate a kidney to his son?

(A) Yes. The state has a compelling state interest in the life of the child that can override Austin's right to refuse medical intervention, as the child will die without the transplant and the risk to the father is far lower.

(B) Yes. A parent owes a special duty to their child, as the child will die without the transplant and the risk to the father is far lower.

(C) No. The state may not override a competent adult's refusal of invasive medical intervention even to save the life of a child.

(D) No. The compelling state interest in the life of the child may override the parent's constitutional right to refuse medical intervention only when the medical intervention also provides benefit to the parent.

192. At the parents' request, can a physician legally declare a baby born with anencephaly, a uniformly lethal congenital absence of major portions of the brain, skull, and scalp, to be dead, in order to donate the baby's organs while they are still suitable for transplant?

(A) Yes. Babies with anencephaly almost always die within days regardless; the end justifies the means.

(B) Yes. Parents can make health care decisions for a child, and this decision could give meaning to the baby's brief life by saving other lives.

(C) No. Like a person in a persistent vegetative state, a baby with anencephaly is permanently unconscious but may still have brain stem functioning.

(D) No. A guardian ad litem, not the parents, must make such a request under the circumstances.

Human Subject Research & Experimental Treatment

193. What is the primary goal of human subject research?
    (A) Improve the health of the patient
    (B) Gain new knowledge for the good of society
    (C) Save other animals from unnecessary experimentation
    (D) Create economic wealth for companies, institutions, and individuals

194. What is "therapeutic misconception" in human subject research?
    ANSWER:

195. A billionaire just self-funded a large research study on inbreeding. What rules likely govern the informed consent required for the study's research subjects?
    (A) The Common Rule
    (B) The Common Rule and state law
    (C) State law
    (D) State law and FDA regulations

196. After receiving disclosure of potential risks, can parents consent to enroll their minor child in an asbestos study that will evaluate how asbestos exposure impacts health over time? The study provides a $5,000 college scholarship for participants.
    (A) Yes, because parents can consent to research on behalf of their minor child.
    (B) Yes, because parents can make health care decisions on behalf of their minor child, weighing risks and benefits under the circumstances.

(C) No, because minors cannot participate in human subject research.

(D) No, because parents cannot consent to research on behalf of their minor child that provides no potential benefit and entails significant health risks.

197. Researchers use existing de-identified DNA and linked same-sex sexual behavior survey responses to determine if certain gene mutations correlate to an increased likelihood of same-sex behavior. The researchers did not interact with the individuals who provided specimens and information. After the research results are published, one of the individuals who supplied DNA and survey responses argues that they should have been told that their DNA and information might be used for research that could exacerbate LGBTQIA+ group-based bias and discrimination. Does federal law require the researchers to disclose the purpose of the research and to obtain informed consent from the individual before use of the individual's DNA and responses?

(A) No, so long as the information and specimens are de-identified and there is no interaction between investigator and individual.

(B) Yes, researchers must obtain HIPAA consent.

(C) Yes, researchers must obtain Common Rule consent.

(D) Yes, researchers must obtain HIPAA and Common Rule consent.

198. Under the Common Rule and FDA regulation, what is the definition and significance of a human research study's being "minimal risk"?

ANSWER:

199. Which of the following is *not* a key criterion for Institutional Review Board (IRB) approval of human subject research?

(A) Risks to subjects are minimized

(B) Risks to subjects are reasonable in light of anticipated benefits, if any, and importance of knowledge reasonably expected to result from study

(C) Research furthers diversity, equity, and inclusion

(D) Selection of subjects is reasonable

200. Individuals who are part of an isolated Native American tribe consent to provide blood samples to a researcher "to study the causes of diabetes" in the tribe. After the research described, the blood samples are de-identified and used by another researcher to study early migration into what is now the United States. The second researcher concludes that people migrated to the isolated area of the tribe from Asia, contrary to the origin story of the tribe. If the individuals who provided blood want to sue, what is the best legal basis?

(A) Failure to disclose the purpose of the migration research pursuant to the Common Rule

(B) Breach of express or implied contract or informed consent pursuant to state law

(C) Failure to obtain consent for disclosure pursuant to HIPAA

(D) Failure to obtain informed consent pursuant to FDA regulations

201. A researcher collects tissue samples along with significant survey data for use in a study on the causes of breast cancer. The consent provides that the survey information and tissue samples may be used in subsequent research on other types of cancer. After the breast cancer research, the data and samples are used in research on the causes of cervical cancer, which can be linked to sexually transmitted infection. Participant data remains identifiable. A participant who provided a tissue sample and survey data is irate. Did the second researcher need to obtain specific consent from the individual prior to research?

(A) Yes, secondary researchers must always obtain specific consent for their particular use of identifiable information or specimens.

(B) Yes, secondary researchers must obtain consent for use of identifiable information or specimens involving sexually transmitted infections or other sensitive research.

(C) No, secondary researchers never have to obtain informed consent.

(D) No, when the initial researcher obtains broad consent, secondary researchers need not obtain participant consent for further research within the scope of the consent.

202. The Bayh-Dole Act attempts to spur an entrepreneurial approach to academic research by giving property rights in the products of such research to researchers and institutions, even when federally funded. How might this approach unintentionally increase research conflicts of interest?

ANSWER:

203. In *Abigail Alliance for Better Access to Developmental Drugs v. Von Eschenbach*, 495 F.3d 695 (D.C. Cir. 2007), the plaintiff sought access to a drug that had not yet been FDA-approved, outside of a clinical trial, after exhausting all other available approved potentially life-saving options. How did the Court rule?

(A) Substantive due process protects a competent adult's right to try unapproved drugs when all other approved options have been exhausted.

(B) History and tradition include government restriction on access to drugs not (yet) shown to be safe and effective, and accordingly, competent adults do not have a substantive due process right to try unapproved drugs.

(C) Equal protection requires that competent adults with conditions that cannot be treated by approved drugs have access to unapproved drugs.

(D) Denial of access to an unapproved drug constitutes cruel and unusual punishment.

204. Under the federal Right to Try Act, which of the following is *not* required to access an investigational medicine not yet approved by the FDA?

(A) A patient must have been diagnosed with a terminal disease.

(B) A patient must have exhausted approved treatment options.

(C) A patient must be unable to participate in a clinical trial involving the investigational medicine.

(D) An investigational drug must have completed Phase I testing and be involved in an ongoing phase II or phase III trial.

205. Despite the federal Right to Try Act and similar state laws, investigational drugs not yet approved by the FDA often remain unavailable to patients. List three common reasons why.

ANSWER:

206. How is the federal Right to Try Act different from the FDA's Expanded Access program?

ANSWER:

Medical Aid in Dying & Other End-of-Life Issues

207. At least ten states allow medical aid in dying, typically through so-called Death with Dignity Acts. Under such statutes, which patients typically have the right to choose to hasten death?
    (A) Competent adults
    (B) Competent adults with a terminal disease
    (C) Competent adults with a terminal disease who are physically and mentally able to self-administer the prescribed drugs that hasten death
    (D) Competent adults over the age of 65 with a terminal disease who are physically and mentally able to self-administer the prescribed drugs that hasten death

208. What practical barrier(s) may prevent a patient who satisfies the stated criteria for medically assisted dying from having access to it? Note that there are five answer choices.
    (A) Providers may be unwilling to prescribe drugs that hasten death, and they are not legally required to do so
    (B) Willing providers may be geographically inaccessible, especially since a second provider is commonly required for confirmation
    (C) This type of care may be financially inaccessible because some insurance, including Medicare, does not pay for drugs that hasten death
    (D) A and B
    (E) All of the above

209. Even with robust procedural protections required by law, some have expressed concern that medical aid in dying might still be tainted by coercion, bias, or lack of choice. Which of the following is *not* a commonly stated concern regarding truly autonomous decision-making for medical aid in dying?
    (A) Inadequate resources hinder the ability of those with disabilities to participate in activities of life.
    (B) Bias and undervaluing of certain characteristics and groups, especially toward dependence and advanced age, cause individuals to believe that they should choose a medically assisted death.

(C) Higher rates of medical aid in dying among traditionally marginalized racial minorities suggest that the practice is a proxy for devaluing these groups.

(D) There is inadequate oversight to ensure that procedural protections contained in law are enforced in practice.

210. What was the Court's holding in *Washington v. Glucksberg*, 521 U.S. 702 (1997), a 5-4 decision on the right to die?

(A) Washington state law prohibiting assisted suicide with no exception for medical aid in dying violates the Equal Protection Clause of the U.S. Constitution.

(B) Washington state law prohibiting assisted suicide with no exception for medical aid in dying violates the Due Process Clause of the U.S. Constitution.

(C) Washington state law prohibiting assisted suicide with no exception for medical aid in dying does not violate the U.S. Constitution because it is narrowly tailored to a compelling state interest.

(D) Washington state law prohibiting assisted suicide with no exception for medical aid in dying does not violate the U.S. Constitution because it is rationally related to a legitimate state interest.

211. The 14th Amendment provides that no state shall "deprive any person of life, liberty, or property, without due process of law; nor deny to any person within its jurisdiction the equal protection of the laws." How does procedural due process differ from substantive due process?

ANSWER:

212. In *Washington v. Glucksberg*, 521 U.S. 702 (1997), what did the Court look to in order to determine the scope of unenumerated liberty interests protected by the U.S. Constitution?

(A) The text of the Constitution

(B) History and tradition

(C) History and tradition, as well as emerging awareness of the dignity and autonomy of affected individuals

(D) None of the above

213. What state interests might support a state law that prohibits medical aid in dying?

ANSWER:

214. In *Vacco v. Quill*, 521 U.S. 793 (1997), what did a unanimous U.S. Supreme Court hold?

(A) New York law criminalizing assisted suicide does *not* violate the Equal Protection Clause, even though state law allows competent adults to refuse or withdraw lifesaving medical treatment.

(B) New York law criminalizing assisted suicide violates the Equal Protection Clause because it allows some to hasten death and not others.

(C) New York law's distinction between ending lifesaving medical treatment and assisting suicide is arbitrary and irrational.

(D) New York law criminalizing assisted suicide faces strict scrutiny because it targets a suspect class.

215. Assume the following patients have reached the terminal stage of their disease and reside in a state that has authorized medical aid in dying. Which patient(s) are *most* likely to be able to hasten death if they so choose?

(A) A patient with amyotrophic lateral sclerosis (ALS) who is mentally capable but can no longer use her hands or swallow

(B) A patient who has Alzheimer's disease and is no longer mentally capable but completed an advance directive requesting medical aid in dying while still capable

(C) A patient who has congestive heart failure and is struggling with depression

(D) A patient of advanced age who has cancer

216. In *Cruzan v. Director, Missouri Department of Health*, 497 U.S. 261 (1990), a case involving a parental request for withdrawal of hydration and nutrition from a patient in a persistent vegetative state, what did the U.S. Supreme Court hold?

(A) The Due Process Clause may protect a liberty interest in refusing life-sustaining medical treatment

(B) The State has an interest in the preservation of human life

(C) A and B, requiring balancing between the individual liberty interest and the state interest

(D) None of the above

217. Courts often treat a competent patient seeking to withdraw life-sustaining care differently from a surrogate seeking withdraw on behalf of a no longer or never competent patient. Which of the following most accurately reflects the reasoning of cases, such as *Bouvia v. Superior Court*, 225 Cal. Rptr. 297 (Ct. App. 1986), involving a competent adult seeking to refuse or withdraw life-sustaining care, including artificial nutrition and hydration?

(A) The state has no interest at stake

(B) The state has an interest in preservation of life and prevention of suicide that outweighs the individual's right to refuse medical treatment

(C) The state has an interest in preservation of life and prevention of suicide but that interest does not outweigh the individual's right to refuse medical treatment

(D) The state may prevail if it shows that its law is rationally related to a legitimate state interest

218. An 84-year-old patient with multiple end-stage conditions is in a persistent vegetative state and needs dialysis three times a week to respond to end-stage renal disease. Providers would like to stop dialysis, which they consider "futile." Relatives wish to continue treatment. The patient does not have an advance directive. It is unclear whether or not the patient can feel pain. The dialysis will remove excess fluid and waste products from the patient's body as intended. The providers maintain that, under the circumstances, this will only prolong the dying process. How should a court respond?

(A) Defer to the surrogate decision-maker, the relatives, who can insist on any care they desire

(B) Defer to the providers, who have the medical expertise to determine futility

(C) Consult state law, especially any state Health Care Decisions Act or futility statute, but also consider common law and constitutional rights to determine who has authority to decide under the circumstances

(D) Consult the hospital ethics committee, and then defer to the providers if the committee agrees with them after allowing 10 days for potential transfer

219. Under the Uniform Determination of Death Act (1980), a physician may declare a patient dead if, in accordance with accepted medical standards, the patient has sustained which of the following?

(A) Irreversible cessation of cardiopulmonary function

(B) Irreversible cessation of all function of the entire brain

(C) A or B

(D) A and B

Topic 25 Questions

Public Health

220. How does public health differ from individual health care decision-making?
ANSWER:

221. What is the legal source of a state's ability to enact public health measures?
ANSWER:

222. Public health measures can be controversial when they trade-off with individual rights. What individual rights are commonly abridged by public health laws?
ANSWER:

223. Which of the following is a public health measure? Note there are five answer choices.
(A) Quarantine order to respond to an infectious disease
(B) Public education on hand washing to combat infectious disease

(C) Mandatory seatbelt law

(D) A and B

(E) All of the above

224. What standard of review did the Supreme Court apply in *Jacobson v. Massachusetts*, 197 U.S. 11 (1905), to determine whether a local Board of Health vaccine requirement impermissibly infringed individual rights protected by the U.S. Constitution?

(A) Strict scrutiny

(B) Intermediate review

(C) Rational review

(D) Has no real or substantial relation to protecting public health, or is, beyond all question, a plain, palpable invasion of rights; arbitrary or so far beyond what was reasonably required for the safety of the public

225. A state adopts a vaccine mandate for public school attendance. What exemption(s), if any, must be included to avoid constitutional infirmity?

(A) Objection based on sincerely held religious belief, observance, or practice

(B) Objection based on conviction that the potential harms of the vaccine outweigh any potential benefits

(C) Individual medical contraindication

(D) All of the above

226. In response to an airborne infectious disease, a city in California issues a public health order that restricts religious gatherings of 10 or more people while allowing Walmart to remain open with social distancing. If a church brings a free exercise case challenging the order, what standard of review should apply?

(A) Strict scrutiny

(B) Intermediate review

(C) Rational review

(D) Has no real or substantial relation to protecting public health, or is, beyond all question, a plain, palpable invasion of rights; arbitrary or so far beyond what was reasonably required for the safety of the public

227. Public health measures are sometimes invalidated under the non-delegation doctrine. What fundamental principle underpins this legal doctrine?

(A) Limited government

(B) Separation of powers

(C) Federalism

(D) Liberty

228. Public health authority can also be constrained by administrative law. What statute typically defines required administrative procedures?

ANSWER:

229. While unfounded myths often overstate the relative risk of vaccination, vaccines can occasionally cause rare side effects. A young woman has an adverse reaction to a recommended vaccine. What is her legal remedy?

(A) Product liability claim against the manufacturer

(B) Malpractice claim against her physician

(C) National Vaccine Injury Program

(D) A and C

230. In 2018, the Surgeon General issued an advisory on e-cigarette use among youth, declaring such use an epidemic and stating that e-cigarette use can lead to addiction and harm to developing brains and lungs. The advisory estimates that, in 2018, one in five high school students used e-cigarettes, a 900% increase in four years. Should youth e-cigarette use be declared a "public health emergency" as that phrase is defined in the Model State Emergency Health Powers Act of 2001?

(A) Yes. Because youth e-cigarette use has been declared an epidemic, it constitutes a public health emergency.

(B) Yes. Because youth e-cigarette use impacts millions, is harmful, and has been declared an epidemic, it constitutes a public health emergency.

(C) No. Youth e-cigarette use is not caused by bioterrorism, natural disaster, or other cause prescribed in the definition.

(D) No. A public health emergency requires a contagious disease and e-cigarette use is not contagious.

Questions

Practice Exam

231. Maria Hernandez is a licensed nurse practitioner within her state of residence and practices at a small five-physician cardiology practice. Nurse Hernandez provides services to patients with chronic and acute heart disease. The Board of Nursing recently sent Nurse Hernandez a letter stating that based on the reports of several patients Nurse Hernandez is providing diagnostic services beyond a nurse practitioner's scope of practice. Specifically, the Board alleges that her diagnostic practices constitute the practice of medicine. If Nurse Hernandez's license is suspended by the Board of Nursing and Nurse Hernandez brings an action in court alleging wrongful revocation of her license, what is her best argument in court?
    - (A) Nurse Hernandez's services have never harmed patients.
    - (B) Nurse Hernandez has had a flawless practice history and has never had any disciplinary actions taken against her prior to this incident.
    - (C) The Board of Nursing refused to review a report submitted by Nurse Hernandez regarding the use of the diagnostic equipment for the purpose of managing a plan of care for patients with chronic heart disease.
    - (D) The Board of Nursing decided to revoke Nurse Hernandez's license despite the fact that the hearing officer recommended a five-year suspension.

232. The Privacy Officer at County Community Hospital has been notified about a ransomware attack that has hit the hospital. An employee clicked a link that she thought was for a software update but was really for a virus. All files on the hospital's server have been frozen and are inaccessible to the hospital, and the attackers are demanding a Bitcoin ransom of 25 Bitcoin (around $500,000). The hospital reports the attack to the FBI and attempts to recover its files through backups. It takes three weeks, and the hospital has to turn away patients. The hospital cannot determine whether any data was accessed by the hackers. Does the hospital have any HIPAA liability for this intentional act by a third party?
    - (A) Yes. Although the hospital did not cooperate with the hackers, it is not clear whether protected health information has been shared. This is likely a presumed breach.
    - (B) Yes. All ransomware attacks are considered HIPAA breaches.

(C) No. There is no HIPAA breach until the hospital is able to determine whether protected health information has been accessed by the hackers.

(D) No. The Office of Civil Rights does not require that ransomware attacks be reported as HIPAA breaches since ransomware attacks are not the fault of the provider.

233. Which of the following would likely not fall under a hospital's duty of care, as described in *Thompson v. Nason Hospital*, 591 A.2d 703 (Pa. 1991)?

(A) Wife is visiting husband in the hospital and wife trips on a loose board on a stairwell and is injured.

(B) Delusional patient ends up jumping out of the hospital window because hospital policy was vague or not followed regarding use of restraints.

(C) Patient is injured as a result of surgery performed by a physician who has been sued for malpractice in excess of five times.

(D) Patient is injured when physician performing surgery accidentally cuts liver duct and bile pours into the abdomen unbeknownst to the nursing staff. Patient is discharged before signs and symptoms appear.

234. What aspect of the Affordable Care Act was upheld as constitutional under Congress's taxing power in *National Federation of Independent Business (NFIB) v. Sebelius*, 567 U.S. 519 (2012)?

(A) The expansion of Medicaid to all individuals earning less than 135% of the FPL

(B) The requirement that individuals who file taxes are required to purchase a health insurance policy with minimum coverage obligations or pay a tax

(C) The obligation of employers to provide health insurance with minimum coverage obligations

(D) The obligation that employers provide subsidies and credits to individuals reimbursable by the federal government

235. Under the Affordable Care Act, insurers can rate (charge based on individual characteristics) individuals on which of the following two things?

(A) Age and sex

(B) Sex and race

(C) Sex and disability

(D) Age and tobacco use

236. A non-profit hospital in Big City is struggling to stay afloat and has been contemplating various options that might boost its revenues. The hospital was originally formed in 1822 with the charitable purpose of "providing inpatient health care needs to the people of Big City." A substantial amount of its business is women's services, and it has considered shutting down the

hospital and converting itself into a birthing center. To do this, it has thought about merging with a for-profit company. Under the transaction, it would sell all or substantially all of its assets other than that equipment used exclusively for women's services (which constitutes about 2% of the hospital's total asset value) to a third party and then merge the nonprofit into a new legal entity co-owned by the for-profit entity. Other than the hospital's Board of Directors, what other approvals might be required by the hospital before the assets can be sold?

(A) The Centers for Medicare and Medicaid Services must first approve the change of ownership to maintain the ability to treat Medicaid patients.

(B) The state Department of Health has to approve any changes that impact the license of any entity licensed in the jurisdiction.

(C) The state's Attorney General is likely required to approve the transaction to ensure that the sale is in the best interest of the general public.

(D) Only the Board of Directors is required to approve the deal; all other agencies impacted, such as the Department of Health, can receive notice only.

237. Same facts as above, but assume that the Board of Directors had a meeting to discuss this potential transaction that lasted approximately 30 minutes. The transaction itself was only discussed for approximately 15 minutes, as the directors did not have any questions following the CEO's presentation recommending the transaction to the Board. The Board unanimously approved the sale and instructed the CEO to proceed with closing. Several residents in the area surrounding the hospital are very upset about the news that the hospital will be closing, as it will mean that the residents must drive over 20 miles to the next closest hospital, which takes approximately 40 to 45 minutes in traffic. If the neighbors file suit to stop the sale or otherwise object to the sale, what duty might they allege the board members breached that would give the neighbors the best chance of success?

(A) Breach of duty of loyalty, because the Board was concerned only about the financial situation of the hospital and failed to consider the health care needs of the people of Big City.

(B) Breach of duty of care, because the meeting was too short to render a decision of this magnitude.

(C) Breach of duty of obedience, because the board failed to focus on how this sale would be in furtherance of the mission of the hospital.

(D) None, as this decision will be protected by the business judgment rule.

238. Dr. Jones is convicted of unlawfully distributing oxycontin to patients not in need of the prescription, which is a Class E felony in his state. He is sentenced to nine months of probation. Dr. Jones primarily served Medicaid patients, and the Court found that the Medicaid program paid over $100,000 for improper prescriptions. The Court further found that Dr. Jones was also using oxycontin during the time, as part of his defense at trial was an impaired mental capacity. What is the most likely response from the Office of Inspector General regarding Dr. Jones's status with federal health care programs?

(A) Dr. Jones will be permissively excluded from federal health care programs for at least three years with the overpayment amount being an aggravating factor.

(B) Dr. Jones will be mandatorily excluded from federal health care programs for at least five years with the overpayment amount being an aggravating factor.

(C) Dr. Jones will be mandatorily excluded from federal health care programs for at least five years with his substance abuse being an aggravating factor.

(D) Dr. Jones will be mandatorily excluded from federal health care programs for at least three years with his substance abuse being a mitigating factor.

239. Sally Smith works as a surgical technician for a large academic medical center. Sally has noticed that, frequently, an attending physician is scheduled for several overlapping surgeries. To maintain this schedule, the attending physician begins the surgery in one room, then leaves the resident physician (a physician still in training during a four-year training period after graduation from medical school) to finish the surgery. Sally knows that the Medicare Conditions of Participation require that a licensed physician (the attending physician) be present during the "key portions" of the surgery, directly supervising the work of the resident, to bill Medicare for the services of the resident. Sally suspects that the hospital is billing for the surgeries as if the attending physician is providing direct supervision for the key portions of the surgeries, but based on the schedule, it seems this is likely impossible. Assuming Sally's suspicions are true, is this a viable claim under the False Claims Act?

(A) No. False Claims Act liability does not extend to violations that allege merely non-compliance with a regulation.

(B) Likely no. Most courts have concluded that implied false certification claims are not viable.

(C) Yes. Implied false certification claims are actionable under the False Claims Act.

(D) Likely yes, so long as Sally can prove that the violation of this implied false certification would be material to the federal government.

240. Metro General Hospital (MGH) is a 200-bed hospital located in Metropolis, a large urban city with a population of more than 250,000. MGH is owned and operated by the City of Metropolis and has been in operation since the early 1900s. It treats any and all residents of the City of Metropolis, regardless of the ability to pay. MGH has meager resources. It provides primary and tertiary care, with very few specialty services. St. Michael's Hospital is a 350-bed academic medical center located just outside the city limits of Metropolis in an affluent suburb. St. Michael's Hospital provides a high level of care and a full range of services, including the state's only Level I Trauma Center, and other quaternary care. St. Michael's also has two other satellite hospitals that are part of its health system that are located within Washington County — the county in which Metropolis is located. St. Michael's is the largest provider in the area, with 55% market share. MGH has been struggling financially and its census has declined

in recent years. It is currently the smallest provider in the market, with only 11% market share. There is a third health system in the county that has two hospitals, which collectively have about 30% market share. St. Michael's is interested in acquiring MGH. You are concerned that this could be problematic under federal antitrust law. Which antitrust law likely presents the biggest risk based on the facts above?

(A) Sherman Act Section 2, because of St. Michael's action in connection with this acquisition.

(B) Sherman Act Section 1, because of St. Michael's and MGH's collective plans to merge.

(C) Clayton Act Section 7, because of the potential of the merger's competitive effects.

(D) None, because of the application of the Noerr-Pennington Doctrine.

241. Same facts as in Question 240 above, but assume that the parties have completed the acquisition and MGH is now part of the St. Michael's system. A few months after the completion of the acquisition, the Federal Trade Commission (FTC) opened an investigation into the merger's competitive effects. Based on the facts, what information, if true, may be the best way for St. Michael's to rebut the presumption that the merger is anticompetitive?

(A) The consolidation of MGH's operations into St. Michael's will result in more efficient and effective operations with lower costs overall for the hospitals, resulting in better consumer pricing.

(B) Patients will be transferred more easily to St. Michael's for specialty services not available at MGH.

(C) MGH's financial position will be stronger because the merger will likely enable MGH to charge higher hospital rates to payors and thus consumers.

(D) MGH serves a market that St. Michael's does not currently have in the urban core, and the merger will offer St. Michael's superior services to more patients.

242. A group of private investors is interested in building a hospital in a growing area south of a major city for residents who do not want to travel into the city for their care. The investors have done market analysis and determined that the average level of income in the targeted area, along with the percentage of individuals who have private commercial insurance, will make this a profitable market. The group is from out of town and is not familiar with the state laws that might impact the building of a hospital in the market. Which state law, if applicable in this state, could have the biggest impact on their plans?

(A) The Corporate Practice of Medicine Doctrine

(B) The State Action Doctrine

(C) A Certificate of Need law

(D) The Stark Law

243. Jane Alvarez needs a hip replacement. Her physician, Dr. Hernandez, schedules Jane for surgery at City Hospital. During the surgery, it is the responsibility of the first assistant, Sally Jones, who is a City Hospital employee, to count the number of sponges being used during the surgery and then to assure they have the same number of sponges at the end of the surgery. Sally gets distracted during the surgery and loses count. She does not want Dr. Hernandez to get mad at her though. So Sally lies and tells Dr. Hernandez that all the sponges are accounted for. Jane has complications from a sponge left in her abdomen and requires follow-up surgery and five additional days in the hospital. Jane would like to file suit against the hospital for her increased medical bill and for her pain and suffering caused by the sponge complications. Will Jane be able to sustain a claim against the hospital?

(A) Yes, because under *Thompson v. Nason Hospital*, Jane could show that the hospital policy requiring the first assistant to count the sponges is ineffective or inadequate.

(B) Yes, because the hospital is vicariously liable for the acts of Sally, the hospital's agent.

(C) Yes, because the hospital is directly liable for the acts of Sally, the hospital's agent.

(D) No. Because Dr. Hernandez is the "captain of the ship," it is unlikely that Jane will be able to sustain this claim against the hospital.

244. Mario Fiorella has been experiencing heart palpitations and is searching for a cardiologist. He has noticed billboards on the highway around his rural town for Miller County Community Hospital, the closest hospital to his home. The image of Dr. Rosalina Rossi, a cardiologist, appears on several billboards with the phrase "Miller Meets Your Heart Needs." There is a caption on the corner of the billboard that reads "Dr. Rosalina Rossi, cardiologist." Mario makes an appointment with Dr. Rossi, who concludes that Mario needs bypass surgery. Dr. Rossi asks Mario where he lives and schedules surgery at Miller County Community Hospital the following week. In addition to privileges at Miller County Community Hospital, Dr. Rossi also has privileges at two other hospitals within the 60-mile radius of Miller County Community Hospital and rents space near each hospital on different days of the week. There is a complication during Mario's surgery, and Dr. Rossi damages Mario's heart, resulting in Mario's needing a pacemaker for the rest of his life. Mario would like to sue Miller County Community Hospital for the damage to his heart and for his additional medical bills. Will Mario be able to sustain a claim against Miller County Community Hospital?

(A) No. The damage was caused by Dr. Rossi's negligence, and the hospital is not liable for Dr. Rossi's acts.

(B) No, unless it can be shown that Dr. Rossi was serving as an employee of Miller County Community Hospital at the time of the surgery.

(C) Yes, if it can be shown that Mario reasonably relied on the Miller County Community Hospital billboard in making his decision to seek care from Dr. Rossi and the hospital.

(D) Yes, because Dr. Rossi had privileges to practice at two other hospitals.

245. Frank Jones presents at the emergency room claiming a work-related injury. This is the third time in six months that Frank has appeared in the emergency room. The nurse is suspicious that Frank is seeking medication for an addiction. The nurse tells the doctor as the doctor is entering the room, "Watch that guy in Room 3. He is here all the time. He just wants drugs to feed his habit. Don't believe a word he says about getting hurt at work." The doctor does a cursory screening of Frank's injuries, denies him any care, and sends him on his way. Frank goes to a neighboring hospital and is diagnosed with a brain bleed. He suffers complications from the brain bleed, requiring several months of rehabilitation. Can Frank sustain a claim against the hospital for violations of Section 504 of the Rehabilitation Act of 1973?

(A) Probably yes, so long as Frank can prove that at least one motivation for the failure to treat was because of Frank's perceived substance use disorder.

(B) Probably yes, so long as Frank can prove that the sole motivation for the failure to treat was because of Frank's perceived substance use disorder.

(C) Probably no, because Frank has no known disability.

(D) Probably no, because Frank was screened appropriately and any failure to treat is mere negligence.

246. After valid informed consent, a 16-year-old patient receives gender-affirming vaginoplasty, a genital surgery, from a general surgeon. Unfortunately, this patient becomes one of the rare one percent of patients who later regrets surgery. Upon becoming a legal adult, the patient decides to sue the surgeon for malpractice. During trial, the patient would like to submit the Endocrine Society's clinical practice guidelines, which recommend delaying gender-affirming genital surgery until the patient is 18 years old. Founded in 1916, the Endocrine Society is one of the leading professional medical organizations involved in gender-affirming care. Should the Court allow this evidence to be admitted?

(A) No, because the general surgeon is not a member of the Endocrine Society nor does she hold herself out as an endocrinologist.

(B) No, because the clinical practice guidelines of the World Professional Association for Transgender Health (WPATH), another leading medical organization for gender-affirming care, suggest that there may be benefit to vaginoplasty performed before age 18, making the Endocrine Society guidelines irrelevant.

(C) No, because clinical practice guidelines are generally not relevant for purposes of establishing the standard of care.

(D) Yes, because the clinical practice guidelines are relevant to, although not dispositive of, the standard of care.

247. In 2005, after watching the movie *Million Dollar Baby*, Kat tells her husband, Harry, that she never wants to be kept alive as a "vegetable." However, in 2010, Kat signs a valid advance di-

rective stating, among other things, that if she is terminally ill or injured, she wants to have life-sustaining treatment. Kat's advance directive is never revoked. Unfortunately, in 2012, Kat is in a car accident and suffers significant permanent brain damage. Physicians opine that Kat needs a ventilator and artificial hydration to live as long as possible. Harry is sure that Kat would not want a ventilator or artificial hydration under the circumstances. Kat's brother, Beau, is equally certain that Kat would want artificial hydration but not a ventilator. Beau also reports that, although not separated, Kat's marriage to Harry is on the rocks, and Beau questions whether Harry has Kat's best interests at heart. If Kat's state follows the Uniform Health Care Decision Act, what care will she receive?

(A) Kat will receive a ventilator and artificial hydration. The physician knows best, and life should always be preserved as long as possible.

(B) Kat will receive a ventilator and artificial hydration because she never revoked her advance directive which calls for life-sustaining treatment.

(C) Kat will receive artificial hydration but not ventilation. Her brother clearly has her best interests at heart, and this is a middle ground given the uncertainty of her wishes.

(D) Kat will not receive either hydration or ventilation because her husband is her default health care surrogate, and he has authority to decide what care she will receive.

248. Jacob is 62 years old, single, has no children, and has an income of $12,000 per year and assets in the bank worth $250,000. Assume that 100% of the FPL for an individual is $13,580 per year. Jacob is a U.S. citizen who lives in a non-expansion state. His employer does not provide health insurance. To which government health insurance benefit is he entitled, if any?

(A) Medicare

(B) Medicaid

(C) Premium tax subsidy to purchase individual insurance

(D) He is not entitled to any government health insurance benefit

249. Hussein has terminal cancer and is in significant pain that is difficult to control effectively without impairing his lucidity. He is affluent, 84 years old, and has lived a good life. He would like to live another 10 years and see his grandchildren happily married, but since that is almost certainly impossible, he would like his family to gather from across the country to usher him into what he believes will be eternal life. In the majority of states, what best describes Hussein's legal rights?

(A) As a competent adult, Hussein may seek and obtain medical aid in dying from his health care physician, just as he would any other prescription medicine.

(B) If Hussein signs a written request, fulfills the waiting period, and has two qualified providers sign off, he will have the choice of medical aid in dying.

(C) Hussein cannot be prescribed medical aid in dying to end his life within hours, but he may be prescribed palliative sedation. Palliative sedation intends comfort not death, but it is likely to result in Hussein's death within a week or so.

(D) Hussein may not be prescribed medication known to hasten death.

250. Once a physician-patient relationship is formed, which of the following best captures the duties a physician owes to a patient, if any?

(A) The physician will owe those duties agreed to between the parties.

(B) Informed consent, confidentiality, professional care, and to act primarily for charitable purpose.

(C) Informed consent, confidentiality, continuing attention, and professional care.

(D) The physician does not owe the patient any duties.

251. Which of the following categories of individuals do *not* receive additional protections for human subject research otherwise subject to the Common Rule?

(A) Prisoners

(B) Children

(C) Terminally ill individuals

(D) Pregnant women

252. Tina, a 25-year-old law student, would like to earn extra money while also making a difference in others' health and well-being. Which one of the following would best enable Tina to legally maximize her extra income?

(A) Donate her eggs for $8,000

(B) Donate plasma twice a week, every week for a year, for a total of $6,000

(C) Donate a kidney for approximately $73,000

(D) None of the above. U.S. law prohibits Tina from selling part of her body for income.

253. Maria is a 45-year-old woman at average risk for breast cancer. In 2022, her doctor recommends a mammogram, which reveals a small lump in her left breast. As a result, the doctor recommends a breast biopsy and discloses the small risk of bleeding and infection and the benefit of ruling out cancer. The doctor also discloses watchful waiting as an alternative. Maria agrees to the biopsy, and after anxious weeks, she is relieved to learn that the lump is benign, non-cancerous tissue. Then she receives a bill for $1,500, despite having health insurance, and learns that U.S. Preventative Services Task Force (USPSTF) guidelines at the time did not recommend mammogram screening until age 50, as younger women have more false positives. Maria is irate, as she would not have consented to the mammogram or later biopsy had she been told about the USPSTF guideline. Does Maria have a viable informed consent claim against her physician for failure to disclose the USPSTF guideline?

(A) No, because informed consent requires disclosure of material risks, benefits, and alternatives, but it does not require the disclosure of specific guideline recommendations, even if prominent.

(B) No, because non-disclosure of the USPSTF guideline did not cause Maria any damages.

(C) Yes, because the USPSTF guideline would be considered material by most patients.

(D) Yes, but only if Maria lives in a subjective causation state.

254. Which of the following is *not* a basis to disqualify an expert in a medical malpractice case in any state?

(A) Specialty of the expert

(B) Licensure of the expert

(C) Active or recent practice of the expert in the subject matter area

(D) Expert regularly testifies for plaintiffs but not for defendants

255. During the declared public health emergency resulting from COVID-19, the Director of the Centers for Disease Control and Prevention (CDC) issued a second nationwide eviction moratorium. The eviction moratorium prohibited tenants who made certain declarations of financial need from being evicted in counties experiencing high levels of COVID-19 transmission. When the U.S. Supreme Court reviewed this moratorium in *Alabama Association of Realtors v. Department of Health and Human Services*, 141 S. Ct. 2485 (2021), what did it hold?

(A) During a public health emergency, the CDC has broad powers to control infectious disease pursuant to the Public Health Services Act, including issuing an eviction moratorium.

(B) No government entity may issue an eviction moratorium without just compensation to property owners, as such would violate the Fifth Amendment Takings Clause.

(C) The federal government lacks authority to issue an eviction moratorium; only states may do so, as the landlord-tenant relationship is the particular domain of state law.

(D) The federal government has authority to issue an eviction moratorium, but no federal agency may issue an eviction moratorium without clear authorization from Congress. The CDC exceeded its statutory authority.

256. The majority of states allow sterilization of intellectually disabled individuals under certain circumstances. What U.S. Supreme Court precedent arguably supports such laws?

(A) Skinner v. Oklahoma, 316 U.S. 535 (1942)

(B) Buck v. Bell, 274 U.S. 200 (1927)

(C) Stump v. Sparkman, 435 U.S. 349 (1978)

(D) Burwell v. Hobby Lobby Stores, Inc., 573 U.S. 682 (2014)

Answers

Introduction: The U.S. Health Care System & Its Challenges

1. **Answer (C) is correct.** The United States spends twice as much on health care as the average developed country per capita, and yet it is the only one of the 38 Organization for Economic Cooperation and Development (OECD) countries that does not provide some form of "universal" access to health care. Roosa Tikkamen & Melinda K. Abrams, *U.S. Health Care from a Global Perspective, 2019: Higher Spending, Worse Outcomes*, COMMONWEALTH FUND (2020). In fact, in 2022, more than 40% of Americans reported having recently delayed or forgone needed medical care due to cost. Alex Montero et al., *Americans' Challenges with Health Care Costs*, KAISER FAM. FOUND. (2022). Despite spending 18% of GDP on health care, the United States ranks roughly 52nd in the world in life expectancy. Twenty-eight million Americans (over 8% of the U.S. population) have no health insurance and cannot afford care. The U.S. system costs more, achieves less based on outcomes data, and leaves more people behind than comparable countries internationally.

   Answers (A), (B), and (D) are incorrect for the reasons set forth above.

2. **Answer**: Avoidable ill health may cause unnecessary pain and suffering, shorten lifespan, and diminish an individual's ability to contribute to work, family, and community. Like education, access to health care is a prerequisite for an individual to be able to realize their full utility in both economic and non-economic terms. In the context of contagious disease, non-diagnosis or non-treatment can result in increased disease spread, thereby impacting not only individual health but public health as well.

3. **Answer (A) is correct.** While health law largely focuses on improving health care, evidence shows that genetics, behavior, and the social determinants of health have a larger impact on health and well-being than access to medical interventions. Social determinants of health include things like economic stability, education, nutrition, housing, transportation, safe neighborhoods, unpolluted air and water, lack of discrimination, and social support. Given that only roughly 15% of health outcomes can be attributable to medical care, policymakers are slowly beginning to discuss the tradeoffs of medical intervention costs with other health outcome drivers and considering a more comprehensive approach.

   Answers (B), (C), and (D) are incorrect for the reasons stated above.

4. **Answer (C) is correct.** Over-reliance on a market-driven approach likely exacerbates health inequities, but racial and other disparities in health are not a driving force in health care market failures. Health care market inefficiency stems primarily from several other factors. First, poor information regarding the price, quality, and benefit of care distorts the market. Often, neither the doctor nor patient knows how much a particular service will cost at the time the service is selected. The highly fragmented insurance system, rife with price discrimination, fuels a lack of price transparency. Even if the price is known, the physician and patient often lack access to reliable empirical evidence on the benefit of care alternatives. Other significant drivers of market failure include concentrated markets with little competition, the moral hazard created by third-party payers and tax subsidies (diminishing patient incentive to price shop), the fact that physicians often serve as suppliers while also heavily influencing consumer choice, and the reality that many patients do not view equivalent providers as interchangeable (patient preference for a stable physician-patient relationship). *See* Brietta R. Clark et al., Health Law: Cases, Materials and Problems 405–08 (9th ed. 2022); *see also* Topic 12: Regulation of Private Health Insurance (defining and discussing moral hazard).

   Answers (A), (B), and (D) are incorrect for the reasons set forth above.

5. **Answer**: The triple aim of health policy reform is improving cost, quality, and access. Donald M. Berwick et al., *The Triple Aim: Care, Health, and Cost*, 27 Health Affairs 759–69 (2008). Cost seeks to reduce the per capita cost of our health care system. Quality strives to augment the patient experience of care. And access aims to improve population health.

   Increasingly, equity is viewed as an equally important aim of health policy reform. Equity focuses on how benefits are distributed within the population. It often seeks to remedy historic and ongoing discrimination and to address health disparities. While a "quality" aim seeks to improve the caliber of care, without regard *to who* receives higher quality care, equity concentrates on ensuring fair allocation of resources and opportunities between groups or individuals.

   In addition to equity, some contend that choice should be a key reform goal. Because patient preferences, values, and lifestyles vary, choice can be an instrumental part of making care acceptable and improving patient satisfaction.

   Reform goals can be in tension and force tradeoffs. For example, a reform that further benefits the already advantaged might satisfy all or part of the triple aim but exacerbate equity concerns. Other times, a proposed reform advances multiple goals simultaneously. Consider a reform that eliminates unnecessary leg amputations. This would improve the quality of care and likely decrease care costs. If decreased amputations also reduce historic racial disparities in amputation, the reform also promotes equity. Policymakers typically find a reform that furthers multiple goals particularly compelling.

6. **Answer**: Insurance is intended to reduce financial uncertainty and spread financial risk of illness, injury, and disease from one individual or entity to all members of a group. Spreading

the risk this way makes loss manageable. Insurance accomplishes this by charging an insurance premium, a known periodic fee, in exchange for agreeing to assume the risk of a large covered loss. The risk-spreading aspect of insurance means that some individuals will pay more for their insurance coverage than they otherwise would for their individual health care needs. Insurance companies typically set premiums (underwrite) based on anticipated claims of the insured, administrative expenses, and profit to the insurance company. There are different ways to define "anticipated claims of the insured." Topic 13: Health Care Markets and Reform compares two of these: experience rating and community rating.

7. **Answer (B) is correct.** Five percent of the American public accounts for half of all health care spending. Emily M. Mitchell, *Concentration of Healthcare Expenditures and Selected Characteristics of Persons with High Expenses*, Agency for Healthcare Res. & Quality: Med. Expenditure Panel Survey (Jan. 2021). Because insurance spreads risks and costs, a large number of relatively healthy, low-risk individuals subsidize the cost of the small number of individuals who have significant health care costs. As discussed in greater detail in Topic 13: Health Care Markets and Reform, the Affordable Care Act's guaranteed issue of coverage coupled with community rating for premiums results in more equitable premiums across the population. However, this approach also results in healthier individuals being charged premiums that exceed their likely financial risk. This may be one reason that adults aged 26–34, who tend to be healthier and lower risk, have the highest uninsured rate. Jennifer Tolbert et al., *Key Facts About the Uninsured Population*, Kaiser Fam. Found. (Dec. 19, 2022).

   Answers (A), (C), and (D) are incorrect for the reasons set forth above.

8. **Answer (D) is correct.** The ACA prohibits consideration of preexisting health conditions but allows premiums to vary according to geography, tobacco use, and age. As a result, states with fewer insurance options and smaller populations tend to have higher premiums. A silver plan in Wyoming for a 40 year old costs more than twice as much as the same plan for a 40 year old in New Hampshire, making it likely that James's insurance premiums will be higher than John's and Robert's because of where James lives. *Average Marketplace Premium by Metal Tier, 2018–2023*, Kaiser Fam. Found. (2023) (a silver plan premium averages $801 in Wyoming versus $317 in New Hampshire). Absent a wellness plan (which could "discount" premiums by up to 30%), there is no premium differential based on lifestyle choices. Age is usually the largest differential, as the ACA allows insurance companies to charge older beneficiaries up to three times as much (although this amount is still less than the expected claims differential for insureds over age 50). 42 U.S.C. §300gg(a)(1)(A)(iii).

   The ACA moved away from actuarial fairness to a community-rating approach for premium-setting. Yet, it retained a system with a significant premium differential based on geography, tobacco use, and age. This approach and these exceptions raise interesting questions: Is residence a choice (like tobacco use is treated) or mostly bad luck (like illness is treated)? Should the ACA allow insurance companies to vary premiums according to more lifestyle choices that impact expected claims? Should the age-based premium differential cap be removed since we will all become older? Setting aside the merits of the three exceptions, is community rating more or less equitable than actuarial fairness? These are the questions that policymakers wrestle with in connection with efforts to improve and reform the health care system.

Answers (A), (B), and (C) are incorrect for the reasons stated above. Answer (A) reflects a pure social-solidarity approach. Answer (B) likely reflects a pure actuarial-fairness approach. Answer (C) would be correct if age was the only relevant factor and geography did not play a role.

9. **Answer (D) is correct.** In 2021, over 70% of non-elderly uninsured Americans were living in a household with at least one full-time worker, and that number climbs to 82% when part-time work is included. Jennifer Tolbert et al., *Key Facts About the Uninsured Population*, Kaiser Fam. Found. (Dec. 19, 2022). Unfortunately, many jobs do not provide health insurance or have unaffordable premiums. This problem was worse before the Affordable Care Act (ACA) imposed fines on large employers failing to offer health insurance or offering insurance coverage with premiums in excess of 9.12% of an employee's income. However, the ACA fines remain less expensive for large employers than offering affordable insurance, and the reforms do not address smaller employers, the self-employed, or part-time workers (even if working multiple part-time jobs). Most uninsured individuals in the United States are part of what is often referred to as the "working poor," especially in non-expansion states.

   These statistics are important when evaluating recent efforts to impose work requirements on state Medicaid programs. It is true that some Medicaid beneficiaries are able to work but do not. However, experts estimate that the percentage of such beneficiaries is in the single digits, after removing those looking for work, in classes, or meeting other work requirement proposal exceptions. If adopted, Medicaid work requirements may incentivize 7% of beneficiaries to seek work or lose benefits, but studies suggest that the cost of this would be loss of coverage for many other beneficiaries who actually meet the requirements but have difficulty consistently complying with the paperwork required to prove it.

   Answers (A), (B), and (C) are incorrect accordingly.

10. **Answer (B) is correct.** While illness may sometimes attempt to reflect functional impairment, any impairment exists independently of our definition of illness. In contrast, the definition of illness plays a significant role in insurance coverage, our understanding and assertion of personal responsibility, and the perceived need for and appropriateness of medical attention.

    Answers (A), (C), and (D) are incorrect for these reasons.

11. **Answer (C) is the best answer.** Our health care system regards preventative care, like well visits, as health care, despite not treating any malady. At the same time, private insurance typically does not cover non-emergency transportation, even though treatment by a doctor located far away may be impossible without it. Most state Medicaid programs do cover some

non-emergency transportation costs, but often not all. Health insurance does not typically extend to social determinants of health, like housing, even though evidence suggests that access to the social determinants of health plays a larger role in positive health outcomes than access to health care providers. Finally, health insurance seldom covers wilderness therapy or other forms of alternative or complimentary medicine, even when some evidence suggests it may be as effective for certain disorders as traditional medicine, with fewer side effects.

Answers (A), (B), and (D) are not the best answer for the reasons set forth above.

Provider Licensing & Discipline

12. **Answer (C) is correct.** If Dr. Carr can show that the Board failed to consider relevant evidence regarding the standard of care that it should have considered, the court may reverse the Board's decision. When disciplinary action is taken against a licensed physician by a board of medical examiners, the physician has the right to appeal such action to state court. The court will review the Board's decision to determine if it is supported by "substantial evidence." *See* In re Williams, 573 N.E.2d 638 (Ohio 1991).

    Answers (A) and (B) are incorrect. These arguments could have and would have been presented to the hearing officer. The court will not re-weigh the evidence presented as the court's review is not *de novo*.

    Answer (D) is incorrect. The makeup of the Board is a public policy matter, and its composition does not determine whether it relied on substantial evidence in rendering its decision.

13. **Answer (A) is correct.** A professional licensing board (here, the Board of Medical Examiners) can take action against (i) individuals who are licensed by the Board (here, physicians), (ii) individuals who are not licensed but are performing services that would otherwise require licensure (e.g., diagnosing patients, prescribing pharmaceuticals, performing surgery, etc.), and (iii) individuals who are licensed in another profession but are acting outside the scope of their practice. This question is an example of an action taken against an individual who is licensed in another profession but is arguably acting outside the scope of her practice. If Nurse Allgood is being actively supervised by a physician and such services are rendered pursuant to such supervision, then she cannot be deemed to be committing the unauthorized practice of medicine. *See* Sermchief v. Gonzales, 660 S.W.2d 683 (Mo. 1983).

    Answer (B) is incorrect. It does not matter if Nurse Allgood has been practicing this way historically. Activities are not "grandfathered in." The scope of practice for certain professions can change over time, and all individuals must comply with current licensing laws, rules, and regulations.

    Answer (C) is incorrect. There is no information in the question that the cease-and-desist letter is a direct result of prescribing controlled substances. Even if Nurse Allgood does not prescribe controlled substances, there may still be a claim under state law that Nurse Allgood is practicing outside the scope of her practice.

    Answer (D) is incorrect. The statement is false as a matter of law, as professional licensing boards do typically have this authority.

14. **Answer (B) is the best answer.** Under *In re Guess*, 393 S.E.2d 833 (N.C. 1990), a licensing board is responsible for determining the scope of unprofessional or unethical conduct and that can be true even if there is no evidence that the practice at issue has caused harm to a patient. Absent legislation to the contrary, a licensing board has the authority to determine that non-conventional practices, such as homeopathic medicine, constitute unprofessional practice.

    Answer (A) is not the best answer. The question relates to the authority of the Board to take this action, not whether the procedure that was followed at the administrative level was proper.

    Answer (C) is incorrect. It is not dispositive that the practice has not harmed patients.

    Answer (D) is incorrect. There is no requirement that a licensing board agree with or accept the recommendation of the hearing officer so long as a board's decision is supported by substantial evidence.

15. **Answer (D) is the best answer.** An individual who receives notice from an administrative agency, like the cease-and-desist letter, can choose to immediately seek a declaratory judgment from a court.

    Answer (A) is incorrect. Because Answer (D) is correct, Answer (A) is incorrect. An individual need not wait to be enjoined before seeking relief in court.

    Answer (B) is not the best answer. While the agency can interpret the law, courts do not automatically give deference to an administrative agency regarding its interpretation of a statute on the scope of its own jurisdiction. *See* State Bd. of Nursing v. Ruebke, 913 P.2d 142 (Kan. 1996). In light of the Board's position in the cease-and-desist letter, Jackie is likely better off seeking a court determination of whether teeth whitening constitutes the unauthorized practice of dentistry.

    Answer (C) is incorrect. State licensing agencies, such as a board of dental examiners, have authority to bring an action against individuals who engage in unauthorized practice of the licensed profession.

16. **Answer (C) is correct.** The Court in *North Carolina State Board of Dental Examiners v. Federal Trade Commission*, 574 U.S. 494 (2015), held that state action immunity under antitrust law only applies to administrative agencies that are "actively supervised" by the state. Therefore, administrative agencies that are not actively supervised by the state, even if considered a state agency, will not be afforded immunity from antitrust laws. Answer (C) is correct because it demonstrates what might be necessary to show active supervision by the state of the activities of the Board.

    Answer (A) is incorrect. In this answer, there appears to be no active supervision or involvement by the state in the activities of the Board.

    Answers (B) and (D) are incorrect. These answers are unrelated to the issue in the question and are not defenses in an antitrust case.

17. **Answer (B) is correct.** The process for a determination regarding the unauthorized practice of medicine by another physician will vary from state to state. In some states, this action is equivalent to an action that a licensing board might take against any individual who is presumed to be practicing without a license, even though the physician is licensed to practice medicine in a different state. For those states, the standard approach for an administrative agency to take is filing an injunction or other action against the provider in a civil or criminal court. *See* Brietta R. Clark et al., Health Law: Cases, Materials and Problems 60 (9th ed. 2022) (addressing the fact that boards must use existing criminal or civil law statutes when unlicensed providers are arguably practicing medicine in the state); Tenn. Comp. R. & Regs. 0880-2-.12(4)(b)(1) (noting that willfully and knowingly practicing medicine without a license is actionable under the Medical Practices Act as a Type A Civil Penalty). In other jurisdictions, the regulatory scheme allows for physicians practicing within another state who are not licensed within that state to be brought before the applicable agency, such as a board of medical examiners, for a hearing. *See* Ohio Rev. Code Ann. § 4778.21; Wash. Rev. Code Ann. §18.130.190(2) (which provides a hearing through the administrative level).

    Answer (A) is incorrect. A licensure agency cannot deny licensure for an individual who has not yet applied for a license in that state. The proper way to address this action is not a denial of licensure, but other administrative action or civil or criminal action.

    Answer (C) is incorrect. While state licensing agencies are required to report disciplinary actions taken against individuals licensed in their state to other states, Dr. Juarez would first have to have been found to have engaged in the unauthorized practice of medicine in the neighboring state in order to trigger disciplinary action in her own state. Note, however, that if Dr. Juarez were found to have engaged in the unauthorized practice of medicine in another state, such conduct could be considered unprofessional in a state in which Dr. Juarez is properly licensed, thus affecting her license in a state in which she is properly licensed.

    Answer (D) is incorrect. This draws a conclusion on the merits of her actions, which cannot be determined based on the facts set forth in the question.

18. **Answer (C) is correct.** A physician or other medical professional who is disciplined by the state licensing board for their respective profession (e.g., Board of Medical Examiners for physicians, Board of Nursing for nurses, etc.) can bring an action in state court against the state licensing board arguing that the disciplinary action was wrongful. *See* In re Guess, 393 S.E.2d 833 (N.C. 1990). When such an action is brought, the state district court will review the decision to determine whether the actions of the licensing board were supported by substantial evidence. This standard is deferential to the licensing board.

    Answer (A) is incorrect. This answer is false. Physicians do have the right to seek review of a state licensing board's disciplinary action.

    Answers (B) and (D) are incorrect. Both answers state the wrong standard of review.

Regulation of Health Care Institutions

19. **Answer (D) is correct.** Nursing homes are required to be licensed within the state in which they are located and are subject to those state laws, rules, and regulations. If a nursing home wishes to provide services to Medicare and/or Medicaid patients, then the nursing home must enroll with those programs and is thus subject to federal laws, rules, and regulations. Those federal laws are monitored by the state licensing agencies, which are responsible for conducting surveys, responding to reports, etc. While nursing homes can seek third-party accreditation, there is no "deeming status" for compliance with applicable federal laws if the nursing home is accredited.

    Answers (A) and (B) are incorrect. Nursing homes can and often are regulated by both federal and state laws.

    Answer (C) is incorrect because federal regulations are monitored by state licensing agencies, not third-party accreditation agencies.

20. **Answer (A) is correct.** The answer here turns on the standard of review for a court's review of the actions of the Departmental Appeals Board (DAB). A court will review whether the actions taken by the DAB were based on substantial evidence. To be successful, a plaintiff must prove that the decision of the DAB was not based on substantial evidence. If the ALJ did not consider any of the evidence that might be presented by the nursing home to defend itself, this would be the best proof.

    Answer (B) is incorrect. The ALJ can weigh the testimony of those experts and other witnesses at the hearing to render its decision. This fails to show that the decision was not based on substantial evidence.

    Answers (C) and (D) are incorrect. These answers do not properly state the standard of review. Both answers are factors that an ALJ could consider as part of the overall determination.

21. **Answer (C) is correct.** CMS issued a final rule on civil monetary penalties imposed against nursing homes that includes a structure for reduction in penalties if self-reported. The rules require that reports be made within 10 days of the date the facility becomes aware of the deficiency, the facility take steps to correct the issue, and the facility waive the right to a hearing.

    Answer (A) is incorrect. There is a mechanism for fine reduction if the rules are followed.

Answer (B) is incorrect. This answer incorrectly states the rule. As set forth above, the rule requires that the report be made within 10 days of the date the facility became aware of the deficiency. This answer incorrectly states that nursing homes can report any time prior to the state Department of Health's or CMS's discovery of the violations.

Answer (D) is incorrect. While CMS will not allow self-reporting for serious violations, these would not rise to the level of serious violations as presented.

22. **Answer (C) is correct.** Nursing homes and skilled nursing facilities are monitored by the applicable state Department of Health or other state agency that is responsible for facility licensure for compliance with state and federal law (as applicable). For those facilities that participate in the Medicare and/or Medicaid programs, the Centers for Medicare and Medicaid Services (CMS) delegates oversight of operations and compliance with applicable Medicare regulations, including conducting of site visits and annual surveys or inspections, to the state licensing body.

    Answer (A) is incorrect. While hospitals are required to seek third-party accreditation and such accreditation deems compliance with applicable Medicare regulations, nursing homes are not required to seek accreditation, and accrediting bodies do not investigate nursing homes on behalf of the federal government.

    Answer (B) is incorrect. CMS delegates authority and oversight for compliance with federal laws to the state licensing board.

    Answer (D) is incorrect. The Medicare Administrative Contractors assist in coverage and claims processing but are not involved in oversight of operations.

23. **Answer (D) is correct.** The most drastic penalty that the federal government can assert for non-compliance is to remove an entity's or provider's ability to participate in Medicare and/or Medicaid.

    Answers (A) and (C) are incorrect. The actions described in these answers can be taken, but they are considered more temporary and less drastic than termination of the provider agreement, which would prevent the facility from taking any Medicare or Medicaid patients (or at least from being able to charge Medicare or Medicaid for services provided to them).

    Answer (B) is incorrect because only a state has the power to revoke a facility's state-issued license.

24. **Answer (A) is correct.** In contrast to Question 23, CMS delegates oversight and monitoring of compliance with federal regulations for hospitals to the Joint Commission. If hospitals are accredited, then the hospital is deemed to comply with Medicare regulations. All periodic and initial inspections and surveys are conducted by the accreditors. Representatives from CMS may also conduct a site visit later, depending on the severity of the complaint.

    Answers (B), (C), and (D) are incorrect. For standard complaints, the Joint Commission is responsible for the investigation of complaints, which it then reports to CMS, as needed.

25. **Answer (B) is the best answer.** Hospitals accredited through the Joint Commission that complete a "deemed status" accreditation survey are determined to have met or exceeded the Medicare and Medicaid requirements without an additional inspection or survey from CMS.

Answer (A) is not the best answer. While this approach provides some *additional* advantages to accreditation, it is not the best answer because the primary driver for hospitals to be accredited through the Joint Commission is the ability to avoid an additional survey from CMS or a state agency for compliance with Medicare and Medicaid regulations.

Answer (C) is incorrect. This is an inaccurate reading of the Joint Commission standards. Medicare and Medicaid regulation requirements are incorporated into the Joint Commission standards; therefore, compliance with the Joint Commission standards amounts to compliance with the applicable federal regulations.

Answer (D) is incorrect. This statement is factually false. Hospitals are not required to be accredited with the Joint Commission. Hospitals can instead pass a state inspection.

Topic 4 Answers

Physician-Patient Relationship: Formation, Duties, & Termination

26. **Answer (D) is correct.** Generally, formation of a physician-patient relationship requires mutual consent. *See, e.g.*, St. John v. Pope, 901 S.W.2d 420, 423 (Tex. 1995). Patient consent (directly or via proxy) to the relationship may not be required in an emergency, for court-ordered treatment, or for an independent medical exam.

    Answer (A) is incorrect. Absent a pre-existing relationship, a physician is not legally obligated to treat a particular patient, even if that patient has significant need and the physician is the only provider available with expertise.

    Answer (B) is incorrect. Physicians have no legal obligation to treat Medicaid patients, and some physicians refuse to do so. Others cap the number of Medicaid patients they will accept. If physicians want to receive payment for the treatment of Medicaid patients, they must enter into a Provider Agreement with their state's Medicaid program.

    Answer (C) is incorrect. Under the Emergency Medical Treatment and Labor Act (EMTALA), a hospital with an emergency room that accepts Medicare generally has a duty to stabilize a patient who presents with an emergency medical condition. 42 U.S.C. § 1395dd(b). A physician who operates a private practice outside a hospital setting does not owe the same duty.

27. **Answer (C) is correct.** Generally, formation of a physician-patient relationship requires mutual consent. Consent may be express or implied based on conduct.

    Answers (A) and (B) are incorrect. Formation of the physician-patient relationship requires neither express consent nor written agreement.

    Answer (D) is incorrect. Under EMTALA, when a patient presents at a hospital, it triggers a hospital's duty to screen the patient and to stabilize the patient if he or she is diagnosed with an emergency medical condition. *Id.* Physicians do not have the same legal obligation at an office practice. A scheduled appointment for a specific medical service may be evidence that a physician has consented to formation of the physician-patient relationship, but a patient unilaterally presenting at the physician's office does not trigger a duty to treat. Lyons v. Grether, 239 S.E.2d 103 (Va. 1977).

28. **Answer (B) is the best answer.** Physicians may generally decline to enter into a physician-patient relationship for any reason (including for no reason), but not for discriminatory reasons. Here, Pat is part of a protected class. Dr. Money cannot legally decline to treat Pat because of Pat's disability. 42 U.S.C. §§12101–12213. Reasonable accommodation and other legal obligations arising under the Americans with Disabilities Act of 1990 (ADA) are discussed in greater detail in Topic 11: Discrimination: EMTALA, Title VI, ADA, GINA, and ACA.

    Answer (A) is incorrect because Answer (B) more fully and accurately states the law.

    Answer (C) is incorrect. Physician offices are considered places of public accommodation pursuant to the ADA and other civil rights legislation.

    Answer (D) is not the best answer. Physicians do not generally have an obligation to enter into a physician-patient relationship with any particular patient. So, while it likely violates the ADA for Dr. Money to refuse to treat Pat based on Pat's disability, Dr. Money remains free to refuse to treat Pat for other non-discriminatory reasons if he can establish that such reasons are not a pretext.

29. **Answer (D) is the best answer.** Forming a physician-patient relationship parallels other contracts, turning primarily on the parties' agreement. However, once a physician-patient relationship is formed, the physician's standard of care and other fiduciary or quasi-fiduciary duties, like confidentiality, typically govern. The parties seldom expressly contract for relationship terms, and even if they attempt to do so, public policy limits their ability to circumvent many professional obligations imposed on physicians.

    Answer (A) is not the best answer for the reasons set forth above.

    Answers (B) and (C) are not the best answer. Both are correct statements of law but less complete than the best answer, Answer (D).

30. **Answer (A) is correct.** While contracts include a duty of good faith and fair dealing and physicians are often described as quasi-fiduciaries, patient suits challenging physician rates as unreasonable have seldom met with success. *See, e.g.*, Armijo v. Affilion, LLC, 854 F. App'x 236, 238–40 (10th Cir. 2021) (concluding that there is no duty under physician standard of care to charge reasonable fees). Meanwhile, a physician owes the patient a duty to maintain confidentiality (Topic 5), to obtain informed consent (Topic 6), to act in accordance with the applicable standard of care (Topic 8), and to provide continuing attention. A physician may also have a duty to avoid, or at minimum to disclose, any potential financial conflict of interest relating to a treatment relationship. Moore v. Regents of the Univ. of Cal., 793 P.2d 479 (Cal. 1990); AMA, Code of Medical Ethics Op. 11.2.2 and 11.2.4 (2016).

    Answer (B) is incorrect. While states vary in the exact wording of the standard of care owed by physicians, all impose some form of duty of reasonable prudence or minimally competent care once a physician-patient relationship is formed. *See* Topic 8: Medical Malpractice.

    Answer (C) is incorrect. Once a physician agrees to undertake treatment of a particular condition, the physician owes the patient a duty of continuing attention until that condition resolves, the patient terminates the relationship, or the physician provides reasonable notice enabling the patient to obtain alternative treatment. Ricks v. Budge, 64 P.2d 208 (Utah 1937). *See* Topic 11: Discrimination: EMTALA, Title VI, ADA, GINA, and ACA.

Answer (D) is incorrect. Pursuant to the Health Insurance Portability and Accountability Act of 1996 (HIPAA) and under common law, with few exceptions, a physician has a duty to maintain the confidentiality of information obtained during the course of medical treatment. *See* Topic 5: HIPAA and Confidentiality.

31. **Answer (C) is the best answer.** Courts have generally, although not uniformly, found exculpatory clauses that prospectively limit physician liability for negligence void as against public policy. *See, e.g.*, Tunkl v. Regents of Univ. of Cal., 383 P.2d 441 (Cal. 1963); Ash v. N.Y. Univ. Dental Ctr., 164 A.D.2d 366, 369 (App. Div. 1990) (state's interest in the health of its citizens and the special relationship between physician and patient make exculpatory agreement unenforceable). Such clauses may be enforceable under narrow circumstances. For example, they have been enforced in situations involving last hope experimental treatment. They may also be enforced when a patient refuses recommended treatment and assumes the risk of an alternative care approach.

    Answers (A) and (B) are incorrect. Courts have deferred to parties' express agreement limiting the scope or duration of the physician-patient relationship. Absent such express agreement, there is an implied agreement that the physician owes the patient a duty of continuing attention. This duty is discussed in the answer to the next question.

    Answer (D) is incorrect. A court would likely enforce a forum selection clause absent evidence that such clause is unreasonable, unjust, or invalid because of fraud.

32. **Answer (C) is correct.** Once a physician-patient relationship is formed, a physician owes the patient a duty of "continuing attention." Accordingly, if a physician wishes to terminate the relationship while the patients has ongoing treatment needs for the same medical problem, the physician must provide the patient with notice and a reasonable opportunity to find another provider. The physician should also help to facilitate the transfer of care to avoid liability for abandonment. While patient complaints may cause a physician to seek termination, the physician cannot actually terminate the relationship without successfully transferring the patient to another provider that the patient accepts or establishing that the patient was given reasonable time and means to make such a transfer. *See, e.g.*, T.L. v. Cook Child.'s Med. Ctr., 607 S.W.3d 9, 56 (Tex. App. 2020).

    Answers (A) and (B) are incorrect. A patient is generally free to terminate the physician-patient relationship at any time, and the relationship terminates automatically when the episode for which the patient originally sought treatment is resolved.

    Answer (D) is incorrect. A physician may terminate a physician-patient relationship after giving notice and a reasonable opportunity to find another provider.

HIPAA & Confidentiality

33. **Answer (C) is correct.** The Health Insurance Portability and Accountability Act of 1996 (HIPAA), as amended, defines a "covered entity" as: "(1) A health plan. (2) A health care clearinghouse. (3) A health care provider who transmits any health information in electronic form in connection with a transaction covered by this subchapter." 45 C.F.R. §160.103. WebMD is an internet website that provides general information regarding medical conditions. It is neither a health plan, a health care clearinghouse, nor a provider and thus does not meet the definition of "covered entity."

    Answers (A) and (D) are incorrect. Both of these answers are providers (Dr. Smith as an individual and Shady Pines Psychiatric Hospital as a facility), which are considered "covered entities."

    Answer (B) is incorrect. Blue Cross Blue Shield of Tennessee is a health plan and is thus a "covered entity."

    Please note that a health care clearinghouse is an entity that processes or facilitates the processing of health care information. Examples would include a billing and collection company or a community health information system.

34. **Answer (D) is correct.** In this scenario, Billing Associates, Inc., is a "business associate" of Seattle Grace Hospital. Under HIPAA, a "business associate" as defined in 45 C.F.R. § 160.103, is directly liable for breaches of "protected health information" to the same extent as a "covered entity."

    Answer (A) is incorrect. This answer does not reflect the current rule under HIPAA. While a "covered entity" might *also* have a breach of contract claim against a "business associate," after the HITECH Act of 2009, breach of contract is no longer the sole remedy under law.

    Answer (B) is incorrect. "Business associates" can also be liable, and the employee would not be considered a member of Seattle Grace Hospital's workforce.

    Answer (C) is incorrect. A "covered entity" is not liable if the "business associate" is responsible for the breach, although there may be some reporting obligations. *See* 45 C.F.R. § 164.504(e)(1).

35. **Answer (B) is correct.** Under HIPAA, one's state is not included as one of the 18 identifiers that constitute "protected health information" because it is considered too generic/vague for purposes of identification.

    Answers (A), (C), and (D) are incorrect. All of these answers are examples of some of the 18 identifiers constituting "protected health information" under HIPAA.

36. **Answer (B) is correct.** Under HIPAA, "covered entities" and "business associates" are only permitted to disclose "protected health information" as permitted under applicable regulations. All other disclosures not specifically permitted pursuant to HIPAA statutes and regulations are prohibited and would be considered a breach. A valid subpoena is a permitted disclosure because HIPAA allows disclosures as "required by law." *See id.* § 164.103 (defining "required by law" to include court orders and subpoenas or summonses issued by a court).

    Answer (A) is incorrect. Although a disclosure would be permitted if disclosed for purposes of treatment, the requested disclosure in this instance was not for the purposes of treatment.

    Answer (C) is incorrect. It does not matter if the disclosure would not be harmful or otherwise might assist the patient; rather, HIPAA requires that any use or disclosure be specifically permitted.

    Answer (D) is incorrect. This answer is not relevant to the question. When "protected health information" is disclosed, it is required that the information be the minimum necessary for the request. In this instance, however, the question is whether the use or disclosure itself is permissible, regardless of the form of disclosure.

37. **Answer (D) is correct.** HIPAA does not provide a private right of action to individuals for breach of its provisions, but individuals in a confidential relationship whose protected health information has been impermissibly used or disclosed may have a state law breach of confidentiality claim. *See* Humphers v. First Interstate Bank, 696 P.2d 527 (Or. 1985).

    Answer (A) is incorrect. HIPAA does not preempt state laws that provide greater restrictions and protections than federal law, unless in conflict.

    Answer (B) is incorrect. It is not always necessary to prove who exactly was responsible for the breach if it is clear from the facts that the information was leaked from a particular source. *See* Doe v. Medlantic Health Care Grp., Inc., 814 A.2d 939 (D.C. 2003).

    Answer (C) is incorrect. The facts do not support an invasion of privacy claim, which relates to prying into one's personal records, not failing to keep one's personal records confidential.

38. **Answer (C) is correct.** Covered entities under HIPAA are not permitted to use or disclose information unless pursuant to a specific permitted use or disclosure. Although frustrating, a patient's self-disclosure as to information in a public forum such as Yelp does not waive any HIPAA obligations, nor does it create a permitted use or disclosure for the covered entity.

    Answers (A) and (B) are incorrect because answer (C) is correct—there is no permitted use or disclosure in this scenario.

Answer (D) is incorrect. The minimum necessary rule only applies to a permitted use or disclosure.

39. **Answer (A) is correct.** This answer requires the reader to apply HIPAA's breach analysis, which is a four-part test: "an acquisition, access, use, or disclosure of protected health information in a manner not permitted under subpart E is presumed to be a breach unless the covered entity or business associate, as applicable, demonstrates that there is a low probability that the protected health information has been compromised based on a risk assessment of at least the following factors: (i) The nature and extent of the protected health information involved, including the types of identifiers and the likelihood of reidentification; (ii) The unauthorized person who used the protected health information or to whom the disclosure was made; (iii) Whether the protected health information was actually acquired or viewed; and (iv) The extent to which the risk to the protected health information has been mitigated." 45 C.F.R. §164.402. Answer (A) applies these four factors to presume this was a breach.

Answer (B) is incorrect. This answer cites a previous definition of "breach" under HIPAA that has since been amended.

Answer (C) is incorrect. An unauthorized use or disclosure is a breach of HIPAA regardless of the number of patients impacted.

Answer (D) is incorrect. HIPAA *presumes* that an unauthorized use or disclosure is a breach, and it is not necessary to prove access for an unauthorized use or disclosure to be considered a breach.

40. **Answer**: Based on the information provided and the daughter's story regarding how Juanita's mother heard that Juanita had been admitted to the hospital for complications in connection with an opioid prescription, it is possible that there is a breach of Juanita's protected health information. Juanita should first confirm whether or not she provided specific permission in her medical record for her provider to leave detailed messages regarding her condition at the phone number provided in her medical record. If no such consent/permission exists, then this phone call and message appear to be a HIPAA breach. Unfortunately for Juanita, HIPAA does not provide a private right of action under federal law. Therefore, Juanita can make a report to the Office for Civil Rights about the potential breach and could also make a report to the state licensing board. Those bodies should investigate the complaint and determine whether any action should be taken against the facility under HIPAA or state licensing laws. If Juanita is still interested in also going after the hospital in court, she could bring a state law breach of confidentiality claim against the hospital. While there is no notation in Juanita's medical record regarding any disclosure, including the message on the machine, and Juanita did not hear the message herself, it may not be necessary for Juanita to provide proof of the message or phone call. In the case of *Doe v. Medlantic Health Care Group, Inc.*, 814 A.2d 939, the District of Columbia Court of Appeals concluded that even though the plaintiff could not pinpoint the exact incident of the breach, the plaintiff had presented substantial evidence concerning the hospital's protocols and the routine failure of employees to comply with the applicable proto-

cols to sustain a claim in court. To be successful in this claim, it would be helpful for Juanita to know what is set forth in hospital protocols regarding the calling of next-of-kin or other relatives when a patient has been discharged and whether such practices are in accordance with hospital policies and communicated to the patients in advance. If Juanita can successfully show that that hospital frequently or uniformly fails to follow its own protocols, then it will not matter whether Juanita can pinpoint who called and left the message for purposes of sustaining a breach of confidentiality claim.

41. **Answer (B) is the best answer.** In *Byrne v. Avery Center for Obstetrics and Gynecology, P.C.*, 102 A.3d 32 (Conn. 2014), the court "concluded that...the HIPAA regulations may well inform the applicable standard of care in certain circumstances." Because providers, as covered entities, are subject to HIPAA, and HIPAA will serve as at least the minimum level of protection that will need to be in place, many state courts will allow HIPAA regulations to serve as evidence of the standard of care with respect to patient records. Therefore, Answer (B) is the best answer because all covered entities will be subject to HIPAA, and this answer is the only one that does not indicate the possibility of other standards that are less restrictive than HIPAA.

Answer (A) is incorrect. This answer states the standard of care that is typical for a medical malpractice claim, which is not the same as a breach of confidentiality claim. Even if this were applied in certain jurisdictions, if such standard of care were less restrictive than HIPAA, then HIPAA would be assessed as the proper standard of care because HIPAA provides the applicable floor.

Answer (C) is not the best answer because Answer (B) is better. Any standards under the Joint Commission are informed by compliance with HIPAA; thus hospitals accredited by The Joint Commission should have policies that comply with HIPAA. Like the comment above regarding Answer (A), if a standard is not as restrictive as HIPAA, then the standard of care will be HIPAA because it is intended to serve as a floor for patient confidentiality.

Answer (D) is incorrect. This answer is not responsive to the question. A breach of confidentiality claim would address whether the hospital complied with the applicable standard in keeping the information confidential in the first place. It would not address the steps that a hospital is advised to take *after* a breach for purposes of complying with Federal Bureau of Investigation guidance.

Topic 6

Answers

Informed Consent

42. **Answer (B) is the best answer.** Informed consent can take many forms, but it most frequently involves at least some oral conversation between physician and patient, as well as the patient's signing a consent form. During the informed consent process, a physician must disclose the nature of the treatment and its material risks, benefits, and alternatives, including non-treatment. For each alternative, the physician should likewise disclose the alternative's material risks and benefits. Ideally, informed consent is an interactive process during which the patient has the opportunity to ask questions and to seek clarification. States have different thresholds for which types of medical intervention requires informed consent, but all states require it for surgery.

    Answer (A) is not the best answer. An advance directive is a legal document completed by the patient to provide instructions regarding what type of medical care should (and should not) be provided to the patient in the future, typically in the event the patient later becomes incapacitated. An advance directive does not necessarily involve communication with a physician, and without more, it is not generally adequate authorization for treatment.

    Answers (C) is not the best answer. Informed patient decision-making is the primary goal of informed consent, but it is not the process itself.

    Answer (D) is incorrect for the reasons stated above.

43. **Answer (C) is the best answer.** Informed consent's primary ethical foundation rests on autonomy and bodily integrity.

    Answers (A) and (B) are not the best answers. While there is some evidence that patients benefit from shared decision-making as a result of higher patient satisfaction, this is not the primary ethical consideration behind informed consent. Likewise, the desire to avoid causing harm to a patient is not the primary motivation. A patient could benefit from a medical intervention despite a failure to obtain informed consent.

    Answer (D) is incorrect. Ethicists define justice in different ways, but to many, it requires providing to each his or her due. Informed consent focuses primarily on permission, not distribution of resources or fairness.

44. **Answer (D) is the best answer.** Today, most informed consent claims sound in negligence, although such claims may also sound in battery when there is a complete absence of consent.

The complete absence of consent required for battery is rare, and it occurs most frequently when a physician accidentally operates on the wrong site, a site to which the patient never consented.

Answer (A) is not the best answer. As noted above, historically, the common law tort basis for an informed consent claim sounded in battery. *E.g.*, Schloendorff v. Soc'y of N.Y. Hosp., 105 N.E. 92, 93 (N.Y. 1914). Although such a claim remains viable, it is rare, and most informed consent claims are based on negligence.

Answer (B) is not the best answer. While most informed consent claims sound in negligence, such claims can also be based in battery if there is a complete absence of consent.

Answer (C) is incorrect. This answer misstates the basis for each tort.

45. **Answer (A) is correct.** Informed consent requires the disclosure of diagnosis (if known) and prognosis, as well as the nature, benefits, and material risks of the proposed treatment and any reasonable alternatives (including non-treatment). This question tests how "material risks" are determined in a physician-based disclosure state. A physician-based disclosure state determines required disclosures based on what a reasonably prudent physician would disclose to a patient under similar circumstances. *See, e.g.*, Culbertson v. Mernitz, 602 N.E.2d 98 (Ind. 1992). Here, the facts state that a reasonable physician would disclose risks 1, 2, and 3. So, these are the required risk disclosures.

    Answer (B) is incorrect. A reasonable patient would consider risk 4 material, and risk 4 is therefore a required disclosure in a patient-based disclosure state. *See, e.g.*, Canterbury v. Spence, 464 F.2d 772 (D.C. Cir. 1972). However, a physician-based disclosure state would only require disclosure of risks 1, 2, and 3 — the disclosures that a reasonable physician regards as material.

    Answer (C) is incorrect. This particular patient regards risk 5 as material, but most physicians and other patients do not. A physician-based disclosure state would ordinarily only require disclosure of risks 1, 2, and 3 — the disclosures that a reasonable physician regards as material. If Patient asks about risk 5, however, the physician will likely have a duty to respond truthfully.

    Answer (D) is incorrect. States do not generally require physicians to voluntarily disclose individual physician risk information as part of informed consent. Brian Murray, *Informed Consent: What Must a Physician Disclose to a Patient?*, 14 AMA J. Ethics 563–66 (2012); *but see* Johnson v. Kokemore, 545 N.W.2d 495 (Wis. 1996) (affirming decision to admit evidence that a neurosurgeon should have disclosed lack of experience and differential morbidity and mortality statistics for an inexperienced surgeon). Here, the physician-specific medical school and licensing exam performance are fairly tangential to the procedure risks. A physician-based disclosure state would only require disclosure of risks 1, 2, and 3 — the disclosures that a reasonable physician regards as material.

46. **Answer (B) is the best answer.** Informed consent requires the disclosure of diagnosis (if known) and prognosis, as well as the nature, benefits, and material risks of the proposed

treatment and any reasonable alternatives (including non-treatment). This question tests how "material risks" are determined in a patient-based disclosure state. Most patient-based disclosure states determine required disclosures based on what a reasonable patient in the plaintiff's position would consider material to the decision under the circumstances. *See, e.g., Canterbury*, 464 F.2d 772. Here, the facts state that most patients would regard risks 1, 2, 3, and 4 as material. So, these risks are required disclosures.

Answer (A) is incorrect. A reasonable patient would also consider risk 4 to be material, and risk 4 is therefore a required disclosure in a patient-based disclosure state.

Answer (C) is not the best answer. This particular patient regards risk 5 as material, but most patients do not. The facts do not say whether or not Quinn shared this idiosyncratic disclosure preference with Doctor. Even if Quinn did, triggering a *duty* to disclose in some patient-based states, Quinn will only be able to satisfy *causation* in the small minority of states that allow subjective decision-causation. Since, at most, this answer would be correct a handful of states, it is not the best answer.

Answer (D) is incorrect. States do not generally require physicians to voluntarily disclose individual physician risk information as part of informed consent. See the answer to Question 45 above. A patient-based decision disclosure state would likely only require disclosure of risks 1, 2, 3, and 4—the disclosures that a reasonable patient regards as material to the decision.

47. **Answer (D) is correct.** To recover, Quinn must show that: (1) Doctor had a duty to disclose risk 3, 2) Doctor breached that duty by failing to make the required disclosure, (3) a reasonable patient (or Quinn in subjective decision-causation states) would have made a different decision regarding the course of treatment if risk 3 had been properly disclosed, and (4) Quinn suffered the injury that should have been disclosed in risk 3. Here, Doctor had a duty to disclose risk 3, and Doctor breached that duty. Patient suffered the undisclosed risk, but the facts do not tell us if a reasonable patient (or Quinn in subjective states) would have made a different decision had risk 3 been properly disclosed.

Answer (A) is incorrect. Because Doctor disclosed the risk that harmed Quinn prior to the procedure (risk 1), Quinn will not succeed with an informed consent claim. Even if Doctor breached disclosure duties by failing to disclose *other* material risks, those breaches did not proximately cause Quinn harm. Of course, Quinn may still have a traditional malpractice claim against Doctor if Doctor breached the standard of care in performing the surgery itself and such breach harmed Quinn.

Answer (B) is incorrect. Because risk 6 is not a required disclosure, Doctor has not breached his or her duty, and Quinn's informed consent claim will fail.

Answer (C) is incorrect. In order to recover, Quinn must show injury-causation.

48. **Answer**: The majority of states require a plaintiff to establish *objective* decision-causation. This requires proof that the physician's failure to disclose resulted in a different decision regarding

the course of treatment than a *reasonable* patient in the plaintiff's position would have made with the required disclosure. Four states allow *subjective* decision-causation. This lower standard requires proof that the physician's failure to disclose resulted in a different decision regarding the course of treatment than the *particular* plaintiff would have made with the required disclosure.

49. **Answer:** To prevail on an informed consent claim, a plaintiff must establish both decision-causation and injury-causation. Decision-causation requires a plaintiff to establish that if a proper disclosure had been timely made, a reasonable patient would have made a different decision regarding the procedure. Injury-causation requires the plaintiff to show that the physician's failure to disclose caused the plaintiff to suffer harm, that is, plaintiff was injured by an undisclosed risk.

50. **Answer (A) is correct.** Because the scope of the duty to disclose turns on what a reasonable physician would regard as material in physician-centered disclosure states, defining the scope of the duty typically requires expert proof. In contrast, states split on whether or not expert proof is required to establish which risks a reasonable patient would consider material in patient-centered disclosure states.

    Answer (B) is incorrect. Generally, once the scope of the physician's duty is defined, it is only a fact question whether or not the physician made the required disclosures. This would hold true in both physician-centered and patient-centered states.

    Answer (C) is incorrect. While decision-causation can require expert testimony, this holds true in both physician-centered and patient-centered states.

    Answer (D) is incorrect. While injury-causation and decision-causation can require expert testimony, this holds true in both physician-centered and patient-centered states.

51. **True.** Informed consent claims do not turn on negligent diagnosis or negligent performance of a medical procedure. Even when properly diagnosed and performed, many medical interventions carry risk. If a physician fails to disclose a material risk of the intervention as required, and the plaintiff shows that a reasonable patient would not have consented to the procedure had the risk been disclosed and that the plaintiff suffered harm caused by the undisclosed risk, the plaintiff can prevail on a breach of informed consent claim.

52. **Answer:** The primary disadvantage of disclosing too many risks to a patient is information overload and obfuscation. More information, if unnecessary, can actually make it more difficult for a patient to exercise autonomy. Providing more information also takes more physician time, which may drive up the cost of health care.

53. **Answer (B) is correct.** In an emergency, consent is implied when the patient is incapable of consent and a proxy is not readily available if delay to obtain consent would increase risk to the patient.

    Answer (A) is incorrect. A physician's duty to obtain informed consent from the patient is non-delegable.

    Answer (C) is incorrect. A physician's informed consent duty is the same regardless of the patient's ability to pay.

    Answer (D) is incorrect. In limited circumstances, such as the emergency discussed above or when informed consent would cause a particular patient more harm than good, a physician may forgo, delay, or alter traditional informed consent.

54. **Answer**: Physician Compare and similar websites presuppose that a patient can effectively shop for health care. While such sites may provide benefit, effectively shopping for health care poses a host of challenges. First, the patient must have a choice of providers. Practically speaking, the patient's choice of provider is often limited by narrow insurance networks, provider availability, and/or the emergency nature of the care. Second, sick patients are not always capable of researching and analyzing different provider options, especially at the time care is needed.

55. **Answer**: Decision aids help a patient think through their own values and how those values link to different treatment options. Decision aids are most useful for preference-sensitive care. Care is preference-sensitive when evidence suggests that two or more alternatives may be equally beneficial, and the best course for a particular patient turns on how the patient values certain risks and benefits. Early cancer screening is an example of preference-sensitive care. Because a patient knows his or her own values better than a physician does, decision aids are especially important when the best care option turns on a patient's values.

56. **Answer (C) is the best answer.** The Physician Payment Sunshine Act requires manufacturers to disclose payments to physicians over $10 and physicians to disclose ownership interests in radiology providers to which the physician refers patients for certain tests. Answer (C) is the best summary of required disclosures.

    Answers (A) and (B) are not the best answers. Each is correct but incomplete.

    Answer (D) is incorrect. All of the other answers contain disclosures required by the Physician Payment Sunshine Act.

Topic 7 Answers

Health Care Decision-Making for Others

57. **Answer (D) is the best answer.** The 1993 Uniform Health Care Decisions Act (UHCDA) defines capacity as "an individual's ability to understand the significant benefits, risks, and alternatives to proposed health care and to make and communicate a health care decision." The 2023 Uniform Health-Care Decisions Act, which has been approved by the Uniform Law Commission but as of July 2023 not yet adopted by any state, proposes a more detailed definition of capacity. Nonetheless, the 2023 Act retains the basic requirements that a patient must be able to understand risks and benefits and to communicate a health care decision.

    Capacity is presumed, but under the 1993 Act, if a patient's capacity is challenged, the primary physician determines capacity unless otherwise stipulated in an advance directive. The 2023 Act expands the list of health care providers who can determine capacity. Capacity is a yes/no question for each particular health care decision, and a patient may have capacity to make one health care decision but not another. Capacity may fluctuate over time. Many scholars advocate "supported decision-making" that empowers patients who may not have capacity to make all health care decisions alone to participate in decisions to the extent of their ability, and such is formally recognized under the 2023 Act.

    Answers (A) and (C) are not the best answers. Each is correct but incomplete.

    Answer (B) is incorrect. While it is certainly true in practice that a patient's capacity is less likely to be questioned when the patient agrees with the provider, the UHCDA standard for capacity does not turn on provider agreement or even the reasonableness of a patient's choice. *See, e.g.*, State, Dep't of Human Servs. v. Northern, 563 S.W.2d 197 (Tenn. Ct. App. 1978).

58. **Answer (D) is the best answer.** The 1993 Uniform Health Care Decisions Act (UHDCA) defines an advance directive as "an individual instruction or a power of attorney for healthcare." The 2023 Act has a similar definition but clarifies that an advance directive may contain both instructions regarding care and designation of an agent, as well as either alone.

    Answers (A) and (B) are not the best answers. Each is correct but incomplete.

    Answer (C) is incorrect. A general power of attorney may appoint an agent to make health care decisions as well as financial ones, but an advance health care directive does not typically authorize an agent to make non-health care financial, business, or real estate decisions. The 2023 UHCDA does authorize a health care surrogate to act on behalf of the patient for health care insurance and benefits but not for other financial decisions.

59. **Answer (A) is the best answer.** The 1993 Uniform Health Care Decisions Act (UHCDA) requires that agents first apply individual instructions and expressed wishes, if known. If unknown, the agent should apply the patient's best interest as determined in accordance with the patient's values, to the extent known. Only if the agent is unaware of instructions, wishes, and patient values does the agent apply a more generalized best interest standard. The 2023 UHCDA follows this same approach. It is important to note, however, that roughly half of U.S. states do not follow the UHCDA in requiring that an agent or surrogate follow all three steps.

    Answers (B) and (C) are not the best answers. A health care agent should rely on instructions and expressed wishes, if any, before considering best interests.

    Answer (D) is incorrect because Answer (A) is correct.

60. **Answer (B) is the best answer.** Under *Cruzan v. Director, Missouri Department of Health*, 497 U.S. 261 (1990), the U.S. Supreme Court largely defers to states regarding the terms and conditions of when a surrogate decision-maker can authorize the withdrawal of life-sustaining care for a no-longer-competent patient. States vary regarding the restrictions, exceptions, and conditions required for such withdrawal. There are only limited facts provided, but it seems unlikely that the spouse's testimony of an oral statement made years ago by itself would constitute "clear and convincing" proof of the patient's wishes, as required in states such as Missouri and Michigan. In contrast, states such as California and New Jersey generally allow a surrogate to make all medical decisions for an incompetent patient, including the withdrawal of life-sustaining treatment, so long as consistent with the patient's known wishes and values. Other states, like New York, defer to an ethics review committee. More generally, some states have recognized a state-based "right to die" pursuant to state common law, statute, or constitution, while others continue to follow a more skeptical approach to withdrawal of life-sustaining care.

    Answer (A) is incorrect. In most cases, states allow health care providers to remove life-sustaining care from an incompetent patient at the direction of the patient's agent, surrogate, or guardian if the requirements of state law are satisfied.

    Answer (C) is not the best answer. Some states require "clear and convincing evidence" that the no-longer-competent patient would have preferred withdrawal of the life-sustaining measures. The standard provided in Answer (C) is the lower "more likely than not" standard common in other kinds of civil cases. Answer (B) is best because it captures significant state variability.

    Answer (D) is incorrect for the reasons set forth above.

61. **Answer (A) is correct.** Generally, an authorized guardian, agent, or default surrogate may make a health care decision for an incompetent patient that fails to maximize likely medical benefit, as long as the decision rests on the patient's advance directive, expressed wishes, or known values. *See, e.g.*, 2023 UHCDA § 21(e). This enables a no-longer-competent patient to retain autonomy and define "beneficence" in accordance with personal values (subjective best

interests), even when contrary to the patient's objective best interests according to the provider or most people.

Answer (B) is incorrect. While a provider should generally defer to an authorized guardian, agent, or default surrogate, the provider is not obligated to render care that is contrary to generally accepted medical standards. *See, e.g.*, 2023 UHCDA § 21(e), (f)(3)(A). A competent patient's ability to select care faces this same limit.

Answer (C) is incorrect. State law does not require a provider to render care that is unavailable, despite a request from an authorized guardian, agent, or default surrogate. *See, e.g.*, *id.* § 21(e), (f)(2). This point may seem obvious, but it was litigated during the COVID-19 pandemic when shortages caused the rationing of certain drugs and other care. Surrogate decision-makers sought to rely on the language of state health care decision laws, setting a default of providing care requested by authorized surrogates with enumerated exceptions, to force providers to prioritize the care of their patients.

Answer (D) is incorrect. Most but not all states require a court order prior to the sterilization of an incompetent person (if they allow such sterilization at all), even after a request from an otherwise authorized health care guardian, agent, or surrogate. NAT'L WOMEN'S L. CTR., FORCED STERILIZATION LAWS IN EACH STATE AND TERRITORY (2022). This is an example of the more general rule that an authorized guardian, agent, or surrogate's decision-making authority can be limited by applicable state law or court order. A provider need not comply with an otherwise authorized request that is contrary to state law or court order. *See, e.g.*, 2023 UHCDA § 21(e), (f)(3)(B). A competent patient faces this same general rule, but often, state laws are more restrictive regarding the availability of certain care for incompetent patients or the proof necessary to obtain same.

62. **Answer (D) is correct.** The Establishment Clause of the U.S. Constitution prohibits the state from establishing a religion. This prohibits unduly favoring one religion over another. Accordingly, courts should not offer more deference to parental decision-making when the parent's view is supported by a "mainstream" or established religion than a less common one. Of course, courts do weigh a parent's right to practice their religion and raise their child in that religion, as discussed in Question 64.

Answers (A), (B), and (C) are incorrect. Courts consider each of these factors. *See, e.g.*, *In re* Phillip B., 156 Cal. Rptr. 48, 51 (Ct. App. 1979) (detailing the factors in overriding a parent's decision). Courts generally will only override a parent's decision if a condition is life-threatening. The court must also be convinced that the benefits of the opposed treatment are substantial (in magnitude and likelihood) and that anticipated risks or side effects are relatively minimal in comparison. In determining the best interests of the child, many states rely on "substituted judgment," attempting to apply the values or interests of the particular minor. This may be impossible for a newborn, but as a minor nears the age of majority, courts often give the minor's preferences more weight. *See, e.g.*, *In re* E.G., 549 N.E.2d 322, 327 (Ill. 1989) (holding that the *parens patriae* authority fades as a minor grows older).

63. **Answer**: When a state seeks to override parental health care decision-making for a particular minor, the state will often rely on its child protective services statutes, especially provisions defining neglect and abuse. Absent abuse or neglect, parents generally can make decisions for their minor children, although there are exceptions, especially if a condition is perceived to be life-threatening and treatable. *E.g.*, *In re* Ariel P., 957 N.Y.S.2d 736, 737 (App. Div. 2013).

    It is worth noting that there has been a recent trend of state legislatures' prohibiting specific care for all minors, further limiting parental decision-making. For example, many liberal states have prohibited sexual orientation change efforts and many conservative states have prohibited gender-affirming care for minors. Such laws have been challenged as violating parents' substantive due process rights, with mixed results.

64. **Answer (D) is the best answer.** The parents have an interest in making health care decisions for their child, and the state has an interest in the life of the child. Generally, courts will defer to parental decision-making, but when the child faces a potentially life-threatening disease or condition, courts will allow the state to intervene when intervention appears to be in the best interests of the child. *See, e.g.*, *In re* I.S., 199 N.E.3d 1130, 1155-56 (Ohio Ct. App. 2022) (upholding court-ordered surgical closing of child's congenital heart condition over mother's religious objections). In potentially life-threatening situations, courts usually intervene to authorize a blood transfusion for a minor over the minor's parents' faith-based objections. The result may be different, however, if the minor also opposes the treatment and the court determines that the minor is a "mature minor" under statute or common law. *In re* E.G., 549 N.E.2d 322, 328 (Ill. 1989) (holding that a mature minor may refuse a life-saving blood transfusion).

    Answers (A), (B), and (C) are not the best answers. While each contains a recognized interest, none of these answers accurately reflect the balance between competing interests under the facts provided. A parent's right to make health care decisions on behalf of a minor child is not absolute, nor is the parent's right to practice their religion and raise their child in that religion. At the same time, often the state's interest in preservation of life will not override parental decision-making, as, for example, when parents decline potentially life-saving treatment for a minor child that has a low probability of success and significant side effects. *See, e.g.*, Newmark v. Williams, 588 A.2d 1108 (Del. 1990) (allowing parents to decline potentially life-saving treatment on religious grounds when the likelihood of success was below fifty percent).

Medical Malpractice

65. **Answer (B) is correct.** While there are exceptions, medical malpractice cases typically require expert testimony on the standard of care and its breach. Zaleskas v. Brigham & Women's Hosp., 141 N.E.3d 927, 942 (Mass. App. Ct. 2020). Some states have codified this requirement. *See, e.g.*, MINN. STAT. §145.682. In fact, more than half require a "certificate of merit," an affidavit signed by an expert and/or attorney in order to state a viable medical malpractice claim.

    Medical malpractice expert testimony often includes evidence of custom and practice, although some courts have concluded that custom and practice is not dispositive of the standard of care. *See* Hall v. Hilbun, 466 So. 2d 856 (Miss. 1985) ("The content of the duty of care may be informed by local medical custom but never subsumed by it."). Jurisdictions vary in whether they define the standard of care based on accepted practice (set by physicians) or on what a reasonably prudent physician should do (giving more latitude to the jury to determine what is reasonable).

    Answer (A) is incorrect. It references lay testimony which is usually not sufficient.

    Answers (C) and (D) are incorrect. Most jurisdictions consider clinical practice guidelines and empirical evidence of efficacy relevant to the standard of care, but not dispositive thereof. *See, e.g.*, Hinlicky v. Dreyfuss, 848 N.E.2d 1285, 1291 (N.Y. 2006). Some courts have even excluded evidence of guidelines. *See, e.g.*, Quigley v. Jobe, 851 P.2d 236 (Colo. App. 1992).

66. **Answer (D) is the best answer.** In most jurisdictions, it is not enough for a plaintiff to establish that his or her physician was below average in skill or knowledge. A plaintiff must generally show that the physician failed to act with "minimally competent" skill and knowledge or acted unreasonably. Hall v. Hilbun, 466 So. 2d 856, 871–72 (Miss. 1985). Similarly, while most jurisdictions have abandoned a strict locality rule, most still use a modified locality rule that accounts for available resources like equipment, staff, diagnostics, and specialists. This requires the use of an expert who is familiar with locally available facilities, resources, and options but not necessarily an expert who practices or has practiced in the same locality. *Id.* Beware, however, that a minority of jurisdictions do still require experts who are licensed in the state or neighboring states, unless the court waives the requirement for just cause. TENN. CODE ANN. §29-26-115(b).

    Answers (A) and (B) are incorrect. In most jurisdictions, it is not enough for a plaintiff to establish that his or her physician was below average in skill or knowledge. A plaintiff must generally show that the physician failed to act with "minimally competent" skill and knowledge or acted unreasonably.

Answer (C) is not the best answer. It is correct but incomplete because it fails to acknowledge how locality can impact the standard of care.

67. **Answer (C) is the best answer.** All jurisdictions consider custom and practice relevant. Some refer to it as dispositive. However, these jurisdictions generally recognize that a physician should not be liable for malpractice if their approach comports with respectable minority practice, reasonable clinical innovation, or certain other defenses.

Answers (A) and (B) are not the best answer. Each is correct but less complete than Answer (C).

Answer (D) is incorrect. Most jurisdictions recognize that a physician who deviates from customary practice is not liable for malpractice if such deviation comports with respectable minority practice or reasonable clinical innovation.

68. **Answer (D) is correct.** Statutes of limitation often bar otherwise viable medical malpractice claims. Each state determines its own statute of limitation for medical malpractice, and as a result, the length varies and can be as short as one year. *See, e.g., id.* § 29-26-116(a) (2023) (medical malpractice statute of limitation runs one year from discovery of the wrongful act). States also vary in how they determine *when* the statute of limitation begins to run. Here, the question states that there is a two-year statute of limitation, and this jurisdiction follows the discovery rule. Accordingly, the two-year statute of limitation begins to run once the plaintiff knows or reasonably should know he was injured. Ezra's suit complies with the statute of limitation because he filed within two years of when he discovered (or reasonably should have discovered) he was injured.

Many states also have a statute of repose for medical malpractice cases. A statute of repose requires that all claims be filed within a specified timeframe from the date of the malpractice, without regard to when discovery of injury occurs. Statutes of repose likewise vary in duration, typically ranging from three to seven years. *See, e.g., id.* § 29-26-116(a)(3) (2023) (three-year statute of repose for most medical malpractice claims). Here, the statute of repose is four years. Because Ezra filed his case less than four years after the alleged malpractice occurred, Ezra's suit is not barred by the statute of repose. Interestingly, some states specifically exempt claims based on unintentionally retained surgical foreign objects from the statute of repose. *See, e.g.*, Cal. Civ. Proc. Code § 340.5 (2023); Tenn. Code Ann. § 29-26-116(a)(4) (2023).

Ezra was 30 years old with presumed capacity. However, it is worth noting that if a patient is a minor at the time of the alleged malpractice or otherwise lacks legal decision-making capacity, the running of the statute is often tolled until majority. *See, e.g.*, Fla. Stat. § 95.051(1)(i) (2023) (tolling statute for minors). The statute of limitation may also be tolled as a result of intentional concealment or fraud. *See, e.g.*, Cal. Civ. Proc. Code § 340.5 (2023).

Answer (A) is incorrect. While Ezra filed suit more than two years after his appendectomy, because this jurisdiction follows the discovery rule, the two-year statute of limitation runs from when Ezra discovered, or reasonably should have discovered, his injury, not from the date on which the alleged malpractice occurred.

Answer (B) is incorrect. There are no facts to suggest that Ezra could have discovered his injury sooner. He did not begin experiencing pain until June 2022, more than two years after his surgery. Given the passage of time, it is hard to argue that a reasonable person would have immediately connected the 2022 abdominal pain to the prior surgery, enabling him to file suit. The June to September 2022 time lag may raise more questions, but these months are irrelevant under the facts, as Ezra filed within two years of June 2022.

Answer (C) is incorrect. While Ezra filed the claim within the four-year statute of repose, which bars claims even if injury has not yet been discovered, Ezra must also meet the two-year statute of limitation.

69. **Answer (D) is the best answer.** Even though the general standard of proof for duty, breach, causation, and damages in a civil negligence case is "more likely than not," most states recognize some form of "loss of chance" in medical malpractice cases when the breach of a duty causes a significant decrease in likelihood of survival. *See, e.g.*, Herskovits v. Grp. Health Coop. of Puget Sound, 664 P.2d 474 (Wash. 1983); *but see* Williams v. Spring Hill Mem'l Hosp., 646 So. 2d 1373 (Ala. 1994). The loss of chance doctrine relaxes the burden of proof for causing the patient's death—but not for proving duty and breach. This avoids the injustice of leaving a patient with less than a 50% chance of survival no possible recovery for malpractice when the malpractice leaves the patient significantly worse off. While allowing such claims, most jurisdictions discount damages to account for the fact that death from disease was more likely than not even absent the malpractice.

Answer (A) is incorrect. If medical malpractice causes a patient's death, the patient's estate may bring suit for the damages the patient suffered before death. The patient's heirs may also be able to assert a wrongful death suit for any damages the heirs themselves suffered as a result of the patient's death, although the loss of chance doctrine is more variable in wrongful death suits than survival actions.

Answer (B) is incorrect. As described above, in most jurisdictions the loss of chance doctrine allows recovery for medical malpractice that causes a significant decrease in likelihood of survival, even if the patient's likelihood of survival without the malpractice was less than 50%.

Answer (C) is not the best answer. This answer is correct but less complete than Answer (D) because, while the majority of jurisdictions allow loss of chance claims to proceed, most states discount damages in loss of chance cases.

70. **Answer (C) is correct.** Most jurisdictions recognize comparative negligence, which apportions fault between the plaintiff and defendant, reducing any damages awarded proportionally.

See, e.g., Ostrowski v. Azzara, 545 A.2d 148 (N.J. 1988). Many of these jurisdictions require that the plaintiff be less than 50% or 51% at fault to recover.

Answer (A) is incorrect. Most jurisdictions have abandoned contributory fault, which bars a plaintiff from recovery if the plaintiff is even partially at fault. However, it is important to note that a minority of jurisdictions continue to follow this approach.

Answer (B) is incorrect. Because a tortfeasor should only be liable for harms they proximately caused, the physician should not be liable for harms the patient negligently brought upon himself.

Answer (D) is incorrect because Answer (C) is correct.

71. **Answer**: There are several reasons why medical malpractice suits do not effectively motivate physicians to provide higher quality care. Michelle M. Mello et al., *Fostering Rational Regulation of Patient Safety*, 30 J. Health Pol., Pol'y, & L. 375 (2005). First, physicians perceive such suits as random. Studies suggest that only 2% of those who experience medical error sue, and less than half of those who sue have what neutral experts regard as a valid claim. Mark Hall et al., Health Care Law and Ethics 271 (9th ed. 2018). So, the connection between the failure to use reasonable care and facing a malpractice suit is tenuous at best. Second, physicians regard malpractice suits as uncontrollable. To err is human, predictable, and often unavoidable. Good systems help, but no matter how hard physicians try, they will sometimes make mistakes because they are human. *Id.* Third, insurance rather than individuals typically pays claims, and insurance premiums are not usually based on claims history of an individual physician (although premiums may be based on incidence of claims by specialty). As a result, physicians do not typically pay more in insurance premiums or judgments when they provide lower quality care. Finally, it may be years between any breach of the standard of care and the payment of a claim. This significant time lag dulls any deterrent effect.

Liability of Health Care Institutions

72. **Answer (B) is correct.** Hospitals can be found directly liable for corporate negligence, *see* Thompson v. Nason Hosp., 591 A.2d 703 (Pa. 1991), or vicariously liable for the acts of their employees, agents, or apparent agents. Nurses are usually hospital employees. Physicians can be employees but are more commonly independent contractors whose acts only create vicarious liability if the physicians are agents or apparent agents of the hospital.

    Answer (A) is incorrect. Successor liability is liability that would apply when one entity acquires another and becomes a successor to any liability that existed prior to the acquisition. Successor liability is not commonly alleged in a hospital negligence action.

    Answer (C) is incorrect. Corporate negligence is effectively a type of direct liability, and thus these are merely two of the same types of liability.

    Answer (D) is incorrect. A hospital can be found vicariously liable for the acts of agents acting on its behalf, including actual agents, implied agents, or apparent agents.

73. **Answer (C) is correct.** A hospital can be found to be vicariously liable for the actions of the members of its medical staff if a plaintiff is successful in proving to a jury that the physician was an agent of the hospital. The facts here are similar to *Scott v. SSM Healthcare St. Louis*, 70 S.W.3d 560 (Mo. Ct. App. 2002), in which the court concluded that there were enough facts that a jury could conclude that the physician who was an employee of an entity with which the hospital contracted was an actual agent of the hospital because of the level of control that the hospital exerted over the physician.

    Answer (A) is incorrect. It is possible under agency theory to hold a hospital liable for the acts of its medical staff members.

    Answer (B) is incorrect. The court in the *Scott* case did not find it dispositive that the physician was technically an employee of a physician group rather than the hospital. Instead, the court found that there were enough facts regarding the hospital's control over the physician that a jury could potentially conclude that the physician was an actual agent of the hospital, even if the physician was also an employee of another company with whom the hospital contracted.

    Answer (D) is incorrect. Terminating the physician from the medical staff does not make the hospital an employer-in-fact.

74. **Answer (B) is correct.** In many jurisdictions, a physician who is working in the emergency room is considered to be an agent of the hospital as a matter of law. *See* Simmons v. Tuomey Reg'l Med. Ctr., 533 S.E.2d 312 (S.C. 2000). States recognize this nondelegable duty because a patient generally cannot select or refuse services of an emergency room physician; rather, these physicians are automatically assigned to a patient. Therefore, there can be no notice to the patient, and the patient is always relying on the hospital's representation of the emergency room physician to the public. As a result, the hospital is prevented from using an independent contractor defense.

    Answer (A) is incorrect. The nondelegable duty doctrine does not apply to all medical staff — only emergency room physicians — and the doctrine is based on apparent agency not actual agency.

    Answer (C) is incorrect. The nondelegable duty doctrine does not dictate the type of employment relationship that a hospital has with its physicians. Emergency room physicians can still be independent contractors or employees. However, when the doctrine applies, a hospital will be liable for acts of its emergency room physicians even if the physicians are independent contractors.

    Answer (D) is incorrect. Agency theory is in fact a product of state law and governed by state law. Many states do prevent hospitals from denying vicarious liability for their emergency room physicians.

75. **Answer (C) is correct.** This is an example of hospital liability due to apparent agency, which turns on the relationship between the hospital and third parties and how the hospital holds out the physicians to the public. A hospital can be liable for a physician's negligence under an apparent agency theory if a reasonable person would have believed that the physician was an agent of the hospital based on the hospital's action or inaction and the plaintiff relied on the hospital for services, rather than on the individual physician. *See* Burless v. W. Va. Univ. Hosps., Inc., 601 S.E.2d 85 (W. Va. 2004)

    Answers (A) and (B) are incorrect. Both of these answers describe a scenario in which the hospital is directly liable due to violations of corporate negligence principles.

    Answer (D) is incorrect. Similar facts have been determined by a court to be sufficient for a jury to conclude that the physician is an apparent agent of the hospital.

76. **Answer (D) is the best answer.** The facts of this question are similar to those of *Darling v. Charleston Community Memorial Hospital*, 211 N.E.2d 253 (Ill. 1965), in which the court held that hospitals are responsible for oversight and monitoring of the physicians practicing within their walls. Even though the physician was negligent, the nurses had an obligation to monitor the physician's orders and ensure that the patient was receiving the proper care, which might include calling in another physician for a second opinion or assistance with a patient.

Answers (A) and (B) are incorrect. Under *Darling*, even if the nurses are not responsible for the underlying negligence, the hospital is vicariously liable for the acts of its nurses and administrators if they fail to act to correct or remedy known negligence of the physician.

Answer (C) is not the best answer. This answer implies that the hospital is *only* liable if the nurses were negligent in counting sponges, one of their personal duties. In reality, the hospital can also be liable if the nurses and administrators failed to monitor the physician.

77. **Answer**: Spring Hill Community Hospital will likely have increased liability risk for either of the proposed initiatives. Under option (a), if the hospital is planning to employ the physicians, then the hospital will be vicariously liable for the acts of those physicians as actual agents of the hospital. In much the same way that a hospital is vicariously liable for the acts of its nurses or other allied health professional staff who are employed by the hospital, if the hospital chooses to employ the physicians it will be taking on vicarious liability for all of the acts of those physicians when acting within the scope of their employment. Spring Hill Community Hospital may also be shown to be vicariously liable for the acts of the physicians under option (b). Although the physicians would not be deemed to be actual agents of the hospital, a jury may still find the hospital to be vicariously liable for the acts of the physicians if it can be shown that they are apparent agents. As mentioned above, a hospital can be liable for a physician's negligence under an apparent agency theory if a reasonable person would have believed that the physician was an agent of the hospital based on the hospital's action or inaction and the plaintiff relied on the hospital for services, rather than on the individual physician. *See Burless*, 601 S.E.2d 85. Under these facts, the biggest concern for the hospital (assuming it is trying to *avoid* liability) is the marketing campaign in which it will advertise for the services *and* potentially include photos of the physicians in the ads. To prove apparent agency in court, and thus that the hospital is vicariously liable, the plaintiff would likely have to show that they saw the ad for the services offered by the hospital, came to the hospital seeking those services, and believed the physicians rendering the services were agents of the hospital. An ad featuring the physician's photos along with the specialty may be sufficient evidence to establish an apparent agency claim. Therefore, the CEO should know that the hospital will be found to be vicariously liable for the negligence of the physicians under option (a) and may be found to be vicariously liable for the negligence of the physicians under option (b).

78. **Answer (B) is correct.** Under *Tunkl v. Regents of University of California*, 383 P.2d 441, hospitals, including non-profit research hospitals, cannot ask patients to sign a complete and total waiver of all liability because it is void as against public policy. While hospitals can seek certain waivers for a patient's assumption of risk (*see, e.g.*, Shorter v. Drury, 695 P.2d 116 (Wash. 1985) (showing a waiver to be enforceable for a situation involving medical assumption of risk for a patient who was Jehovah's Witness)), it is not permissible to ask a patient, especially in the emergency room context where the contract is one of adhesion, to sign a waiver releasing the hospital from all liability.

Answer (A) is incorrect. This answer fails to recognize the above-cited exception in which more limited waivers involving an assumption of risk are legally enforceable.

Answer (C) is incorrect. Complete waivers releasing from all liability are generally unenforceable as void against public policy.

Answer (D) is incorrect. While the patient signed the form, this is nevertheless unenforceable as a contract of adhesion.

Hospital Privileges & Other Labor & Employment Issues

79. **Answer (A) is correct.** Some states still have, either via statute or more commonly under common law, a Corporate Practice of Medicine doctrine that prevents physicians from being employed by a corporation, which is defined as any company that is not owned and operated directly by licensed physicians. *See* Berlin v. Sarah Bush Lincoln Health Ctr., 664 N.E.2d 337 (Ill. App. Ct. 1996) (outlining the basic underpinnings and rationale of a typical Corporate Practice of Medicine doctrine under state common law). The prohibition is generally for the purpose of guarding against a situation in which a physician is beholden to two principals — the physician's own medical judgment *and* the directives of the corporation (which may be contrary to the decision of the physician in the physician's medical judgment). The model described in the question is a common model used for getting around Corporate Practice of Medicine prohibitions in which a physician is employed by or the owner of a physician professional corporation or other physician-owned legal entity. That entity then contracts with the hospital to render services to the hospital, oftentimes on an exclusive basis. Note that some states will have statutory exemptions for hospitals or certain types of hospitals from a Corporate Practice of Medicine doctrine. *See* Berlin v. Sarah Bush Lincoln Health Ctr., 688 N.E.2d 106 (Ill. 1997) (noting on remand that the Illinois Supreme Court had reversed *Berlin v. Sarah Bush Lincoln Health Center*, 664 N.E.2d 337, in part because under Illinois law a "licensed hospital, whether for-profit or nonprofit, is exempt from prohibition of Corporate Practice of Medicine, and therefore, such hospital may employ licensed physicians to provide medical services."). Many states will exempt entities such as hospitals because such entities are subject to their own licensure rules.

    Answer (B) is incorrect. This answer is not precisely responsive to the question and not a true statement in that a hospital does not have *absolute* authority over its medical staff. Moreover, this would not explain why it would be illegal for the hospital to employ Dr. Jones.

    Answer (C) is incorrect. The Physician Self-Referral Law, also known as the Stark Law, does not prohibit physicians from being employed by a hospital and actually has a specific exception for this purpose.

    Answer (D) is incorrect. A right-to-work state, which relates to the obligation to join a union in a state, is unrelated to the facts as presented.

80. **Answer (C) is correct.** Hospitals are afforded a large amount of control over members of their medical staffs. A majority of state courts, when reviewing claims for adverse action by a medical staff member whose privileges have been adversely affected, will review such a decision by a hospital only for purposes of determining whether the hospital has followed the process set forth in its own medical staff bylaws. *See* Molleston v. River Oaks Hosp., Inc., 195 So. 3d 815 (Miss. Ct. App. 2015). Thus, most courts will only review whether the physician received due process; they will not review the merits of an adverse action.

    Answers (A) and (B) are incorrect. These are standards that are applied by a minority of jurisdictions that will review the merits of the decision of the hospital's medical staff and/or Board of Trustees to determine whether it was arbitrary and capricious or based on substantial evidence. *See* Sokol v. Akron Gen. Med. Ctr., 173 F.3d 1026 (6th Cir. 1999).

    Answer (D) is incorrect. This is not a standard of review that courts use to analyze adverse actions against physicians by a hospital.

81. **Answer (A) is correct.** Hospitals that take adverse action against a physician on the basis of a quality concern are generally afforded protection under the federal Health Care Quality Improvement Act of 1986 (HCQIA). 42 U.S.C. §11101 *et seq*. Under HCQIA, credentialing decisions are presumed to comply with the law, but they can be rebutted if plaintiffs prove by a preponderance of the evidence that (1) the hospital did not act in the reasonable belief that the action was in furtherance of quality health care, (2) the hospital did not make a reasonable effort to obtain the facts of the matter, (3) the hospital did not afford the physician adequate notice and hearing procedures and such other procedures required by fairness under the circumstances, or (4) the hospital did not act in the reasonable belief that the action was warranted by the facts known after such reasonable effort to determine the facts and after meeting the procedural requirements. Based on the facts, the decision is based on quality concerns presented by the current arrangement, and the manner in which the privileges were revoked was consistent with the bylaws and provided proper notice. It is thus likely that the hospital will be able to assert immunity under HCQIA.

    Answer (B) is incorrect. Potential liability is not a defense for these types of claims. It possibly justifies the hospital's decision, but the standard of review does not speak to whether the decision was meritorious or justified.

    Answer (C) is incorrect. This answer is not a true statement. Even if there are quality concerns with a physician, a hospital must follow the process set forth in its medical staff bylaws for the purpose of taking an adverse action against a physician on its medical staff.

    Answer (D) is incorrect. This answer is not factually accurate. Closing the medical staff is not an absolute defense.

82. **Answer (B) is correct.** The facts here show an action taken by the hospital that is economic in nature and is considered "economic credentialing." Although the American Medical Association discourages this practice, it is not illegal for hospitals to take actions against physicians on

their medical staff in the interest of financial considerations. *See* Mahan v. Avera St. Luke's, 621 N.W.2d 150 (S.D. 2001). *But see* Baptist Health v. Murphy, 373 S.W.3d 269 (Ark. 2010) (finding that the hospital's conflicts of interest policy was overly restrictive and thus unconscionable).

Answer (A) is incorrect. A "clean sweep" provision refers to a provision set forth in an exclusive contract that requires all physicians providing services under the contract to voluntarily relinquish their privileges upon termination of the contract. The facts do not support this scenario.

Answers (C) and (D) are incorrect. The hospital's action does not represent a due process violation (but could be deemed unconscionable, *see Murphy v. Baptist Health*, set forth above) nor is this considered a restrictive covenant, which is typically a provision under a contract setting forth limitations on present or future rights to practice within a certain geographic area.

83. **Answer (D) is correct.** Under *some* state laws, there is an exception to the general rule that at-will employment relationships can be terminated at any time and for any reason for individuals who are terminated in retaliation for reporting compliance or legal concerns, otherwise known as whistleblowing. For example, in the case of *Turner v. Memorial Medical Center*, 911 N.E.2d 369 (Ill. 2009), the court set forth a three-part test to determine whether an at-will employee can sustain a retaliatory discharge claim under Illinois state law: (1) employer discharged the employee; (2) in retaliation for the employee's activities; and (3) the discharge violates a clear mandate of public policy.

    Answers (A), (B), and (C) are incorrect. Each describes types of claims that are more commonly applied outside the at-will employment context and are not applicable to this question.

84. **Answer (C) is correct.** A labor organization is afforded the same protections under the National Labor Relations Act as an organization that is organized as a formal union. *See* New York Univ. Med. Ctr. v. NLRB, 156 F.3d 405 (2d Cir. 1998); Bellevue Psych. Hosp. v. Leavitt, 443 F.3d 163 (2d Cir. 2006).

    Answer (A) is incorrect because Answer (C) is correct.

    Answer (B) is incorrect. While the statement in the answer is true, it is unrelated to the question, which is whether a labor organization has the same protections as a union.

    Answer (D) is incorrect. This answer is not factually true and not responsive to the call of the question.

85. **Answer (B) is correct.** Under the National Labor Relations Act, supervisors are prohibited from being part of a union. *See Oakwood Healthcare, Inc.*, 348 N.L.R.B. 686 (2006). *Oakwood Healthcare* provides some information about how to assess who may qualify as a supervisor under the law and sets forth that a position is considered supervisory when the person must use independent judgment in connection with the assignment of tasks under their role. The facts in Answer (B) are consistent with this definition.

Answers (A), (C), and (D) are incorrect. These examples do not represent actions or skills that require the staff member to use independent judgment in the assignment of tasks to other workers, and therefore these roles would not be considered supervisory.

86. **Answer (B) is the best answer.** Under the American with Disabilities Act (ADA), an employer may reassign a disabled employee to a different job if the employee's disability presents a direct threat to the health and safety of others that cannot be ameliorated through other reasonable accommodation. Estate of Mauro v. Borgess Med. Ctr., 137 F.3d 398 (6th Cir. 1998). Therefore, if the hospital can show that a surgical assistant with narcolepsy that is not well-controlled presents a direct threat to the health and safety of others, this is a defense to the employee's claim that reassignment to the position of scheduler was a demotion in violation of the ADA.

Answer (A) is incorrect. Offering an employee with a disability a different job can be, but is not always, a reasonable accommodation under the law. If the other job is inferior to the current job, then such other job may not be considered a reasonable accommodation and thus may not be a defense. Simply offering someone another job is not necessarily a reasonable accommodation.

Answer (C) is not the best answer. As stated in Answer (B) above, the hospital's best defense is to prove that the employee's condition presents a direct threat to the health and safety of the employee or others when performing the essential job functions of a surgical assistant. If the hospital is not able to prove this, then the hospital can attempt to argue that the reassignment to scheduler is not a demotion. "Reassignment is an accommodation of last resort that is considered only if there are no other effective accommodations that would enable an employee with a disability to perform the essential functions of their current job or if all other possible accommodations would impose undue hardship." U.S. Dep't of Just., Off. of the U.S. Att'ys, Reasonable Accommodation Policy and Procedure 6(F) (July 3, 2023). Here, this argument is unlikely to succeed given the very different roles and responsibilities of a scheduler versus a surgical assistant, which is a skilled job, but it may be the hospital's only remaining defense if the hospital is unable to establish the direct threat defense.

Answer (D) is incorrect. The ADA applies regardless of whether an employee is under a contract or at will.

Discrimination: EMTALA, Title VI, ADA, GINA, & ACA

87. **Answer (A) is the best answer.** The facts as described are a clear violation of the Emergency Medical Treatment and Active Labor Act (EMTALA), 42 U.S.C. §1395dd, which requires hospitals that are enrolled as providers with Medicare and have emergency departments to screen all patients who present on the hospital campus for an emergency medical condition, without regard to payment. Under the law, a hospital is prohibited from delaying the screening for any reason related to the patient's ability to pay. The hospital is not permitted to pause the screening to seek a pre-authorization.

    Answers (B), (C), and (D) are not the best answer. Each might be a state law claim that Ms. Davis could consider pursuing, but it is less clear that she would be successful on any of these claims. Given that this was a requirement under Ms. Davis's insurance, it is possible that the hospital would not be found liable in any of these state law claims or perhaps only partially liable because the hospital was merely acting pursuant to procedures established by the insurance policy. Also, when Ms. Davis presented to the emergency room, she had no prior physician-patient relationship with any physicians in the hospital.

88. **Answer (C) is correct.** While EMTALA requires that the screening take place, EMTALA is not intended to serve as a federal malpractice statute. Therefore, while the screening may have led to an incorrect diagnosis or perhaps even have been negligent, it is likely not a violation of EMTALA as long as the screening itself was equivalent to the screening that is given to other patients in the emergency room with similar symptoms. *See* Baber v. Hosp. Corp. of Am., 977 F.2d 872 (4th Cir. 1992).

    Answers (A) and (B) are incorrect. As stated above, EMTALA is not intended to be a federal malpractice statute for federal negligence claims, and these claims relate to the physician's negligence. It should be noted that it may be possible for a plaintiff to claim that the screening was so cursory or inadequate that it was the equivalent of not having been screened at all, but the facts here do not seem to rise to that level, and Answer (C) tells you to assume that the screening was consistent with screening given to other patients with similar presentation. *See Baber*, 977 F.2d 872.

    Answer (D) is incorrect. This answer is factually wrong. EMTALA does create a private right of action against the hospital (although not against physicians).

89. **Answer (A) is correct.** Under *Ricks*, 64 P.2d 208, a physician cannot terminate a patient unless (1) the condition no longer requires attention, (2) the patient fires the physician, or (3) the physician withdraws and provides reasonable notice so as to enable the patient to secure other medical attention. Unless the physician has met one of these three conditions, the physician could be found to have abandoned the patient. Based on the facts, the gangrene was a result of the diabetes, which was an ongoing condition for which Dr. Hudson was treating Noah. Although Dr. Hudson did withdraw, a court would likely view this notice to be insufficient given that Dr. Hudson did not warn Noah of the gangrene and the need to seek immediate medical treatment for the condition, nor did the physician continue treatment until a new doctor-patient relationship could be established.

Answer (B) is incorrect. Breach of contract would not be the best claim. It may be harder to prove a breach of the parties' agreement, and damages from a breach of contract claim may not provide as much compensation to Noah. In this type of case, breach of contract damages are typically only expectation damages, the amount necessary to place Noah in the position he would have been in had the breach not occurred. Typical tort damages in the context of a negligence action will compensate an individual to return them to where they were before the injury. Such tort damages would include the cost of the surgery, costs for additional care required to correct the negligence, pain and suffering, etc.

Answer (C) is incorrect. Individual physicians in their offices do not have EMTALA obligations.

Answer (D) is incorrect. This answer shows a standard negligence claim, which would likely be more difficult to prove than an abandonment claim. It is not clear that Dr. Hudson was negligent in his care of Noah or that his prior treatment was the proximate cause of Noah's injuries.

90. **Answer (D) is correct.** As mentioned above, a physician can withdraw from providing treatment to a patient *if* the physician provides meaningful notice. Based on these additional facts, it is likely that Dr. Hudson will be able to show that he provided reasonable notice to Noah to seek care from another provider and that Noah must have been receiving such care because Dr. Hudson transferred Noah's medical records to another provider.

Answer (A) is incorrect. Dr. Hudson is obligated to take Noah in the position that Noah is in for purposes of treating Noah. Dr. Hudson cannot just abandon the patient and has an ongoing duty to treat the condition. *See id.* It is worth noting, however, that while courts do not permit consideration of *pre-treatment* lifestyle choices, they may allow an argument that *post-treatment* patient conduct, such as failure to follow physician's instructions, contributed to the patient's injury. *See Ostrowski*, 545 A.2d 148. This would not relieve Dr. Hudson of his duty of continuing attention, but it might result in the apportionment of damages. For more discussion on comparative fault, see Question 70.

Answer (B) is incorrect. Dr. Hudson was treating Noah for his type two diabetes and that would mean ongoing treatment for known complications from diabetes, such as gangrene.

This should be one of the things that Dr. Hudson is looking for in his treatment of Noah's chronic condition.

Answer (C) is incorrect. Dr. Hudson had discovered the gangrene and thus had an obligation to notify Noah.

91. **Answer (B) is correct.** The physician's animus in this question seems related to the patient's neighborhood and the fact that he believes people from that neighborhood are drug-seeking. Combined with the fact that sickle cell anemia disproportionately impacts minority populations, one could infer from the comments that the patient was being discharged due to his race.

Answer (A) is incorrect. Title VI of the Civil Rights Act prohibits discrimination on the basis of race, not disability.

Answer (C) is incorrect. The physician was clear that he was discharging the patient because of where he lives. This in combination with the patient's sickle cell anemia diagnosis could be evidence of discrimination on the basis of race.

Answer (D) is incorrect. Proximate cause does not matter in the context of a claim under Title VI.

92. **Answer (D) is correct.** Based on the facts, at least some of the reason that the patient has been discharged may be due to his race. Under the Rehabilitation Act, to prove discrimination, the plaintiff must show that the patient's disability/disease is the *sole* reason for the discrimination. 29 U.S.C. §794(a). In contrast, the Americans with Disabilities Act allows for a claim of discrimination to be sustained if at least one of the reasons for the discrimination was the disability/disease. 42 U.S.C. §12182(a)-(b).

Answer (A) is incorrect. The ADA allows a mixed-motive discrimination claim.

Answer (B) is incorrect. Proper screening matters for an EMTALA claim, but not for a claim under the ADA or the Rehabilitation Act. Moreover, the patient appears to have a viable ADA claim.

Answer (C) is incorrect. Race appears to be one of the multiple reasons the patient was denied care. Given that, the estate does not have an action under the Rehabilitation Act as set forth above.

93. **Answer (C) is the best answer.** Section 1557 of the Affordable Care Act prohibits discrimination on the basis of race, color, national origin, age, disability, or sex in covered health care programs or activities. 42 U.S.C. § 18116. At enactment, many believed that Section 1557 created a single standard for all types of health care discrimination claims and overrode the Supreme Court's holding in *Alexander v. Sandoval*, 532 U.S. 275 (2001) that disparate impact claims were not actionable under Title VI. Contrary to initial thoughts, most courts have instead interpreted Section 1557 to simply carry over existing standards and enforcement

mechanisms under each of the various civil rights statutes, resulting in variation. Thus, disparate impact claims may be permitted for certain types of discrimination under Section 1557 and not others. While there is a current circuit split, "at least four circuits have recognized a disparate impact theory based on lack of meaningful access under Section 504, and by extension, Section 1557." BRIETTA R. CLARK ET AL., HEALTH LAW: CASES, MATERIALS AND PROBLEMS 389 (9th ed. 2022). So, the best legal strategy for the patient here would be to proceed under the Rehabilitation Act and Section 1557.

Answer (A) is not the best answer. As noted above, *Alexander*, 532 U.S. 275, is a case that pre-dates the enactment of Section 1557 and prohibits disparate impact claims under Title VI of the Civil Rights Act. This case did not impact the ability to bring a disparate impact claim for discrimination on the basis of disability under Section 504 of the Rehabilitation Act, a different federal law.

Answer (B) is incorrect. As stated above, most courts recognize a disparate impact claim for violation of Section 504 of the Rehabilitation Act. In contrast, most courts have limited Title VI claims to intentional discrimination, not allowing disparate impact claims. *See, e.g.*, Southeastern Penn. Transp. Auth. v. Gilead Scis., 102 F. Supp. 3d 688 (E.D. Pa. 2015).

Answer (D) is incorrect. The facts do not support a sex discrimination claim. Moreover, if a sex discrimination claim is based on Title IX, it requires intentional discrimination, not merely disparate impact. *See* Briscoe v. Health Care Serv. Corp., 281 F. Supp. 3d 725, 738–39 (N.D. Ill. 2017). Finally, as discussed above, most courts recognize a disparate impact claim for violation of Section 504 of the Rehabilitation Act.

94. **Answer (D) is the best answer.** Courts have generally held that states are not obligated under the U.S. Constitution to provide police, fire, or other safety services, including medical care. *See* Wideman v. Shallowford Cmty. Hosp., 826 F.2d 1030 (11th Cir. 1987). Courts have recognized, however, that states may be obligated to provide medical care when the state has a "special custodial relationship" with the patient, such as if the patient is an inmate in the state's prison system. *Id.* If the state has exercised a significant degree of custody and control over the individual and then places that individual in a position of danger, then it has an obligation to render care. In this instance, Ms. Jackson has no special custodial relationship with the state and thus has no action under the 14th Amendment to the U.S. Constitution. But Ms. Jackson may have other claims available to her, including possible claims under EMTALA or applicable state or local law.

Answer (A) is incorrect. For the same reasons that Answer (D) is correct, Answer (A) is incorrect. Courts have consistently held that there is no right under the 14th Amendment to the U.S. Constitution for medical services and treatment.

Answer (B) is incorrect. Similar to Answer (A), courts have also found that there is no constitutional right that obligates the states to provide emergency services such as ambulance drivers and emergency medical technicians.

Answer (C) is not the best answer. While Answer (C) is correct for most citizens, Answer (D) is a better choice because it more completely states the law. There are instances in which the state has a special custodial relationship with a patient that requires the state to provide certain medical services and treatment because of the custody and control that the state exerts.

95. **Answer (C) is correct.** In *Lovell v. Chandler*, 303 F.3d 1039 (9th Cir. 2002), the court found that when a state's Medicaid program extended eligibility to individuals under a new program, restricting such program only to non-disabled individuals violated the ADA because it discriminated on the basis of disability. While the state was not required by federal law to extend these coverage benefits, once the state undertook to extend eligibility to certain individuals, it was obligated to do so in a non-discriminatory manner. The same analysis also applies under Section 1557 of the ACA which prohibits discrimination on the basis of disability in programs receiving federal funding, like Medicaid.

Answer (A) is incorrect. Although the state's action was not in violation of the Social Security Act, once the state extended benefits beyond the minimum requirements, it was obligated to do so in a non-discriminatory manner under the ADA and Section 1557 of the ACA. Therefore, it is not enough that the state simply complied with the Social Security Act.

Answer (B) is incorrect. While it is true that a state is not obligated to provide Medicaid services, all states have chosen to provide Medicaid coverage for residents of their state. Once a state has undertaken the obligation to provide Medicaid, the state is obligated to comply with federal law governing the Medicaid program. *See* Health & Hosp. Corp. of Marion Cty. v. Talevski, 599 U.S. ___, 143 S. Ct. 1444 (2023). Again, though, the issue here was not a failure to meet the Medicaid requirements under federal law but rather a failure to provide such benefits in a non-discriminatory manner under the ADA and Section 1557 of the ACA.

Answer (D) is incorrect. While states are required to meet minimum thresholds, they have great flexibility to determine eligibility beyond those minimum obligations. For example, Alabama sets the income eligibility threshold for Medicaid for parents (in a family of three) with a minor child at 18% of the federal poverty level (FPL) or less, whereas Tennessee sets its income eligibility threshold for that same population at 82% of the FPL or less. *See Medicaid Income Eligibility Limits for Adults as a Percent of the Federal Poverty Level*, KAISER FAM. FOUND. (Jan. 1, 2023).

96. **Answer (C) is correct.** The Genetic Information Nondiscrimination Act of 2008 (GINA) prohibits certain discrimination based on genetic information in health coverage and employment. GINA does not bar discrimination based on genetic information or a manifested medical condition in life, disability, or long-term care insurance. AMA, GENETIC DISCRIMINATION (2013). Accordingly, Ella may be charged a higher premium based on her genetic information for any life, disability, or long-term care insurance, but she may not be charged a higher premium for health coverage. Some states provide more robust protection from discrimination

based on genetic information that could impact premiums for life, disability, or long-term care insurance, but this question focuses on GINA alone.

Answer (A) is incorrect. GINA prohibits discrimination based on genetic information in health coverage, and Ella may not be charged a higher premium for health insurance based on her genetic information.

Answers (B) and (D) are incorrect. GINA does not prohibit discrimination based on genetic information in life, disability, or long-term care insurance, and under federal law, Ella may be charged a higher premium based on her genetic information for each of these insurance types.

Regulation of Private Health Insurance

97. **Answer (C) is correct.** The Affordable Care Act (ACA) did not take on meaningful tort reform but instead focused its attention on what is referred to as the triple aim: improving the quality of care, lowering the cost of care, and improving population health through greater access and comprehensive benefits.

Answers (A), (B), and (D) all incorrect. These answers all reflect goals of the ACA.

98. **Answer**: Dante has a few options available to him, and some are dependent on his financial situation and what he can afford. First, it is possible that Dante qualifies for Medicaid in his state. If Dante goes onto healthcare.gov or a state exchange, if applicable, Dante should be able to share his annual income, and this will determine his eligibility for Medicaid in his state. The state of Kentucky has expanded its Medicaid program, and thus Dante would be eligible for state Medicaid if his income is less than 138% of the FPL. If Dante does not qualify for Medicaid in his state, then he should be able to go onto healthcare.gov or a state exchange and purchase a plan on the exchange. If Dante earns in excess of 100% but less than 400% of the FPL, then he will be eligible for premium-assistance tax credits and cost-sharing subsidies. Lastly, Dante could attempt to purchase a private insurance plan through an insurance company. If Dante buys a private insurance plan that is not offered through the health insurance exchanges, such a plan does not have to comply with the Affordable Care Act. This means that the insurance company can deny Dante for pre-existing conditions or charge him a substantially higher premium if the insurance company deems Dante to be high risk. Under the Tax Cuts and Jobs Act of 2017, there is no penalty for Dante's *not* having health insurance. So, if Dante does not purchase health insurance at all, there is currently no penalty that is owed.

99. **Answer**: The Governor's proposals show the contrast between an "open marketplace" model in option one versus an "active purchaser" model in option two. In an open marketplace model, the state can create minimum obligations, and the onus is on the insurer to ensure that it meets minimum obligations to be eligible for the exchange. These exchanges usually benefit from increased competition, thereby ideally driving down prices. The open marketplace also requires less active management because the criteria are established up front, and the management consists primarily of assuring compliance with the obligations. Alternatively, option two is what is considered an active purchaser model. Under this model, the state solicits proposals and then selects certain insurers from among those proposals. This requires more active management by the state at the beginning of the process. This process can also reduce costs

as a result of the state's selecting only those insurers that offer products with lower premiums or other cost-saving measures. The federal exchange established under the ACA, healthcare.gov, adopts an open marketplace model, and all insurers that meet the necessary minimum requirements can be qualified health plans offered on the marketplace.

100. **Answer (A) is correct.** The requirement that employers provide birth control is part of preventative and wellness services. 124 Stat. 119. Coverage of birth control as an essential health benefit (regardless of category) has been controversial and contains many exceptions.

Answers (B), (C), and (D) are all incorrect. While these are in fact three categories of the ten essential health benefits, birth control is not part of any of these services.

101. **Answer (C) is correct.** Under the ACA, certain individuals are eligible for premium assistance subsidies and/or cost-sharing reduction payments on a sliding scale based on income level. To access these subsidies and cost-sharing reduction payments, the individual is required to purchase a silver plan, as all such benefits are only available through silver plans.

Answers (A), (B), and (D) are incorrect. While these metal tiers are plans available on exchanges, an insured cannot access the subsidies and cost-sharing reduction payments through these tiers.

102. **Answer (C) is correct.** The case of *King v. Burwell* asks whether premium assistance tax credits are available to individuals who purchase health insurance through healthcare.gov, a federal health insurance exchange, as opposed to a state-operated exchange. This was because of certain language in the ACA indicating that the subsidies may only be available through a "State Exchange." The court found that the language was ambiguous, and if Congress had intended to require states to set up their own exchanges in order to allow their residents to have access to the subsidies, then Congress would have said so more explicitly.

Answers (A), (B), and (D) are all incorrect. These ACA issues were litigated in other cases.

103. **Answer (D) is correct.** Under the ACA, in 2023, large employers are prohibited from charging their employees a premium for health insurance that is in excess of 9.12% of the employee's household income. Dep't of Health & Hum. Servs., *Affordable Coverage*, HealthCare.gov (last visited July 31, 2023). If the employer is found to be charging employees more than 9.12% of their household income for health insurance premiums, then the employer is subject to a fine by the federal government. 26 U.S.C. § 4980H.

Answer (A) is incorrect. This answer misstates the threshold, which is not related to the increase year over year, but to the premium charged as a percentage of the employee's household income.

Answer (B) is incorrect. The ACA penalizes large employers that simply pass on high costs of insurance to their employees by charging employers a fine if premiums are in excess of 9.12% of employee's household income.

Answer (C) is incorrect. This answer confuses to whom the law is directed. Frank is required to purchase health insurance or pay a tax penalty (although the current tax penalty is $0). Frank's employer, however, has a separate obligation to ensure that Frank's costs in purchasing insurance are affordable. This employer provision was included to ensure that employers do not simply make their insurance unaffordable to push employees to the exchanges.

104. **Answer (B) is correct.** The No Surprises Act of 2020 generally prohibits balance billing, which is the practice of billing the patient for the difference between the amount the health care provider charges and the amount paid by insurance, for out-of-network charges for emergency services and for out-of-network charges by providers rendering care at an in-network hospital. CMS, *No Surprises: Understand Your Rights Against Surprise Medical Bills*, CMS: Newsroom (Jan. 3, 2022). The Act applies to charges incurred at inpatient hospitals, critical access hospitals, hospital outpatient departments, and ambulatory surgery centers, but it does not apply to charges incurred at physician's offices. This federal law supplements but does not supplant state surprise billing laws that may provide even greater consumer protection. Here, the emergency medical technician selected an out-of-network hospital for Chloe's emergency care. Chloe will be responsible for any cost sharing associated with an in-network hospital provider, but she cannot be balance billed for out-of-network charges. Oliver intentionally selected an in-network hospital for his non-emergency procedure, but he likely does not control all of the providers who render care within that hospital. He cannot be balance billed for out-of-network charges associated with a radiologist or anesthesiologist who provides additional services as part of his in-network hospital visit. Oliver could be balance billed for a surgeon or other provider he specifically selected.

Answer (A) is incorrect. While Chloe and Oliver could have been balanced billed in many states before the No Surprises Act of 2020 took effect, balance billing is no longer permissible under these circumstances.

Answers (C) and (D) are incorrect. Even though Chloe's care was emergency and Oliver's care was elective, neither had a choice of provider. Chloe did not choose the hospital. Oliver chose the hospital but did not choose the individual radiologist. Under these facts, neither could be balance billed.

Health Care Markets & Reform

105. **Answer (B) is correct.** Prior to the ACA, insurance companies used experience rating to guard against the potential for large claims from a high-risk individual. They rated a potential beneficiary based on the individual experience of that beneficiary: health history, family health history, pre-existing conditions, sex, race, etc. — any factors making that individual more likely to incur higher health expenses. Insurance companies selling non-compliant ACA plans may still follow this rating approach today.

    Answer (A) is incorrect. Community rating is the process set forth by the ACA, which does not take into account the individual experience of each beneficiary but looks at the entire community and allocates costs and expenses across the entire population to guard against high risks. Under this rating system, healthy people may pay a higher premium than they would in an experience-rated system in order to offset the equal amount paid by higher-risk individuals who will likely incur higher insurance expenses.

    Answers (C) and (D) are incorrect. These answers are not entirely responsive to the facts and will offer the insurance company less control over high-risk individuals. Moral hazard is the concept that individuals who have insurance are more likely to use it than those who do not. To prevent overuse or encourage thoughtful use of insurance coverage, insurance companies will charge co-pays, deductibles, and co-insurance to insured individuals. While these cost-sharing techniques might discourage use overall, they won't specifically target high-risk individuals more than low-risk individuals. Adverse selection is the concept that those who are most in need of insurance — high-risk individuals — are those most likely to seek it out. Insurers will guard against adverse selection by advertising and trying to sell policies in places and to people who are more likely to be low-risk, thereby creating favorable selection. Insurers want to guard *against* adverse selection, not use it for purposes of lowering costs.

106. **Answer (C) is correct.** Insurers use cost-sharing mechanisms to discourage individuals from overutilizing health insurance and health services. These techniques are designed to make the insured more thoughtful about visiting the doctor because they will owe money. Stop-loss insurance is not an example of a cost-sharing obligation. Rather, stop-loss insurance is a type of insurance that insurers or self-insured employers might purchase to ensure that their overall expenses do not exceed a set amount (e.g., an insurer might have stop-loss insurance for total claims in excess of $10,000,000). While stop-loss insurance helps the insurer guard against runaway costs, it does not deter individual overutilization of services.

Answers (A), (B), and (D) are incorrect. Co-pays, co-insurance, and deductibles are all types of cost-sharing obligations designed to deter over-utilization.

107. **Answer (A) is the best answer.** Managed care as a concept emerged in the 1970s and 1980s as a way for insurers to guard against exponential increases in the cost of care reimbursed on a cost basis. To guard against these costs, insurers began inserting themselves into the delivery of care by controlling when, how, and in what amount care is provided to patients. Thus, managed care controls a combination of payment for care and the delivery of that care.

Answer (B) is not the best answer. Not all controls under managed care plans are limitations on services, so the answer is incomplete compared to Answer (A).

Answer (C) is incorrect because it is incomplete. Controlling who a patient visits is merely one mechanism that managed care companies use to control the delivery of care.

Answer (D) is incorrect. These are simply two tactics that managed care companies use to control costs and delivery of care.

108. **Answer (B) is correct.** Utilization review is a technique used by insurance companies to review the use of services by their insureds. Typically, utilization review is retrospective, and therefore, similar to the facts of the Question, it involves a situation in which the insurance company reviews care *after* it has been rendered and makes a determination on whether such care was within the policy limits. The other answers describe other insurance control mechanisms, but these mechanisms are not consistent with the facts of this particular question.

Answer (A) is incorrect. Capitation is a mechanism by which the insurance company determines, in advance, a set price that it will pay to a provider for each insured member who is assigned to that physician. The physician will receive the "capitated" payment (usually per member, per month) regardless of whether or how many services the physician renders to the insured in a given time period.

Answer (C) is incorrect. This answer describes a process in which each insured is assigned a primary care provider and that provider is responsible for all referrals for services that the insured might need. The insured cannot seek care other than through a referral from the primary care physician.

Answer (D) is incorrect. This answer describes a mechanism in which the insurance company seeks pricing for applicable services from several different providers and will only reimburse based on a specific reference point (often the lowest price or the average price).

109. **Answer (C) is correct.** First under HIPAA with commercial group plans and then under the ACA in the individual market, insurers in these markets are no longer permitted to deny coverage to individuals for pre-existing conditions in most instances (certain exceptions apply based on timing of when insurance is acquired on the commercial group market).

Answers (A), (B), and (D) are all incorrect. HIPAA and the ACA did not curb adverse selection, community rating, or moral hazard, all of which remain commonly used practices today. See Answer 105 above for an explanation of these terms.

110. **Answer (A) is the best answer**. Insurance based on actuarial fairness looks at the cost of insurance based on actual usage and dictates the applicable price to be charged for a premium based on that use. Distributive justice, in contrast, focuses on fairness and equity for populations and sets premiums so that all share in the overall expenses of health care, regardless of whether certain segments of the population are heavier users. A distributive justice approach presupposes that no one chooses to get sick, and thus no one should be punished for needing greater access to services. While this is similar to experience rating versus community rating, actuarial fairness and distributive justice focus on average expenses for categories such as sex. It is statistically true that women over their lifetimes tend to utilize more health services than men, which is largely a result of child-bearing responsibilities. *See* Klea D. Berkis et al., *Gender Differences in the Utilization of Health Care Services*, 49 J. FAM. PRACT. 147 (2000). Experience rating can look at groups but can also look at the individual experience of a single individual to increase the premium expenses for that single individual.

Answer (B) is incorrect. The ACA does not have provisions for nor does the question describe a model in which insurers are not subject to adverse or favorable selection.

Answer (C) is not the best answer. While the ACA moves away from actuarial fairness and away from experiencing rating, the question specifically mentions the move from higher premiums "due to average higher usage of services" for a category such as women. For that reason, Answer (A) is a better answer.

Answer (D) is incorrect. Techniques to guard against moral hazard are still commonly used.

Topic 14 Answers

Employee Retirement Income Security Act (ERISA)

111. **Answer (A) is correct.** Express preemption is under Section 514 and sets forth that all state laws relating to employee benefit plans are preempted by federal law under the Employee Retirement Income Security Act (ERISA), 29 U.S.C. § 1001 *et seq.*, unless directed toward insurance.

Answer (B) is incorrect. Section 502, which is also under ERISA, is considered complete preemption because it preempts a state court from hearing any claims that could have been brought as federal ERISA claims. State courts are thus required to remove to federal court any claim that could have been brought as a federal ERISA claim, even if brought as a state law claim.

Answer (C) is incorrect. This answer incorporates Answer (B), which is wrong because Section 502 preemption is not express preemption but rather is considered complete preemption.

Answer (D) is incorrect because Answer (A) is correct.

112. **Answer (D) is correct.** ERISA is not applicable to this claim because Sally purchased her insurance through healthcare.gov. ERISA only applies to claims against an employee benefit plan, and a plan purchased through healthcare.gov is a private plan.

Answers (A), (B), and (C) are incorrect because ERISA does not apply.

113. **Answer (C) is the best answer.** Answer (C) is correct because this state law relates directly to the appeal process for denial of an employee benefit plan claim. ERISA has a provision for timely appeal of denial of claims by employee benefit plans, and therefore this claim could have been brought as an ERISA claim; the state law is preempted by ERISA.

Answer (A) is incorrect for the reasons set forth above. ERISA preempts the state law.

Answer (B) is not the best answer because the facts do not indicate whether the employer has a self-insured plan, and the "deemer" clause only comes into play if the plan is self-insured. Section 502 complete preemption is a better answer because it applies regardless of whether it is a self-insured plan.

Answer (D) is not the best answer. It is not clear that this would be removable under Section 514 express preemption because the law does seem to be directed toward insurance, as it is specific to health insurance policies in the state. This will likely be "saved" under Section 514 unless it is a self-insured plan and the deemer clause governs.

114. **Answer (B) is the best answer.** As stated above, the "deemer" clause will apply if a plan is self-insured because all self-insured plans are governed by ERISA in federal court.

Answer (A) is incorrect. As discussed above, ERISA preempts this state law.

Answer (C) is not the best answer. Once it is established that a plan is self-insured, then all actions against self-insured plans are required to be heard only in federal court, without the need to go through a preemption analysis under Section 502. Application of the "deemer" clause is an easier analysis for purposes of removal because the parties are not required to go into an analysis regarding the claim itself and whether it could have been brought as an ERISA claim.

Answer (D) is not the best answer. Similar to Answer (C) above, once it is established that a plan is self-insured, then all self-insured plans are in federal court without the need to go through a "saved" preemption analysis under Section 514. Thus, the "deemer" clause analysis is easier as set forth above.

115. **Answer (A) is correct.** Answer (A) sets forth the test that is applied by *Gobeille v. Liberty Mutual Insurance Co.*, 577 U.S. 312 (2016), which held that a law is determined to relate to an employee benefit plan if it has "reference to" ERISA plans or if the law has an impermissible "connection with" ERISA plans. To determine whether a law has an impermissible connection with ERISA plans, the Court established the following test: (1) whether the state law governs a central matter of plan administration or interferes with nationally uniform plan administration, or (2) whether acute economic effects of the law force an ERISA plan to adopt a certain scheme of substantive coverage or restrict its choice of insurers.

Answer (B) is incorrect. This is the test that applies under Section 514 when a court is trying to determine whether a state law is "saved" from preemption, because laws that govern insurance are saved from preemption. The inquiry in this question and in *Gobeille* is an earlier one asking whether the law even relates to an ERISA plan.

Answer (C) is incorrect. Whether a law interferes with the uniform plan is a question that is typically asked in the context of analyzing whether a law is preempted under Section 502 and thus not properly heard in a state court. This is a different inquiry than whether the law relates to an ERISA plan.

Answer (D) is incorrect. This is similar to the inquiry described in Answer (B) above and goes to whether or not a particular law may be "saved" from preemption under Section 514. Before one can analyze whether a state law is saved from preemption, one first must establish that it relates to ERISA at all.

Medicare & Medicaid

116. **Answer (C) is correct.** Medicare is a federal program providing public health insurance to most Americans aged 65 or older and to younger Americans with a disability, end-stage renal disease, or amyotrophic lateral sclerosis (ALS). Medicare eligibility does not require limited economic means, although income can impact premiums.

    Answers (A) and (B) are incorrect because Medicare is a federal program, not a joint federal-state program like Medicaid.

    Answers (B) and (D) are incorrect because Medicare does not means-test income or assets.

117. **Answer (A) is correct.** Medicare has four parts: Part A (hospital insurance), Part B (physician's office insurance), Part C (Medicare Advantage Plan), and Part D (prescription pharmaceutical insurance). Traditional Medicare includes Medicare Part A and Part B. Those enrolled in traditional Medicare may add an optional Medicare Prescription Drug Plan (Part D), which covers some prescription drugs. Alternatively, beneficiaries may enroll in a Medicare Advantage Plan that includes prescription drug coverage. Either way, Medicare beneficiaries have the ability to include coverage for some medically necessary prescription pharmaceuticals.

    Answers (B), (C), and (D) are incorrect. Generally, Medicare does not cover hearing aids, long-term nursing home care, eye exams, or dental care, even though such coverage would address many of the commonly unmet needs of Americans of advanced age.

118. **Answer (D) is the best answer.** In *National Federation of Independent Business (NFIB) v. Sebelius*, 567 U.S. 519 (2012), the Court upheld most, but not all, of the ACA. The Court determined that the individual mandate falls within Congress's authority to tax, but it held that requiring states to expand Medicaid to cover all low-income individuals or lose future federal Medicaid funds is coercive and exceeds congressional authority. Medicaid is a joint federal-state program providing public health insurance to certain low-income Americans.

    Answer (A) is incorrect. The Supreme Court upheld most, although not all, of the ACA.

    Answers (B) and (C) are not the best answers. Each correctly states one of the Court's conclusions, but only Answer (D) captures both.

119. **Answer (B) is correct.** None of these individuals appears eligible for Medicaid at present. They all make in excess of 138% of the FPL for a single individual household, as $400 per week for four weeks a month adds up to $1,600 per month. Abdul is also not eligible because he is a foreign national in the United States on a student visa. Don is also not eligible because he lives in a non-expansion state and is not categorically eligible.

    Answers (A), (C), and (D) are incorrect for the reasons stated above.

120. **Answer (A) is correct.** Because their income is above 100% but below 400% of the FPL, all qualify for a premium tax credit under the ACA. 42 U.S.C. §§ 18071(b)(2), 18081(a)(2). The American Rescue Plan made these subsidies more generous, and the Inflation Reduction Act extended the subsidy enhancements through 2025. Individuals who are lawfully present recent immigrants, such as Abdul on a student visa, may qualify for premium subsidies even though they are not eligible for Medicaid.

    Answer (B) is incorrect because all are eligible for a premium subsidy.

    Answers (C) and (D) are not the best answer because they each list some but not all of those eligible for a premium subsidy under the facts.

121. **Answer (C) is correct.** Brett and Cai are now eligible for Medicaid: they are U.S. citizens, they live in expansion states, and their households are below 138% of the FPL. In expansion states, Medicaid eligibility turns on modified adjusted income, not assets, so Cai's assets are irrelevant.

    Answers (A) and (B) are incorrect. Abdul is still not eligible because he is a foreign national in the United States on a student visa, and Don is still not eligible because he is not categorically eligible in most non-expansion states as a non-elderly adult with no children and no disability.

    Answer (D) is incorrect. It correctly states that Brett is eligible but fails to recognize that Cai is also eligible.

122. **Answer (B) is correct.** All four gentlemen now have incomes below 100% of the FPL. The ACA does not generally provide a premium subsidy to individuals with income below that threshold because such individuals are supposed to be eligible for Medicaid. *Id.* §§ 18071(b)(2), 18081(a)(2). Recognizing that lawfully present recent immigrants are generally not Medicaid-eligible, the ACA created an exception to the premium subsidy income floor for this group. Abdul will qualify for a subsidy despite having an income below 100% of the FPL because he is a lawfully present recent immigrant.

    Answers (A), (C), and (D) are incorrect. Brett, Cai, and Don will not qualify for a premium subsidy because their income is below 100% of the FPL and they are not lawfully present recent immigrants. *Id.* §§ 18071(b)(2), 18081(a)(2). Brett and Cai do not need a subsidy because they qualify for Medicaid. However, Don is not eligible for Medicaid or for the premium subsidy. When the Supreme Court ruled in *NFIB v. Sebelius*, 567 U.S. 519, that the federal government could not force states to expand Medicaid to all low-income adults as a condition of participation in the program, the ACA's drafting structure created a coverage gap in non-expansion states for non-categorically eligible individuals with income below 100% of the FPL who are not lawfully present recent immigrants. Don falls within this coverage gap.

123. **Answer (D) is the best answer.** Brett and Cai and their minor children are eligible; they are U.S. citizens, they live in expansion states, and now that their household size is two, their income is below 138% of the FPL. For parents, eligibility turns on income, not assets. So Cai's assets are irrelevant. Don's child is also eligible, but Don likely remains ineligible because, while being a parent of a minor child who is eligible may make him categorically eligible, it is unlikely that he meets income eligibility based on current state thresholds. Even non-expansion states provide minor children with Medicaid eligibility at this income level. We would need immigration status information on Abdul's child to determine his or her Medicaid eligibility.

Answer (A) is incorrect. Abdul is not eligible for Medicaid because he is a foreign national in the United States on a student visa. Don is not eligible because his income is too high to qualify in non-expansion states.

Answer (B) is not the best answer. It does not include Brett and Cai who are eligible, and we do not have enough immigration information to determine if Abdul's child will be eligible.

Answer (C) is incorrect. As mentioned above, while being a parent makes Don categorically eligible, the majority of non-expansion states set income eligibility for caretaker parents below 50% of the FPL. The most generous non-expansion state, Wisconsin, sets income eligibility at 100% of the FPL. Here, 100% of the FPL for a household of two is $18,310. If Don works 40 hours a week at $10 an hour for 52 weeks a year, he will earn $20,800 in a year, too much income to be eligible for Medicaid in any non-expansion state.

124. **Answer (C) is the best answer.** As U.S. citizens, Brett, Cai, and Don will be Medicare-eligible based on their age so long as they qualify to receive social security benefits. Individuals must earn 40 social security credits to qualify for social security benefits. An individual earns a credit by working and paying social security taxes. Given the income described in the facts, Brett, Cai, and Don will qualify for Medicare so long as they worked for at least ten years.

Answer (A) is not the best answer. Non-citizens can qualify for Medicare if they are permanent residents and have paid into the social security system long enough to qualify for social security benefits. If Abdul becomes a permanent resident, sometimes called obtaining a green card, he could qualify for Medicare. However, a student visa is not sufficient to qualify for Medicare, and nothing in the facts suggests that Abdul applied for and received permanent resident status.

Answer (B) is incorrect. As U.S. citizens, Brett, Cai, and Don will be Medicare-eligible based on their age so long as they qualify to receive social security benefits.

Answer (D) is not the best answer. While the answer correctly states that Brett is Medicare-eligible, it fails to recognize that Cai and Don are also eligible.

125. **Answer (C) is correct.** Federal law requires that a Section 1115 waiver be an "experimental, pilot, or demonstration project" and that the project "promotes the objectives" of Medicaid. 42 U.S.C. § 1315. During the Trump administration, CMS approved 13 state waivers imposing a work requirement for Medicaid eligibility. Courts invalidated these waivers, finding that CMS failed to consider if a work requirement promotes Medicaid's objectives. *See, e.g.*, Gresham v. Azar, 950 F.3d 93, 102 (D.C. Cir. 2020). The U.S. Supreme Court granted certiorari, but the Biden administration then withdrew all work requirement waivers that had not expired and asked the Court to vacate the judgments and remand the cases for dismissal as moot. The Court granted the Biden administration's request, leaving the permissibility of a Section 1115 waiver to impose a Medicaid work requirement unresolved. Arkansas v. Gresham, 142 S. Ct. 1665 (2022).

Answers (A) and (B) are incorrect. Effectiveness is not expressly required by law. Since Section 1115 waivers are for experimental projects, states may not yet know whether the projects will prove effective. It is worth noting, however, that CMS retains discretion to grant or to deny a waiver that complies with code requirements.

Answer (D) is incorrect. Federal law requires that a project be experimental and promote the objectives of Medicaid, as set forth in Answer (C).

126. **Answer (D) is correct.** Dentures are an optional Medicaid benefit. Just over half of state Medicaid programs cover them. Some optional Medicaid benefits are covered by all 50 state programs, like prescription drugs.

Answers (A), (B), and (C) are incorrect. All of these services are mandatory Medicaid benefits.

127. **Answer (D) is correct.** Answer (D) states one of the factors for granting a preliminary injunction, not one of the requirements for an individual to be able to bring a claim to enforce a provision of the Medicaid Act. In contrast, Answers (A), (B), and (C) set forth the three requirements that must be satisfied for a particular provision of the Medicaid Act to confer a private right of action pursuant to 42 U.S.C. § 1983. Answer (A) quotes the first requirement, as amended in *Gonzaga University v. Doe*, 536 U.S. 273, 287 (2002). Answers (B) and (C) quote the second and third requirements from *Blessing v. Freestone*, 520 U.S. 329, 340–41 (1997). As a result of these three requirements, courts have interpreted certain provisions of the Medicaid Act to be enforceable by individual beneficiaries in private litigation, whereas other provisions may only be enforced by the Department of Health and Human Services (HHS).

Answers (A), (B), and (C) are incorrect. As set forth above, each answer states one requirement for a provision of the Medicaid Act to create a private right of action.

128. **Answer (A) is correct.** In *Armstrong v. Exceptional Child Center, Inc.*, 575 U.S. 320 (2015), the U.S. Supreme Court held that there is no private enforcement of the Medicaid requirement mandating reimbursement rates high enough to enlist a sufficient number of providers. HHS

could enforce this plan requirement, although the mechanisms to do so are problematic as they involve defunding the entire state Medicaid program.

Answer (B) is incorrect. The majority of circuit courts have held that a beneficiary can enforce the "free choice of provider" provision. *See, e.g.*, Planned Parenthood Ariz., Inc. v. Betlach, 727 F.3d 960, 967–68 (9th Cir. 2013); Planned Parenthood of Ind., Inc. v. Comm'r of Ind. St. Dep't Health, 699 F.3d 962, 968 (7th Cir. 2012); Planned Parenthood So. Atl. v. Baker, 941 F.3d 687, 697–701 (4th Cir. 2019); *but see, e.g.*, Does v. Gillespie, 867 F.3d 1034, 1040–46 (8th Cir. 2017); Planned Parenthood of Greater Tex. Family Planning & Preventative Health Servs., Inc. v. Kauffman, 981 F.3d 347 (5th Cir. 2020).

Answer (C) is incorrect. Most courts have held that a beneficiary can sue to enforce the reasonable promptness requirement. *See, e.g.*, Waskul v. Washtenaw Cnty. Cmty. Mental Health, 979 F.3d 426, 445–48 (6th Cir. 2020); *but see* Nasello v. Eagleson, 977 F.3d 599, 602 (7th Cir. 2020).

Answer (D) is incorrect. Most courts have held that a beneficiary can enforce the mandatory categories of benefits. *See, e.g.*, *Waskul*, 979 F.3d 426, 445–48.

Structure & Governance of Health Care Entities

129. **Answer (B) is correct.** Boards of directors for nonprofits are subject to the same standard of review under a liability claim as boards of directors for for-profit entities — gross negligence. *See* Stern v. Lucy Webb Hayes Nat'l Training Sch. for Deaconesses & Missionaries, 381 F. Supp. 1003 (D.D.C. 1974). Unlike trustees of a trust that owe a higher standard and could be liable for acts of simple negligence, courts will require proof of gross negligence to establish liability of directors of non-profit entities.

 Answer (A) is incorrect because Answer (B) describes the correct standard.

 Answers (C) and (D) are incorrect. The directors in the question can be found liable for gross negligence, which is a lower standard than either willful neglect or intentional misconduct.

130. **Answer (C) is correct.** Directors of a non-profit corporation have three fiduciary obligations: duty of care, duty of loyalty, and duty of obedience. *See, e.g.*, Manhattan Eye, Ear & Throat Hosp. v. Spitzer, 715 N.Y.S.2d 575 (Sup. Ct. 1999); Stern v. Lucy Webb Hayes Nat'l Training Sch. for Deaconesses & Missionaries, 381 F. Supp. 1003 (D.D.C. 1974). The facts described here portray self-dealing, which if not disclosed can be considered a violation of a director's fiduciary obligation of the duty of loyalty.

 Answers (A) and (B) are incorrect. Issues related to self-dealing arise under the duty of loyalty, not the duty of care or the duty of obedience.

 Answer (D) is incorrect. Non-management is encompassed under the duty of care and is not exemplified by the facts in the question.

131. **Answer (D) is correct.** The duty of obedience is a fiduciary duty unique to directors of non-profit boards that requires directors to consider the mission of the entity as the primary focus of the directors in the context of decision-making. Answer (D) describes a situation in which the directors are making a decision on the basis of the mission of the entity overall, which is the financial stability of the main hospital.

 Answer (A) is incorrect. The directors in this answer are not focusing on the needs of the community and must consider the needs of the community as part of their duty of obedience, above financial-only considerations.

Answer (B) is incorrect. The directors must consider the mission of the organization and how selling it for a mall would impact the overall mission to provide health services to the community. *See Manhattan Eye, Ear & Throat Hosp.*, 715 N.Y.S.2d 575.

Answer (C) is incorrect. The purpose of the purchase in this answer does not seem consistent with the mission of the organization and could be an activity that would otherwise be taxable because it is inconsistent with the mission of the organization overall.

132. **Answer (C) is correct.** Medicare beneficiaries are assigned to Accountable Care Organizations (ACOs) by attribution based on a plurality of primary care visits that a patient has within the previous 12 months. 42 C.F.R. §425.10 *et seq.* This means that a Medicare beneficiary can go to any physician that the beneficiary wants, at the beneficiary's choosing, regardless of ACO affiliation. Therefore, Answer (C) is *not* an attribution of the Medicare Shared Savings Program.

Answers (A), (B), and (D) are incorrect because they are all requirements under the Medicare Shared Savings Program.

133. **Answer (B) is correct.** Under *In re Caremark International Inc. Derivative Litigation,* 698 A.2d 959 (Del. Ch. 1996), once a board of directors of a health care entity, whether for-profit or non-profit, becomes aware of a compliance issue, the board is required to implement a new or existing compliance plan and take appropriate steps to correct the fraud. If fraud has occurred in the past, then the directors are on notice that such fraud could occur again and must have a compliance plan in place that they implement appropriately and expediently.

Answer (A) is incorrect. Whether the company has admitted fault is not a defense for purposes of the shareholder derivative action, which relates to a failure to monitor a claim as a result of the monies paid to settle the case.

Answer (C) is incorrect. The directors could still be liable despite already having a compliance plan in place if they were aware of the fraud and failed to implement the compliance plan.

Answer (D) is incorrect. It is not enough to fire someone who may have been partially responsible for the fraud. The directors are required to implement a compliance plan that will help to identify a root cause for the fraud and, ideally, prevent issues in the future, beyond one employee.

134. **Answer (A) is correct.** Under most state statutes, a non-profit company requires approval of its Board of Directors and the state Attorney General for major decisions, including a sale of all or substantially all of its assets. The Attorney General typically stands in the role of shareholder for purposes of protecting the assets of the "owners" of the non-profit organization, which is the general public.

Answer (B) is incorrect. Non-profit organizations do not have shareholders.

Answer (C) is incorrect. Officers of a corporation (non-profit or for-profit) are responsible for implementing decisions of the Board of Directors but do not have independent judgment authority beyond that delegated by the Board of Directors to make decisions on behalf of the corporation.

Answer (D) is incorrect. Most states require approval of the Attorney General in addition to the Board of Directors.

135. **Answer (B) is the best answer.** The duty of obedience is the fiduciary duty that requires directors of a non-profit organization to consider the mission as the prime driver of decisions in connection with the organization. Thus, it is often referred to as the concept of "mission primacy." *See Manhattan Eye, Ear & Throat Hosp.*, 715 N.Y.S.2d 575.

Answer (A) is incorrect. This answer describes a situation in which a non-profit organization is creeping away from its mission into other ventures.

Answer (C) is not the best answer. The duty of obedience is a type of fiduciary duty that is owed by non-profit directors. So this answer is not as precise as Answer (B).

Answer (D) is incorrect. While this answer describes what the duty of obedience encompasses, it is not the common phrase utilized by courts.

Tax-Exempt Health Care Organizations

136. **Answer**: Although for-profit hospitals and non-profit hospitals are both subject to the same laws and regulations in connection with hospital operations, including Medicare Conditions of Participation and applicable state licensure laws, for example, there are some key distinctions that could impact operations and sustainability for the Sisters of the Divine Mission Hospital. First, the primary difference between a non-profit entity and a for-profit entity is that a for-profit entity is organized and exists for the benefit of its shareholders. All profits derived from operations of the entity may inure to the shareholders. In contrast, a non-profit organization is organized for the benefit of the public and the profits derived from operations must inure back into the charitable mission of the entity and not to any private individual or entity (e.g., a shareholder). This does not mean that a for-profit entity cannot use profits to support operations and improve facilities (rather than pay a dividend). It just means that whether to use the profits in that manner instead of for the purpose of issuing dividends is a decision for the entity's directors and shareholders. States and the federal government are willing to forgo the collection of taxes (income tax, sales tax, property tax) for non-profit entities because they are providing a service that relieves the government of having to provide the service itself. That means, though, that the non-profit entity is obligated to provide services in accordance with its charitable purpose in order to be provided with the tax exemption that is afforded to it. In the specific problem at hand, Sisters of the Divine Mission Hospital has a charitable purpose obligating it to provide services to the "poor and downtrodden." This means that beyond obligations under the Emergency Medical Treatment and Active Labor Act (EMTALA), Sisters of the Divine Mission Hospital may have additional obligations to treat certain types of indigent patients in furtherance of its charitable mission. To the extent it is providing services to more individuals who are underinsured or without an ability to pay, it is likely that this could result in smaller margins for this hospital versus the for-profit. Non-profit, tax-exempt hospitals do not necessarily have access to capital in the same way as for-profit hospitals. A for-profit hospital has investors (new and existing) who may be willing to make additional monetary investments in the entity. This can be done in both public and private markets. In contrast, a non-profit hospital cannot seek investor funding — it can seek donations from the public or obtain tax-exempt bond financing. This could impact Sisters of the Divine Mission Hospital's ability to raise capital to compete with the funding sources that may be available to the for-profit hospital. Although there are some advantages of for-profit status, the fact that a hospital is beholden to shareholders can impact operations and operational choices. In contrast, the non-profit hospital will be able to make decisions that are in furtherance of the mission regardless of whether there may be a different decision that would be more financially

beneficial. In all, Sisters of the Divine Mission Hospital's mission to treat the "poor and downtrodden" could require it to treat a higher percentage of low-income individuals. But both hospitals will follow substantially the same laws, rules, and regulations in connection with operation of services.

137. **Answer**: A non-profit, tax-exempt entity that has ownership in a for-profit entity can maintain the distribution from such joint venture as tax-exempt so long as the non-profit, tax-exempt entity has sufficient control over the operations of the entity. These facts are similar to the case of *Redlands Surgical Services v. Commissioner of Internal Revenue*, 113 T.C. 47 (1999), *aff'd per curiam*, 242 F.3d 904 (9th Cir. 2001), in which the IRS concluded that the non-profit, tax-exempt entity owner did not have sufficient control over the subsidiary joint venture with a surgical company to allow the income to be treated as tax-exempt. Relying on Revenue Ruling 98-15 ,the court concluded that although the parties to the joint venture had equal board control and veto power, the non-profit, tax-exempt entity holding company that owned the joint venture (and thus its only operations) did not have sufficient control over the joint venture to maintain its tax-exempt status. Although the hospital in this question has its own operations, and thus the revenue from the joint venture will only constitute a portion of the total revenues of the hospital, if the hospital wants to ensure that the proceeds will be treated as tax-exempt, the hospital should set up the company with control over the joint venture. In Revenue Ruling 98-15, this includes control over contracting, control over decision-making beyond simply veto power, and the ability to make decisions based on the mission of the organization over financial considerations.

138. **Answer (D) is correct.** Following the establishment of the Medicare and Medicaid programs, the IRS began to use the "community benefit" standard, which basically examines whether the entity can demonstrate the services and benefits that it is providing to the community. Examples that historically were considered as constituting "community benefit" were open emergency rooms, willingness to hire any physicians, a community-led board of directors, and use of excess funds for research, education, and teaching. *See* IHC Health Plans, Inc. v. Comm'r, 325 F.3d 1188 (10th Cir. 2003).

    Answer (A) is incorrect. Although the IRS considers whether the entity's actions are for the purpose of fulfilling its mission, the IRS does not apply a primary purpose test for purposes of considering tax-exemption more generally.

    Answer (B) is incorrect. Mission primacy is a fiduciary obligation of the directors on the Board of Directors, but this is not a test that the IRS uses for this purpose.

    Answer (C) is incorrect. The charitable trust doctrine is not applicable here. This doctrine applies to charitable institutions and requires that gifts/donations provided for specific or restricted use can only be used for that purpose.

139. **Answer (C) is correct.** Although the IRS has started to take a more aggressive stance in the past few years regarding the need for federally tax-exempt entities to provide some amount

of charity care, the IRS still applies the community benefit standard, which does not require a certain level of charity care to be met as a threshold matter. Answer (C) is an example of the community benefit standard.

Answer (A) is incorrect. While Congress and the IRS have discussed whether a minimum level of charity care should be required for tax-exempt entities, the IRS currently does not have a minimum requirement.

Answer (B) is incorrect. Hospitals are not prohibited from having a policy to not ask individuals up front whether they require financial assistance, but the IRS does not count "bad debt" (debt that has become uncollectible and is therefore written off) as constituting "charity care" services.

Answer (D) is incorrect. The IRS does not consider bad debt to be part of "charity care."

140. **Answer (B) is correct.** State property tax exemption is often subject to a five-part test, known as the *Korzen* test: (1) no capital, capital stock, or shareholders; (2) earns no profits or dividends, but derives funds mainly from private charity and holds them in trust for its exempt purpose; (3) dispenses charity to all who need it and apply for it; (4) does not provide gain or profit to any individual; and (5) does not appear to place any obstacles in the way of those who need and would avail themselves of the charitable benefits it dispenses. *See* Provena Covenant Med. Ctr. v. Dep't of Revenue, 925 N.E.2d 1131 (Ill. 2010). Based on this test, Answer (B) makes state property tax exemption less likely because it conflicts with factor (5), in that the hospital creates a barrier for those who need and may want charitable services. Specifically, the hospital requires a patient to know of the availability of the discount and request assistance prior to receiving services in order to be eligible for financial assistance.

Answers (A), (C), and (D) are incorrect because they are all consistent with criteria that courts have found to have satisfied at least one of the factors above.

141. **Answer (D) is correct.** Federally tax-exempt organizations are prohibited from providing benefits to private individuals; rather, such profit/benefit should inure only back into the mission of the organization. I.R.C. § 501(c)(3). Because the discount will apply to any physician, regardless of whether the physician has privileges, this is an example of private benefit to outsiders.

Answers (A) and (B) are incorrect. An Excess Benefit Transaction and private inurement are both situations in which the tax-exempt organization provides a benefit to a "disqualified individual" (as defined by I.R.C. § 4958(f)(1)(A)) or an insider. An "insider" is typically a key individual such as a chief executive officer or a director who is in a position of influence. In the facts, although some physicians may have influence, the intention is to benefit any outsiders of the organization, not insiders.

Answer (C) is incorrect. Private benefit provided to the organization can jeopardize its tax-exempt status if done so frequently so as to eclipse its primary charitable purpose. Private benefit is not considered tax fraud.

142. **Answer (B) is correct.** As stated above, when a benefit transaction involves an individual who is considered an insider or person of influence, it is an example of private inurement. The facts make it clear that the benefit is being provided to someone who is a top referrer to the hospital and thus in a position of influence.

    Answer (A) is incorrect. The penalty associated with a finding of private inurement is revocation of the organization's tax-exempt status, but the penalty associated with a finding of private benefit is not revocation unless there is such a substantial amount of private benefit that the organization's primary purpose can no longer be said to be for the charitable purpose. Therefore, Answer (A) is not the correct answer.

    Answer (C) is incorrect. The facts here do not rise to the level of tax fraud.

    Answer (D) is incorrect. This answer is not responsive to the question and does not provide an example of the above facts; tax-exempt bond financing is a financing mechanism available only to tax-exempt organizations to finance large capital projects.

143. **Answer (C) is correct.** Excess Benefit Transactions, an alternative enforcement mechanism imposed by the IRS when the IRS finds private inurement, impose sanctions and penalties on the individuals who are involved in transactions that provide excess benefit to certain insiders in the organization, known as "disqualified persons." This enforcement mechanism provides for a "rebuttable presumption of reasonableness," which allows the transaction to be presumed permissible if the terms of the transaction are approved by a board of directors or a committee appointed by the board composed entirely of individuals who (1) have no conflicts of interest under the transaction, (2) have obtained and relied upon appropriate comparability data before making their decision, and (3) have adequately documented the basis for their decision. *See* 26 C.F.R. § 53.4958-6. Based on the facts, this transaction seems to qualify for the presumption.

    Answer (A) is incorrect. The Chair would qualify as a "disqualified person" under applicable regulations.

    Answer (B) is incorrect. Just because the Chair is willing to pay the money back does not impact whether it is an excess benefit transaction.

    Answer (D) is incorrect. Approval by the "organizational managers" would not change the analysis that this is an excess benefit transaction. Approval by the organizational managers will only impact who will have to pay penalties.

144. **Answer (B) is correct.** When an entity initially seeks federal tax-exempt status, the entity can complete a standard online form to be granted this status in which the entity attests to its compliance with IRS requirements for tax-exempt entities. The requirements under Section 501(c)(3) are that an "organization must be organized and operated exclusively for exempt purposes set forth in Section 501(c)(3), and none of its earnings may inure to any private shareholder or individual. In addition, it may not be an action organization, i.e., it may not attempt to influence legislation as a substantial part of its activities and it may not participate

in any campaign activity for or against political candidates." Whether an entity complies with these requirements is determined retrospectively once an entity begins operations. Entities are not required to take any specific actions initially other than completing the online form.

Answer (A) is incorrect. Non-profit hospitals must develop a charity care policy to ensure compliance with federal and state rules and regulations for tax-exempt and non-profit entities, respectively. However, the IRS does not require submission or approval of a charity care policy as a condition for its granting tax-exempt status.

Answer (C) is incorrect. Hospitals are required under Section 501(r)(3)(A) to complete a community health needs assessment every three years. This is a process that will begin after the hospital has established its entity and once it begins its operations. It is not required to be submitted or completed prior to operations or as a condition precedent to receiving tax-exempt status.

Answer (D) is incorrect. This response is factually incorrect. Organization as a non-profit legal entity is governed by state law and operates to extend any tax benefits for entities in connection with state property, sales, and excise taxes. An entity that is organized as a non-profit entity within a state can but is not obligated to also apply for federal tax exemption. Likewise, organizations that are not recognized as state non-profit entities can still be eligible for federal tax-exempt status. For example, a neighborhood association may not organize as a legal entity under state law but can apply for federal tax exemption.

145. **Answer (D) is correct.** There is no purpose listed under federal law that is specific to the rendering of health care services or public health as a purpose for which tax exemption would be granted. Most hospitals that are not organized for another purpose, such as a religious organization or educational institution, qualify under the general category of "charitable" purpose. Providing health care services to those without an ability to pay may qualify under the "charitable" purpose category.

Answers (A), (B), and (C) are all incorrect. "Religious," "scientific," and "educational" are each unique purpose categories eligible for tax-exempt status under federal law. Some hospitals operated by religious orders may be organized for religious purposes. Similarly, teaching hospitals or research hospitals may be organized as either educational institutions or scientific research institutions, respectively.

Topic 18

Answers

Fraud & Abuse

146. **Answer (C) is the best answer.** The federal Anti-Kickback Statute makes it illegal to pay or receive any remuneration (directly or indirectly, overtly or covertly) for referring, purchasing, or ordering goods, facilities, services, or items that are paid for by federal health care programs. The two largest federal health care programs are Medicare and Medicaid. Based on the facts, unless the arrangement is revised to meet a safe harbor, the proposed discount likely violates the Anti-Kickback Statute if one purpose of the discount is to induce referrals reimbursable by federal health care programs. 42 U.S.C. § 1320a-7b. Federal regulations found at 42 C.F.R. § 1001.952 set forth all applicable safe harbors. These safe harbors establish criteria for certain arrangements/transactions that, if followed by the parties, will insulate an arrangement that would otherwise violate the Anti-Kickback Statute from liability.

    Answer (A) is incorrect. The legality of the arrangement is not assessed based on the severity of the discount but rather on whether the discount—of any level—was for the purpose of inducing referrals.

    Answer (B) is incorrect. This answer misapplies the test under the Anti-Kickback Statute. It is not whether the inducement was the "primary" purpose but rather whether it was one of the purposes.

    Answer (D) is not the best answer because the motivation does not need to be the primary purpose but rather needs to be just one purpose.

147. **Answer (A) is correct.** The Physician Self-Referral Law, otherwise known as the Stark Law (42 U.S.C. § 1395nn), was enacted following a report concluding that physicians who have an ownership position in the laboratory company to which they referred their patients were more likely to order lab tests than physicians without an ownership position. In response, Congress enacted the Stark Law to ensure that physicians make referrals based on medical judgment because such referral is best for the patient and not because the physician stands to gain financially.

    Answer (B) is incorrect. Self-referral refers to a scenario in which a physician refers a patient for other items or services for which the physician will also benefit financially, but the Stark Law is not limited to only situations in which physicians have referred patients to themselves.

    Answer (C) is incorrect. There is no requirement under the law that physicians can only make referrals to other physicians, although the law itself only governs referrals that physicians make to other physicians or the physicians' family members. While making a referral because it is medically appropriate will contribute to better quality care and promote patient safety, the focus of the law was to curb referrals that physicians were making because such referrals resulted in financial gain for the physicians.

Answer (D) is incorrect. The law stops short of making ownership a prohibition.

148. **Answer (D) is the best answer.** Both the Stark Law and the Anti-Kickback Statute operate by creating a broad prohibition against certain arrangements/transactions but also creating safe harbors (as they are called under the Anti-Kickback Statute) or exceptions (as they are called under the Stark Law). If the criteria in such safe harbors and/or exceptions are followed, the applicable law allows an otherwise prohibited transaction to go forward. While the Anti-Kickback safe harbors and Stark Law exceptions do not totally align, many safe harbors and exceptions contain similar criteria. Under the facts, the hospital will do a one-time purchase and sale of the physicians' practice. This will be an "isolated transaction" in which the hospital will pay the physicians a one-time fee (either in lump sum or installments). The transaction will also involve employing the physicians on a continuing basis. The employment exception under the Stark Law is an easier exception to meet and most closely defines the current relationship that exists between the hospital and the physicians. Therefore, the purchase documents must meet the isolated transactions exception and the employment arrangement must meet the employment exception under the Stark Law.

Answers (A) and (B) are not the best answer. Each answer is correct but incomplete.

Answer (C) is not the best answer. The Stark Law only requires the parties to meet one exception per transaction (note that the asset purchase of the practice is a *different* transaction than the employment arrangement). If the physicians are employed, then the employment exception should apply and Stark Law would not require that the employment arrangement also meet the personal services exception. The personal services exception is also a more difficult exception to meet under the Stark Law, requiring a writing, for example, and thus it would be better for the parties to meet the employment exception based on these facts. If the physicians were going to be independent contractors of the hospital and not employees, then it would be necessary for the parties to meet the personal services exception. Regardless, the parties would also need to meet the isolated transaction exception, making Answer (D) the best answer.

149. **Answer (C) is correct.** Under applicable Medicare billing regulations, when submitting claims or bills for services to the federal government, physicians are required to certify that the services for which the claim is being sought were medically necessary. Only required lab work is considered medically necessary.

Answer (A) is incorrect. As mentioned in the above-stated regulation — a physician may only submit claims for services that the physician certifies are medically necessary at the time rendered.

Answer (B) is incorrect. As established in the regulations set forth above, physicians must certify medical necessity prior to billing for a service.

Answer (D) is incorrect. This answer is not factually true. Federal regulations allow blood work to be billed separately from physician services and do not require the entire panel to be run if only certain tests are necessary.

150. **Answer (B) is correct.** Hospitals are paid for care provided to Medicare patients based on what is referred to as a "diagnosis related group" or "DRG," which is an established rate that is paid for the entire episode of care based on the specific diagnosis and severity of the particular patient. Thus, the hospital will be paid more for the same diagnosis if the patient is considered more specialized or required more care than another patient with the same diagnosis. It is illegal for hospitals to document a higher severity of diagnosis simply to garner the higher DRG payment, which is known as DRG Creep.

    Answer (A) is incorrect. The Medicare Secondary Payor rule is for purposes of charging other forms of insurance first and Medicare second, if applicable. The facts do not support this response.

    Answer (C) is incorrect. "Upcoding" is generally the term for behavior similar to DRG Creep. It describes when physicians code for an outpatient visit at a higher level of care and complexity than was necessary. Physicians bill for outpatient visits based on the service rendered but can classify that service on a five-point scale for purposes of complexity of the service. The higher the complexity, the higher the payment. Because the facts here show an inpatient hospital scenario and not a physician outpatient visit, this behavior is known as DRG Creep.

    Answer (D) is incorrect. There are not sufficient facts to say that the services were unnecessary. There are only sufficient facts to show that the services were billed at a higher rate than allowed.

151. **Answer (D) is correct.** The Civil Monetary Penalties law, among other things, prohibits persons, including hospitals, from offering inducements to beneficiaries that may influence the beneficiary's choice of providers. 42 U.S.C. § 1320a-7a(a)(5). Under this fact pattern, the hospital is offering beneficiaries an inducement to encourage them to come to its institution, which is in violation of this law without an applicable exception.

    Answers (A), (B), and (C) are all incorrect. This law prohibits these activities regardless of payor or policies regarding charity care.

152. **Answer (A) is correct.** In this scenario, Dr. Brown is ordering X-rays, for which the federal government is paying her, but because of the quality of the image, the X-ray fulfills no diagnostic purpose. Ordering the X-ray then, when she does not use it for diagnostic purposes, is the equivalent of a worthless service.

    Answer (B) is incorrect. Upcoding is when a physician codes (on a scale of one through five) for a higher level of care than was rendered during the visit. In the facts of this question, the physician is not claiming a higher level of service than was provided. Rather, she is claiming that she rendered a service that was necessary and appropriate, but it could not have been either given that it had no diagnostic value.

Answer (C) is incorrect. Even if her care is still appropriate and the patient is still being well treated because of the referral, billing for a worthless service is considered improper under applicable regulations.

Answer (D) is incorrect. This answer does not appear to be true — she is unable to use it for diagnostic purposes, which would be the purpose of ordering an X-ray.

153. **Answer (A) is the best answer.** For the Stark Law to apply, the parties to the transaction must meet the definition of a "financial relationship." A "financial relationship" is defined under 42 U.S.C. § 1395nn as when a physician *or physician's "immediate family member"* (emphasis added) has either an ownership or investment interest in the entity or a compensation arrangement with the entity. Under the facts, the physician's wife (the physician's immediate family member) has an ownership position in a staffing company that then contracts with a radiology practice. This creates a compensation arrangement. The ownership position of the physician's wife is imputed to the physician and therefore the arrangement will be required to meet an exception in the same way it would if the physician held the ownership position himself.

Answer (B) is not the best answer. The Stark Law is only violated if an exception does not apply. This answer provides an explanation for why the Stark Law may be implicated, but is not a complete answer because it fails to recognize that compliance with an exception would make this arrangement permissible under the Stark Law.

Answer (C) is incorrect. While it is true that radiologists typically do not have private patients, physicians can still refer patients for services at the radiology center. These services will constitute "Designated Health Services" under the Stark Law and thus requires the arrangement to meet an exception.

Answer (D) is incorrect. Because the physician's ownership is imputed to his immediate family member, the arrangement between the staffing company and the radiology practice constitutes a compensation arrangement under the Stark Law and thus the Stark Law is implicated. The arrangement must meet a Stark exception to be legally permissible. The fact that the payment is fair market value and does not vary with the volume or value of referrals might enable this arrangement to meet an exception, but this arrangement is still a "financial relationship" under the Stark Law.

154. **Answer (C) is the best answer.** Under applicable definitions in the Stark Law, the arrangement will not be considered an indirect ownership or investment interest, which constitutes a "financial relationship," if there is (1) an unbroken chain of persons or entities having ownership or investment interests between the referring physicians and the entity furnishing designated health services (DHS) *and* (2) the entity furnishing the DHS has actual knowledge of, or acts in reckless disregard or deliberate ignorance of, the fact that the referring physician has some ownership or investment interest (though indirectly) in the entity furnishing the DHS. *See* 42 C.F.R. § 411.354(b)(5)(i). Here, it does not appear that the entity furnishing the

DHS — the sleep lab — has actual knowledge of the relationship with Dr. Jones or is acting in reckless disregard or deliberate ignorance of the relationship. Therefore, this relationship as described does not meet the definition of an "indirect ownership or investment interest" and the Stark Law does not apply.

Answers (A) and (B) are incorrect because Answer (C) is correct. The Stark Law is inapplicable based on the facts.

Answer (D) is not the best answer. The rationale behind the regulation is likely to exempt ownerships or investment interests that are so far afield that it is unlikely that the physician is making referrals because of a financial interest. This answer is not as good as Answer (C), though, because it does not describe the regulation and the criteria for how an indirect ownership or investment interest is defined. The regulation does not simply state that relationships that are too attenuated are exempt, but it instead requires that the DHS entity have no actual knowledge of the relationship or not act in reckless disregard or deliberate ignorance of the relationship, as set forth in Answer (C).

155. **Answer (C) is correct.** There are many exceptions under the Stark Law, which generally prohibits a physician from referring to an entity for the furnishing of "designated health services" with which the physician has a "financial relationship." A financial relationship under the law includes any payment of remuneration — whether in cash or in kind. Under this fact pattern, any payment made by the hospital to physicians will constitute a financial relationship and would require compliance with a Stark Law exception. The described arrangement is intended to be covered by the "nonmonetary compensation" exception because a free lunch will constitute a financial relationship between the parties and a free lunch is not monetary compensation but in-kind compensation. Under the exception, hospitals can provide certain nonmonetary compensation to physicians who refer to the hospital if below a certain monetary threshold, which threshold is reset on an annual basis. *See id.* § 411.357(k).

Answer (A) is incorrect. This exception will not work because the lunch will be offered to physicians who are not currently on the medical staff. This exception under the regulations is limited to only members of the hospital's medical staff.

Answer (B) is incorrect. The "professional courtesy" exception is designed to address situations in which physicians provide medical services free of charge or at a highly discounted rate to friends or family members of other physicians with whom they have a referral relationship for DHS. Therefore, this answer would be inapplicable as it is not considered professional courtesy to provide lunch.

Answer (D) is incorrect because Answer (C) is correct.

156. **Answer (D) is correct.** Ambulatory Surgery Centers (ASCs) are paid based on a composite rate, and therefore services rendered at an ASC are not considered "designated health services" (DHS) under the Stark Law. *Id.* § 411.351. For that reason, the Stark Law does not apply when the referral is for services rendered at an ASC.

Answers (A) and (B) are incorrect because answer (D) is correct. Because the referral in this question is a referral for services rendered at an ASC, the Stark Law does not apply.

Answer (C) is incorrect. Because the referrals are not referrals for DHS, it does not matter whether Dr. Hernandez is making them. Therefore, the Stark Law is inapplicable.

157. **Answer (A) is correct**. Because the relationship is between the hospital and a referring physician, it is likely that the physician is making referrals for inpatient hospital services in addition to any referrals for services at the ASC. Therefore, this arrangement, unlike the arrangement in the previous question, needs to meet an exception under the Stark Law. One of the criteria for compliance with a Stark Law exception will be that the arrangement must be in place for at least one year.

    Answer (B) is incorrect. This answer is not factually true. The role of a medical director is administrative, and medical directors do not typically have private patients *in their role* as medical directors.

    Answers (C) and (D) are incorrect. Some plastic surgery is covered by and billed to federal health care programs. Therefore, although plastic surgery services are often not covered and would not be considered DHS under the Stark Law, this is not a blanket rule as some plastic surgery services are DHS. Because some plastic surgery may be DHS, then Answer (D) is also incorrect.

158. **Answer (C) is correct**. Dr. Yang's relationship with the DME company is not a "financial relationship" under the Stark Law because Dr. Yang's joint ownership of Medi-Waste does not give Dr. Yang an ownership position in or compensation from the DME company. The Stark Law is not implicated (and neither is the Anti-Kickback Statute) and Dr. Yang can continue to make referrals.

    Answer (A) is incorrect because Answer (C) is correct. This is not a financial relationship under the Stark Law.

    Answer (B) is incorrect. This arrangement does not provide any remuneration to Dr. Yang in exchange for his referrals and thus this is not a financial relationship under the Stark Law.

    Answer (D) is incorrect. This answer is incorrect for two reasons: (1) certain types of DME are included in the definition of DHS, and (2) whether the services are DHS does not matter if there is no financial relationship.

159. **Answer (A) is correct**. The facts here closely resemble the arrangement in *United States ex rel. Drakeford v. Tuomey Healthcare System, Inc.*, 675 F.3d 394 (4th Cir. 2012). Based on the facts as described, it is likely that the physicians are getting paid in excess of fair market value because they are being compensated for the fair market value of their services *and*, in addition, sharing in a portion of the profits of the entity through their productivity bonus. This arrangement constitutes illegal remuneration under the Stark Law *and* the Anti-Kickback Statute.

Answer (B) is incorrect. A court would likely find that at least one purpose for paying the physicians in excess of the fair market value for their services was to induce referrals to the hospital. Because the compensation is in excess of fair market value, no exceptions or safe harbors are available.

Answer (C) is incorrect. Even though the flat-fee compensation was set at fair market value, when the total compensation with productivity bonus is considered, the arrangement appears to exceed fair market value and is not commercially reasonable.

Answer (D) is incorrect. Medicare does cover pregnancy and birth for women who might otherwise qualify for Medicare due to having a qualified disability, a diagnosis of ALS, or end-stage renal disease, and the Anti-Kickback Statute applies to all federal health care programs (including Medicaid), not just Medicare.

160. **Answer (C) is correct.** Under applicable regulations, there is a provision under the space rental exception that allows the contract to be in a "hold over" status if the arrangement has expired and has not yet been renewed. *See* 42 C.F.R. § 411.357(a)(7).

Answer (A) is incorrect. The regulation was amended to allow for an expired lease to not be considered non-compliant if it meets certain criteria.

Answer (B) is incorrect. It does not matter if the arrangement constitutes a financial relationship or payment relationship between the parties if the parties meet an exception under the Stark Law.

Answer (D) is incorrect. This answer is not factually true. The relationship as described would constitute a financial relationship under the Stark Law.

161. **Answer (C) is correct.** Under the federal False Claims Act, a whistleblower or *qui tam* relator cannot sustain a False Claims Act case unless the whistleblower is disclosing information not otherwise publicly disclosed. Under the law, a court is required to dismiss a whistleblower's claim "if substantially the same allegations or transactions as alleged in the action or claim were publicly disclosed...." 31 U.S.C. § 3730(e)(4).

But, according to the facts, the congressional hearing was about billing irregularities generally in the industry and not specific to the company. This has been commonly interpreted to not constitute "substantially the same allegations or transactions as alleged in the action or claim."

Answer (A) is incorrect because Answer (C) is correct. The information is likely not specific enough to have constituted public disclosure.

Answer (B) is incorrect. It is not necessary to prove original source if the information was not publicly disclosed.

Answer (D) is incorrect. The rule does not require that the disclosure be before the full Congress as opposed to a committee.

162. **Answer (A) is correct.** In contrast to the question above, the information that was publicly disclosed in the article is likely sufficiently detailed that the court will dismiss this case.

Answer (B) is incorrect. The facts state that the relator did not voluntarily disclose the information to the government prior to the public disclosure. Note that under the "original source" definition in 31 U.S.C. § 3730(e)(4), even if information has been publicly disclosed, the whistleblower/*qui tam* relator may still have standing if they were an original source. The definition of "original source" is "an individual who either (i) prior to a public disclosure under subsection (e)(4)(A), has voluntarily disclosed to the Government the information on which allegations or transactions in a claim are based, or (2) who has knowledge that is independent of and materially adds to the publicly disclosed allegations or transactions, and who has voluntarily provided the information to the Government before filing an action under this section." Thus, even if the relator were the original source of the information in the article, they were required to voluntarily disclose this information to the government prior to the filing of the claim.

Answer (C) is incorrect. The facts indicate that the fraud referenced is specific to the company and involves client stories. This is likely enough to show sufficient specificity.

Answer (D) is incorrect. This answer is why the relator does not qualify as an "original source" of the information. But this is an exception to the public disclosure bar, and thus the case would be dismissed under the reasoning in Answer (A) above.

163. **Answer (A) is the best answer.** Since Medicare transitioned to paying hospitals largely based on a patient's diagnosis related group (DRG) — a form of bundled payment for all services provided based on an estimate as to anticipated costs of the patient's diagnosis — hospitals have struggled to align their financial incentives with the financial incentives of physicians. This is because physicians are generally paid based on a fee-for-service system, which encourages the physicians to provide as many services as possible to maximize payment, which is contrary to the fixed-fee DRG model. To better align hospital incentives under the DRG system with physician incentives under the fee-for-service system, hospitals often seek approval of gainsharing arrangements in which a hospital can share any savings it realizes from physicians who are working to reduce unnecessary expenses and services. The practice of gainsharing was long prohibited but was sanctioned in specific form under the Medicare Shared Savings Program under the ACA. The OIG has also taken certain measures in recent years to enable more gainsharing programs, so long as the OIG feels confident that it is preventing these programs from denying or restricting necessary care to patients.

Answer (B) is incorrect. Gainsharing programs are not required to be organized through specific legal entities and do not involve working with third-party payors for contracting purposes. Under the Medicare Shared Savings Program, accountable care organizations are required to be organized as a legal entity, but there are many gainsharing programs that have been approved by the OIG that do not contain these formal limitations.

Answer (C) is not the best answer. Although the OIG had prohibited gainsharing over the years because of fears that it would lead to the reduction or elimination of services, gainsharing is generally understood to be for the purpose of better aligning hospital and physician incentives, enabling the hospital to incentivize physicians to work closely with the hospitals to realize savings that do not compromise patient care. As is evident from the Medicare Shared Savings Program, not all gainsharing programs will necessarily result in the reduction or limitation of necessary services.

Answer (D) is incorrect. This description is not gainsharing. Physicians may join together in organizations such as independent practice associations for the purpose of having greater bargaining power against third party payors. There are significant antitrust implications in organizing in this manner, but this does not describe gainsharing, which involves payment between hospitals and physicians.

Antitrust

164. **Answer (C) is correct.** Monopolization, or attempting to monopolize, is illegal under Section 2 of the Sherman Act but is not one of the *per se* violations listed in Section 1 of the Sherman Act.

 Answers (A), (B), and (D) are all incorrect. Each answer is a *per se* violation of Section 1 of the Sherman Act.

165. **Answer (B) is correct.** Section 2 of the Sherman Act and the Clayton Act are both implicated in this scenario. Section 2 of the Sherman Act involves the activity of a single actor/entity in a market that possesses sufficient monopoly power and uses that power to willfully restrain trade and monopolize the market. When one company uses its market power to buy up competitors, this can implicate Section 2 of the Sherman Act. Because the company is proposing a merger and/or acquisition, this also implicates the Clayton Act, which is a law specifically addressing mergers and acquisitions that, when implemented, have the effect of substantially lessening competition or tend to create a monopoly.

 Answer (A) is incorrect. Section 1 of the Sherman Act is not implicated, as it requires a meeting of the minds between two parties. There are not sufficient facts from which to conclude that the larger hospital is conspiring with the smaller hospital chain to unreasonably restrain trade.

 Answer (C) is incorrect for the same reasons that answer (A) is incorrect.

 Answer (D) is incorrect. The entity seems to have sufficient market power to implicate Section 2 of the Sherman Act.

166. **Answer (C) is correct.** A claim for an antitrust action under Section 2 of the Sherman Act requires that the entity have possession of monopoly power (the ability to control prices or exclude competition) and willful acquisition and maintenance of such power (not just growth). The facts here indicate that the non-profit hospital organization already has a 68% market share, so it has sufficient market share to wield market power. The facts also indicate that it is making threats against insurers to induce the insurers to give the non-profit hospital better rates than its small competitors in an effort to weed them out. This would likely prove the elements of a Section 2 claim.

 Answer (A) is incorrect. The company already has 68% of the market, which is over two-thirds of the market, and the company is looking to acquire more. This represents sufficient market power.

Answer (B) is incorrect. Section 2 of the Sherman Act only requires the action of one party. Thus, in determining whether there has been a violation of Section 2 of the Sherman Act, it does not matter if the insurers agree to the company's requests. That would be more applicable for a claim under Section 1 of the Sherman Act.

Answer (D) is incorrect. The concept of *per se* antitrust violations is an aspect of Section 1 of the Sherman Act and not Section 2.

167. **Answer (D) is correct.** The facts of this problem closely resemble *In re Michigan State Medical Society*, 101 F.T.C. 191 (1983). Although the *Michigan State* court did not recognize the actions of the physicians as constituting a group boycott, the facts here indicate that everyone was told to participate in the refusal to sign the contract, which can constitute a group boycott. It does not matter if the boycott is successful, only that it took place.

    Answers (A), (B), and (C) are incorrect. These answers are all other types of *per se* violations of Section 1 of the Sherman Act, but they are not examples of the actions of the physicians in the question.

168. **Answer (A) is correct.** Any claim under Section 1 of the Sherman Act that does not constitute a *per se* violation is analyzed under the Rule of Reason test. Rule of Reason requires balancing to determine whether the pro-competitive benefits of an action outweigh any anti-competitive harms.

    Answer (B) is incorrect. The Noerr-Pennington Doctrine is a judicially created defense for entities against antitrust liability when their actions are for the purpose of influencing legislation.

    Answer (C) and (D) are incorrect. These are court-applied tests, but not in the context of analyzing a Sherman Act Section 1 claim.

169. **Answer (B) is correct.** The Clayton Act analyzes the impact of mergers and acquisitions on a particular market to determine whether such merger has the effect of substantially lessening competition. In analyzing claims under the Clayton Act, the Federal Trade Commission and courts look at two factors: (1) the product market and (2) the geographic market. Answer (B) shows an analysis of the product market and the geographic market.

    Answer (A) is incorrect. This answer identifies the product market but fails to identify the geographic market. The number of facilities will not help in identifying market share without a definition of the geographic area.

    Answers (C) and (D) are incorrect. The information in these answers will not be helpful in identifying the proper product and geographic markets.

Controlling Reproduction: Contraception, Sterilization, & Abortion

170. **Answer (D) is correct.** Generally, federal funds may not be used to sterilize anyone under the age of 21. 42 C.F.R. § 50.203(a).

 Answers (A) and (B) are incorrect because of the sterilization age restriction. However, it is also a condition of using federal funds for sterilization that the individual be mentally competent. *Id.* §§ 50.203(b), 50.206. Moreover, family planning services are usually cost-effective government expenditures.

 Answer (C) is incorrect. Family planning is a mandatory benefit under Medicaid. Under ACA Medicaid expansion, states must cover sterilization. Under traditional Medicaid, states have discretion to define what family planning services to cover, but even traditional Medicaid states have generally opted to cover sterilization.

171. **Answer (C) is correct.** Many young women with decisional capacity report that a provider has refused their sterilization request. Providers express reluctance to sterilize in light of high incidence of future regret among younger women and the availability of long-acting reversible contraceptives. Nonetheless, the American College of Obstetricians and Gynecologists, the leading professional organization for gynecologists, counsels that providers should respect a competent adult woman's choice to sterilize in accordance with state law, even if young. *Sterilization of Women: Ethical Issues and Considerations*, AM. C. OBSTETRICIANS & GYNECOLOGISTS 3 (2020). Some states require that a woman be at least 21 years of age to consent to sterilization, and generally, federal funds cannot be used for sterilization prior to age 21.

 Answer (A) is incorrect because the ACA requires that most insurance plans cover certain voluntary sterilization procedures for women.

 Answer (B) is incorrect because a competent adult has the right to make his or her own medical decisions regardless of who pays for the care or obtains the insurance.

 Answer (D) is incorrect because, legally, the decision to be sterilized rests with the individual seeking sterilization. Practically speaking, a fiancé may influence the decision, but legally, the fiancé's permission is not required.

172. **Answer (D) is the best answer.** In order to use federal funds to pay for a sterilization, a woman must execute a consent form at least 30 and no more than 180 days before the procedure. 42 C.F.R. § 50.203(d). Because Isa did not execute the consent form 30 days before her hospital visit, federal funds cannot be used for her sterilization during this hospital visit. Medicaid requires pregnancy-related coverage 60 days postpartum, and it allows states to provide pregnancy-related coverage up to 12 months postpartum. American Rescue Plan Act of 2021, H.R. 1319. If Isa returns to seek sterilization after her waiting period has run but before her pregnancy-related Medicaid eligibility expires, Medicaid will cover the procedure.

    Answers (A) and (B) are not the best answer. While Isa is presumed competent and the sterilization would be cost-effective, federal law prohibits the use of federal funds for sterilization outside strict informed consent parameters. The federal government's strict rules were enacted to combat historic abuses but are often criticized as creating an unnecessary barrier to sterilization desired by low-income women. Some states choose to fund such sterilizations using exclusively state or other non-federal funds.

    Answer (C) is incorrect. Federal law requires continued Medicaid eligibility 60 days postpartum, and the majority of states extend Medicaid cover 12-months postpartum.

173. **Answer (D) is the best answer.** Most states allow a person who is not mentally competent to be sterilized pursuant to a court order that sterilization is in the person's best interest or meets certain mandatory criteria. However, two states ban such sterilizations. *See, e.g.*, Alaska Stat. § 13.26.316(e)(2). In contrast, other states have held that sterilization remains a constitutional right for a mentally incompetent patient when the procedure is in his or her best interest. *See, e.g.*, *In re* Valerie N., 707 P.2d 760 (Cal. 1985). Federal funds may not be used to sterilize an incompetent person. 42 C.F.R. § 50.203(b).

    Answers (A) and (B) are not the best answer. States vary regarding the burden of proof required to establish that sterilization is in a patient's best interest, if such sterilization is ever authorized without personal consent. Most states require clear and convincing evidence or other heightened proof. *See, e.g.*, Motes v. Hall Cnty. Dep't of Family & Children's Servs., 306 S.E.2d 260, 262 (Ga. 1983) (requiring clear and convincing evidence).

    Answer (C) is not the best answer. Even disability rights organizations that oppose existing laws allowing "forced" sterilization generally oppose blanket bans on sterilization because some disabled persons want to be sterilized and should have such a right. *See* Nat'l Women's L. Ctr., Forced Sterilization of Disabled People in the United States 15 (Jan. 24, 2022).

174. **Answer (A) is the best answer.** The majority decision eschewed the Fourteenth Amendment due process argument and instead found a right to marital privacy in the "penumbras and emanations" of the First, Third, Fourth, and Fifth Amendments, as well as the Ninth Amendment declaration that people retain rights not specifically enumerated in the Constitution.

    Answers (B) and (C) are not the best answer for the reasons set forth above.

    Answer (D) is incorrect because an equal protection argument was not raised in this case.

175. **Answer (C) is the best answer.** In *Eisenstadt v. Baird*, 405 U.S. 438 (1972), the U.S. Supreme Court held that the Constitution also protects the right of unmarried couples to buy and use contraceptives without governmental interference. Relying on *Griswold*'s holding that married couples enjoy a constitutionally protected right to use contraceptives without governmental intrusion, the Court reasoned that equal protection under the 14th Amendment requires that states accord unmarried couples the same right to privacy.

    Answer (A) is not the best answer because the Ninth Amendment was not the primary basis for the Court's holding in *Griswold* or *Eisenstadt*.

    Answer (B) is not the best answer because 14th Amendment substantive due process was not the primary basis for the Court's hold in *Griswold* or *Eisenstadt*. Although, a year later in *Roe v. Wade*, 410 U.S. 113 (1973), the Court relied primarily on 14th Amendment substantive due process for the right to privacy.

    Answer (D) is not the best answer because the Court has never adopted a procreative justice approach. While the Court described procreation as a fundamental right in *Skinner v. Oklahoma ex rel. Williamson*, 316 U.S. 535 (1942), the Court has always construed that right as a right to be free from governmental intrusion, not as a positive right.

176. **Answer (D) is the best answer.** In *Roe*, the U.S. Supreme Court held that the 14th Amendment's Due Process Clause protects a woman's right to choose abortion pre-viability. 410 U.S. 113 (1973). *Roe* adopted a trimester-based test which was later modified by *Planned Parenthood of Southeast Pennsylvania v. Casey*, 505 U.S. 833 (1992), to focus on viability and undue burden. After close to 50 years, *Roe* was overruled by *Dobbs v. Jackson Women's Health Organization*, 142 S. Ct. 2228 (2022), but even before *Dobbs*, access to abortion was limited by federal and state laws restricting use of government funding for abortion.

    Answers (A), (B), and (C) are not the best answer. While the Court cited cases such as *Griswold v. Connecticut*, 381 U.S. 479 (1965), suggesting a right to privacy based in each of these amendments, the Court ultimately held that the 14th Amendment's Substantive Due Process Clause protects a woman's right to choose abortion pre-viability.

177. **Answer (A) is correct.** Each state determines what constitutes a person within the meaning of the law. Homo sapiens, regardless of characteristics, are usually considered "persons" when they reach a pre-determined stage of development. In contrast, other sentient animals such as great apes do not usually enjoy most legal rights, despite the ability to communicate and reason. In terms of the required stage of development, some states confer "personhood" as soon as an egg is fertilized. *See, e.g.*, KAN. STAT. ANN. § 65-6732. Others require a live birth, at least for full personhood. *See, e.g.*, N.Y. PUB. HEALTH LAW §§ -2599aa, -2599bb (McKinney 2019). Many states fall in between.

    Answers (B), (C), and (D) are incorrect. Moral philosophers sometimes describe consciousness, the ability to communicate, the ability to reason, self-awareness, and/or self-motivated activity as characteristics that make someone or something a moral agent entitled to higher status or special rights. In most instances, the law disregards these characteristics, although some are relevant to decisional capacity determinations.

178. **Answer (D) is the best answer.** *Dobbs* proclaims that states are free to define personhood through the democratic process and that substantive due process rights only protect rights rooted in the nation's history and tradition that are essential components of ordered liberty. 142 S. Ct. 2228, 2239–58. Yet *Dobbs* also states that it does not overturn existing contraception precedent. *Id.* at 2291–94. It is difficult to reconcile these statements, as some states define personhood as beginning at fertilization. So far, existing law has been construed to prohibit governmental interference with procreative freedom prior to *pregnancy*, but the landmark Supreme Court contraceptive cases—*Griswold* and *Eisenstadt*—involved condoms, which act prior to *fertilization*, not oral contraceptives, IUDs, or IVF. So, it is difficult to know how the law may develop in the future.

Answer (A) is not the best answer. Some states define personhood as beginning at fertilization. If not limited by the Constitution, these states may eventually permit condom use but prohibit IUDs, IVF, emergency contraceptives, and birth control pills. To date, no state has gone this far, but since *Dobbs* expressly takes no position on when life begins, it is not clear that any such law would be held unconstitutional. Nonetheless, this is not the best answer since *Dobbs* declares that it leaves contraceptive precedent undisturbed and Answer (D) is the best answer.

Answer (B) is not the best answer. Most scientists agree that prior to implantation, a woman is not "pregnant" and therefore cannot abort. This reasoning could be used to restrict *Dobbs* to the abortion context and leave any contraceptive choices and IVF constitutionally protected from governmental interference. If *Dobbs*'s dicta on contraception can be trusted, this is the most likely result. Yet, because the Court allows states to define when life begins and some states have chosen fertilization, not implantation, Answer (D) is the best answer.

Answer (C) is not the best answer. It is correct that the Court differentiated action intending a harm from action foreseeing the same harm in *Washington v. Glucksberg*, 521 U.S. 702 (1997). Many philosophers support such distinction, known as the doctrine of double effect. Nonetheless, given political realities, it is unlikely that the Court would conclude that states can constitutionally prohibit embryo disposal after IVF but not IUDs and birth control pills. While perhaps less likely, because this answer is also possible, Answer (D) is the best answer.

179. **Answer (C) is the best answer.** In *Burwell v. Hobby Lobby Stores, Inc.*, 573 U.S. 682 (2014), the U.S. Supreme Court held that the Religious Freedom Restoration Act of 1993 (RFRA) requires an exemption to the ACA's contraceptive coverage mandate for a closely held corporation whose owners have a religious objection to contraceptives, as there is a less restrictive means of furthering the government's interest.

Answer (A) is incorrect because the ACA contraceptive mandate has always provided an exemption for certain religious non-profit employers. 42 U.S.C. § 300gg-13(a)(4); Little Sisters of the Poor Saints Peter & Paul Home v. Pennsylvania, 140 S. Ct. 2367 (2020).

Answer (B) is incorrect. Under *Hobby Lobby*, the Court held that religious accommodation under RFRA extends to closely held corporations. In contrast, publicly traded corporations cannot claim religious accommodation.

Answer (D) is not the best answer. It is true that a health insurance issuer is legally required to provide all FDA-approved contraceptives, as prescribed, directly to covered women at no cost after receiving Form 700 providing the issuer with notice of a religious objection. However, the facts do not mention Form 700 or notice of objection to the Secretary of HHS. Further, completing Form 700 alone would not be enough to avoid a fine if the corporation did not qualify for religious accommodation.

180. **Answer (D) is correct.** An individual is presumed to have capacity unless an appropriate professional properly determines that the individual lacks capacity to a reasonable degreee of certainty. 2023 UHCDA. No court has required clear and convincing evidence of capacity in a caesarean section case. Moreover, because a surrogate should authorize care based on the mother's subjective best interest, the surrogate may consider the unborn child if consistent with the mother's values.

Answer (A) is incorrect. The balancing suggestion in Answer (A) reflects the reasoning of cases like *Burton v. State*, 49 So. 3d 263 (Fla. Dist. Ct. App. 2010) (a pregnant woman's right to refuse medical intervention may be overridden if there is a sufficiently compelling state interest and the intervention is narrowly tailored). However, other states have taken a different approach.

Answer (B) is incorrect. Answer (B) reflects the reasoning from Judge Belson's decision concurring in part and dissenting in part in *In re A.C.*, 573 A.2d 1235, 1253–59 (D.C. 1990) (allowing forced intervention if a pregnant woman's capacity is unclear and her prior instructions have been ambivalent because she owes a special duty to her viable fetus and a caesarean section does not significantly increase risk to her). However, other states have taken a different approach.

Answer (C) is incorrect. Answer (C) reflects the reasoning from the majority decision in *In re A.C.*, 573 A.2d 1235 (D.C. 1990), that no balancing of interests is appropriate when a competent pregnant woman refuses surgical medical intervention. *See also In re* Baby Doe, 632 N.E.2d 326 (Ill. App. Ct. 1994) (woman's right to refuse invasive medical treatment is not diminished during pregnancy). However, other states have taken a different approach.

Assisting Reproduction

181. **Answer (B) is the best answer.** Generally, abortion bans prohibit a provider from terminating a "pregnancy." Because pregnancy generally requires a fertilized egg within the body, by definition, in vitro blastocyst embryos likely cannot be "aborted." *See, e.g.*, Mo. Rev. Stat. § 188.015 (2019) (limiting definition of abortion to an embryo or fetus "in the womb"). This does not mean, however, that the intentional destruction of an embryo could not result in other criminal or civil charges. While perhaps unlikely politically, if the blastocyst embryos are considered "persons," then intentionally destroying them could potentially lead to other legal jeopardy. *See, e.g.*, Tex. Penal Code Ann. § 1.07(a)(26) (defining an individual to include any human life at any stage of development after fertilization).

    Answer (A) is not the best answer. As discussed above, it is likely that destroying in vitro embryos does not violate the abortion ban, but this is not the best answer because it fails to capture the other potential risks raised by destruction of the blastocyst embryos if those embryos are treated as persons.

    Answer (C) is not the best answer because, as discussed above, the abortion ban likely does not apply to the in vitro blastocyst embryos.

    Answer (D) is not the best answer for the reasons set forth above and because carrying the genetic mutation for Huntington's disease is not a fatal fetal anomaly. While Huntington's disease can shorten a person's life, it does not cause the person's death in utero or within 28 days of birth.

182. **Answer (E) is correct.** The individual who gives birth and that individual's spouse are presumptive parents. Uniform Parentage Act § 204 (2017). Parentage is also presumed if a couple marries after birth and asserts parentage or resides in a household together with the child for the first two years of the child's life, holding the child out as their own. *Id.*

    Answers (A), (B), (C), and (D) are not the best answer because they are incomplete.

183. **Answer**: A person who provides a gamete for, or consents to, assisted reproduction by another, with the intent to be the parent of the intended child, is the parent of the resulting child.

184. **Answer (C) is the best answer.** Pursuant to Section 804(a)(2) of the Uniform Parentage Act, a gestational surrogate has "no claim to parentage of a child conceived by assisted reproduction under the agreement." Chris and Sara are the babies' genetic parents, making Susan a gestational surrogate.

Answers (A) and (B) are incorrect. While a traditional or genetic surrogate has up to 72 hours after birth to withdraw consent to the surrogacy agreement, a gestational surrogate may not terminate the agreement after embryo transfer. *Compare* UNIFORM PARENTAGE ACT § 808(a), *with* § 814(a). Moreover, the Act only uses the best-interests-of-the-child approach to adjudicate parentage in limited circumstances involving a genetic surrogate, not a gestational surrogate. *Compare id.* § 812(b), *with* § 816(d). See Judge Kennard's dissent in *Johnson v. Calvert*, 851 P.2d 776 (Cal. 1993), for an argument that the best interests of the child should decide parentage.

Answer (D) is not the best answer. The intent of the parties only governs if the parties' surrogacy agreement fails to comply with the requirements of the Act. UNIFORM PARENTAGE ACT § 812(b). See *Johnson v. Calvert*, 851 P.2d 776, for an argument that intent should determine parentage, at least in genetic surrogacy cases.

185. **Answer (C) is correct.** Per *Davis v. Davis*, 842 S.W.2d 588 (Tenn. 1992), absent prior agreement, a court should consider the relative interests of the parties. Generally, the interests of the party seeking to avoid procreation trump, unless the other party has no other reasonable alternative to achieve parenthood.

Answer (A) is incorrect. While a mother can consent to medical procedures involving her body, she does not have unilateral authority over a pre-embryo located outside of her body. In this regard, it is interesting to consider how assisted reproduction equalizes decision-making authority between intended parents.

Answer (B) is incorrect. In *Davis*, the court concluded that a pre-embryo merits "special respect" but is not a person and that "the state's interest in potential human life is insufficient to justify an infringement on the gamete-providers' procreational autonomy." Arguably, *Dobbs* calls this result into question, especially when coupled with Tennessee's Personhood Statute and post-*Davis* amendment to its state constitution.

Answer (D) is incorrect under *Davis* and *Szafranski v. Dunston*, 34 N.E.3d 1132 (Ill. App. Ct. 2015). However, in *A.Z. v. B.Z.*, 725 N.E.2d 1051 (Mass. 2000), the court refused to enforce an agreement that would have bound an ex-husband to become a parent against his will as contrary to public policy.

Organ Transplantation

186. **Answer (B) is the best answer.** The National Organ Transplant Act of 1984 charges the U.S. Department of Health and Human Services (HHS) with creating an Organ Procurement and Transplant Network (OPTN) for obtaining and distributing organs in the United States. HHS contracts with United Network for Organ Sharing (UNOS), a nonprofit, to manage the OPTN. Among other things, UNOS policies determine how to match an organ with an individual on a transplant waiting list. It is worth noting, however, that in 2023 the Health Resources and Services Administration (HRSA) announced a network modernization initiative that plans to seek more contract solicitations and to pursue innovation through continuous competition. HRSA, *Organ Procurement and Transplantation Network Modernization Initiative* (May 2023). While it is too early to know the results of this initiative, UNOS is unlikely to enjoy its current monopoly in the future. At present, UNOS is the best answer.

    Answer (A) is incorrect. State governments regulate many aspects of organ transplantation through state anatomical gift acts, but in an effort to aid uniformity and fairness, key policies and distribution decisions are set at the federal rather than state level. Despite these efforts, in reality, the waiting times for organs vary significantly by geographic region.

    Answer (C) is incorrect. Medicare and Medicaid set standards for payment of organ transplants through their programs and require hospitals which receive program funds to alert an organ procurement organization when a patient dies (or whose death is imminent). Nonetheless, Medicare and Medicaid do not control the retrieval and distribution of organ transplants more generally.

    Answer (D) is incorrect. Doctors and hospitals determine which patients to list on an organ transplant waiting list, perform the transplants, and care for patients involved in transplants. Hospitals play a critical role in our organ transplant system but are not generally responsible for macro policy decisions.

187. **Answer (D) is correct.** Social worth criteria, like professional contributions or celebrity status, are not considered in prioritizing organs. There are other characteristics, like ethnicity and socioeconomic status, which are not considered by themselves but can have a significant impact on priority for other reasons. For example, certain ethnicities correlate with more difficulty in finding a close organ match. Likewise, if a transplant or aftercare is not fully covered by Medicaid, Medicare, or other insurance, then lower socioeconomic status may correlate to more difficulty obtaining an organ. Wealth might also advantage an applicant by enabling them to join multiple geographic lists as a result of the ability to travel easily to other locations.

Answers (A), (B), and (C) are incorrect because anticipated compliance with aftercare, risk of graft failure, and support system can all be factors in priority for organ donation.

188. **Answer (C) is correct.** While many state laws require paid leave for living donors, others do not, and there is no federal law on this issue. Among states that provide paid leave, there can still be significant variation. For example, Colorado provides up to two days paid leave while California provides up to thirty days.

Answers (A), (B), and (D) are incorrect because each paraphrases part of the National Organ Transplant Act (NOTA). Interestingly, in *Flynn v. Holder*, 684 F.3d 852 (9th Cir. 2012), the plaintiff challenged the Act's including bone marrow within the definition of an organ, in light of changes in how bone marrow is extracted today as compared to when NOTA was enacted. The court agreed and held that given the type of tissue (renewable) and how it was removed (peripheral blood stem cell apheresis), bone marrow extracted this way should not be considered an organ for purposes of the ban on compensation for transfer. While this result may be sound policy, it is not clear that it comports with the plain language of NOTA. For paid leave, many states treat bone marrow donation differently than other types of organ donation.

189. **Answer (D) is correct.** Unless expressly stipulated, no person other than the donor may revoke the donor's anatomical gift. There is an exception to this general rule for unemancipated minors.

Answers (A) and (B) are incorrect. While Sammah's husband is her surrogate, he cannot revoke her anatomical gift. Clear and convincing evidence is not required to donate.

Answer (C) is incorrect. While others cannot revoke Sammah's gift unless she expressly authorizes them to do so, she is free to revoke or alter her anatomical gift instructions at any time.

190. **Answer (A) is correct.** Presumed consent assumes that all individuals are willing to donate their organs after death and creates a system to allow the minority who oppose donation a means to opt out. Countries like Norway, France, Italy, Singapore, and Columbia have adopted variations of an opt-out system. Some U.S. states used to have presumed consent for corneal donation, although most have curtailed the practice.

Answer (B) is incorrect. The current U.S. system generally requires an opt-in, affirmative authorization for donation by the donor or the donor's representative.

Answer (C) is incorrect. Presumed consent avoids the need for potential donors to affirmatively register.

Answer (D) is incorrect. Presumed consent does not force anyone to donate an organ, although it does shift the burden to those who oppose organ donation to take steps to affirmatively opt out.

191. **Answer (C) is correct.** While courts have sometimes overridden a pregnant woman's refusal of medical intervention to save the life of her fetus, no similar precedent exists to compel a competent adult to undergo unwanted medical intervention, like a transplant, to save the life of their child outside of pregnancy. Answer (C) actually parallels the holding of *In re Fetus Brown*, 689 N.E.2d 397 (Ill. Ct. App. 1997), a pregnancy case rejecting the balancing-of-interests approach. State-compelled surgery for the benefit of another may raise significant due process and bodily integrity concerns.

Answer (A) is incorrect. This answer reflects the test offered by Florida for involuntarily forcing medical intervention on a pregnant woman for the benefit of her fetus. *Burton*, 49 So. 3d 263 (Fla. Dist. Ct. App. 2010) (considering involuntary inpatient treatment). It has not been adopted or applied to organ transplantation.

Answer (B) is incorrect. Some argue that parents owe a special duty to their child that justifies sacrifice, or, at minimum, balancing interests. This is more of a moral argument than a constitutional one. No court has used this reasoning to order an unconsented organ donation.

Answer (D) is incorrect. This reflects the test offered by Georgia for involuntarily forcing medical intervention on a pregnant woman. Jefferson v. Griffin Spalding Cnty. Hosp. Auth., 274 S.E.2d 457 (Ga. 1981) (overriding refusal of blood transfusion). It has not been adopted to force organ donation.

192. **Answer (C) is correct.** This question is based on *In re T.A.C.P.*, 609 So. 2d 588 (Fla. 1992). Babies born with anencephaly who do not meet the definition of whole brain death cannot be declared dead under current law.

Answer (A) is incorrect because the fact that a person will die soon does not enable a physician to declare them dead in advance of meeting the criteria for death.

Answer (B) is incorrect because a parent may not determine a child's death, nor is declaring death a patient health care decision.

Answer (D) is incorrect because declaring death is not a patient health care decision.

Human Subject Research & Experimental Treatment

193. **Answer (B) is the best answer.** When properly conducted, human subject research can be justified to advance knowledge for societal benefit.

   Answer (A) is not the best answer. Some, but not all, human subject research may provide direct benefit to a participant, but that is not the research's primary goal. Often, human subject research involves no potential direct benefit to participants. Even research that potentially could provide significant benefit to a participant often does not. This may occur when a drug or device being researched ends up not being safe or effective for a particular purpose, for example. It also commonly occurs when a participant is in the control group or receives a placebo.

   Answer (C) is incorrect. Human subject research does not generally aim to benefit other species. In the United States, the Animal Welfare Act regulates the treatment of other animals in research.

   Answer (D) is not the best answer. Research may provide monetary gain, but that should not be its primary goal. The Common Rule and other regulations are designed to ensure that human subject research targets new knowledge and potential societal benefit.

194. **Answer**: Therapeutic misconception refers to the common misunderstanding by research participants that research is intended to provide direct benefit to them, even after being told the contrary. This problem can be especially acute when the participant has a pre-existing doctor-patient relationship with the physician conducting the research.

195. **Answer (C) is correct.** State law governs human subject research that occurs within the state.

   Answers (A) and (B) are not the best answer. Because the study does not appear to be federally funded, the Common Rule does not apply unless state law specifically requires compliance with federal standards. Universities or other institutions like hospitals also sometimes require compliance with the Common Rule regardless of funding source.

   Answer (D) is incorrect. FDA regulations will not apply unless a drug or device will be submitted to the FDA for its approval.

196. **Answer (D) is correct.** For human subject research, minors enjoy heightened protection under the Common Rule and common law. *See, e.g.*, 45 C.F.R. § 46.406(a) (2023) (generally only funding research on children that offers no direct benefit if the research poses only "a minor increase over minimal risk"); Grimes v. Kennedy Krieger Inst., Inc., 782 A.2d 807 (Md. 2001) (finding a special relationship between researchers and minor participants engaged in non-therapeutic research). Parental consent is generally considered insufficient if the research poses a serious health risk and offers no direct benefit to the child.

    Answer (A) is not the best answer. While it is generally true that parents can consent to therapeutic research on behalf of their minor child, the research described is not therapeutic, and it poses more than a minor increase over minimal risk to the child.

    Answer (B) is not the best answer. While it is generally true that parents can make health care decisions on behalf of their minor child, the research described is not therapeutic, and it poses more than a minor increase over minimal risk to the child.

    Answer (C) is incorrect. Minors can participate in human subject research under proper circumstances.

197. **Answer (A) is correct.** Research utilizing fully de-identified information or specimens and no interaction with investigators does not fall within the definition of "human subject research" triggering Common Rule protection. 45 C.F.R. § 46.102(e)(1) (2023). Likewise, HIPAA does not limit use of properly de-identified information since it is not considered "protected health information." *Id.* § 160.103 (2023). FDA regulation would not apply because no drug or medical device is at issue.

    This problem is loosely based on the so-called "gay gene study" published in 2019, which generated significant controversy. Even when disclosure and consent are required, the Common Rule and other consent protections focus primarily on individual health risk and pay less attention to potential group-based harms or bystander risk.

    Answers (B), (C), and (D) are not correct for the reasons set forth above. In addition, researchers may not always meet the definition of "covered entities" pursuant to HIPAA.

198. **Answer**: A study is minimal risk if the "probability and magnitude of harm or discomfort anticipated in the research are not greater in and of themselves than those ordinarily encountered in daily life or during the performance of routine physical or psychological examinations or tests." *Id.* § 46.102(j) (2023); 21 § C.F.R. 56.102(i) (2023). Minimal risk research enjoys increased regulatory flexibility. For example, within listed categories, minimal risk research may be approved through expedited IRB review procedures (i.e., by the board chair or designee rather than full board review).

199. **Answer (C) is correct.** While IRBs protect the rights and well-being of human subject research participants and consider equitable selection of subjects, they are not primarily responsible for diversity, equity, and inclusion of clinical research itself, which has historically been lacking.

    Answers (A), (B), and (D) are incorrect, as each is an essential factor in IRB approval.

200. **Answer (B) is the best answer.** The individuals who provided blood may have a state law claim if they can establish that the first researcher breached an express or implied agreement to use the samples only for purposes of diabetes research or breached a state-law informed-consent obligation. The Common Rule and HIPAA would not require disclosure of the purposes of the second study and consent thereto because the blood samples are de-identified and there is no interaction with the second investigator. 45 C.F.R. §§46.102(e)(1), 160.103 (2023). However, neither the Common Rule nor HIPAA preempts state laws that provide additional protections to research subjects. This question is loosely based on a dispute between the Havasupai Tribe and Arizona State University. Havasupai Tribe v. Arizona Bd. of Regents, 204 P.3d 1063 (Ariz. Ct. App. 2008).

    Answers (A), (C), and (D) are incorrect. Research utilizing fully de-identified specimens and no interaction with investigators does not fall within the definition of "human subject research" triggering Common Rule protection. 45 C.F.R. §46.102(e)(1) (2023). Likewise, HIPAA does not limit disclosure of properly de-identified information since it is not considered "protected health information." *Id.* §160.103 (2023). The FDA only regulates research relating to drugs and devices. Moreover, even if an individual had been able to establish breach of the Common Rule or HIPAA, there is no private right of action to enforce either. *See* Payne v. Taslimi, 998 F.3d 648 (4th Cir. 2021) (holding there is no private right of action to enforce HIPAA); 45 C.F.R. §46.103 (2023) (describing IRB and other government agency enforcement of the Common Rule).

201. **Answer (D) is correct.** The Common Rule allows for broad consent to secondary research under certain circumstances. 45 C.F.R. §46.116(d) (2023). Here, the participant consented to subsequent research on other types of cancer, which would include cervical cancer.

    Answer (A) is incorrect. The Common Rule allows for broad consent to secondary research under certain circumstances and does not always require specific consent. *Id.* §46.116(d) (2023).

    Answer (B) is incorrect. The Common Rule allows for broad consent to secondary research under certain circumstances, and while certain vulnerable populations enjoy heightened protections, research on stigmatized conditions does not trigger additional protections.

    Answer (C) is incorrect. While the Common Rule allows for broad consent to secondary research under certain circumstances, secondary research must still meet Common Rule consent requirements. Some research conducted pursuant to the Common Rule is done with narrow consent, without authorizing future secondary research of identifiable information or specimens. Even if a research participant authorizes broader secondary research, any secondary research must fit within the scope of the broad consent.

202. **Answer**: The Bayh-Dole Act creates a significant profit motive for researchers and research institutions. This has benefit, but, at times, the profit motive may also create tension with the protection of human subjects or the credibility of the research.

203. **Answer (B) is correct.** Because the United States has restricted access to unsafe or ineffective drugs since its founding, the court determined that there is no substantive due process right for a competent adult to have access to unapproved drugs. After *Abigail Alliance for Better Access to Developmental Drugs v. von Eschenbach*, 495 F.3d 695 (D.C. Cir. 2007), most states and ultimately the federal government passed Right to Try laws that provide a pathway for competent adults who have exhausted all approved drugs and cannot participate in a clinical trial to seek access to unapproved drugs. As a practical matter, access to unapproved drugs remains limited primarily due to cost and manufacturer willingness to supply the drugs.

    Answer (A) is incorrect. The court reached the opposite conclusion based on the United States' long history and tradition of allowing the government to restrict access to drugs based on safety or efficacy.

    Answer (C) is incorrect. There is no suspect class here, and the government can establish that restricting access to drugs until they are shown to be safe and effective passes rational review. The government has an interest in protecting people from being exploited by unsafe and ineffective drugs that can cause harm.

    Answer (D) is incorrect. Denial of access to drugs that have not been FDA-approved is not punishment.

204. **Answer (A) is correct.** To be eligible to legally access an investigational medicine not yet approved by the FDA, a patient must be diagnosed with a life-threatening disease or condition, but the patient need not have reached the point of terminal illness.

    Answers (B), (C), and (D) are incorrect because all are required for eligibility pursuant to the Right to Try Act. In addition, a patient or the patient's representative must provide written informed consent and the investigational drug must be the subject of an active investigational new drug (IND) application that has not been placed on clinical hold.

205. **Answer**: First, Right to Try laws do not require pharmaceutical manufacturers to provide investigational drugs or biologics to patients. These are really "right to ask" laws. Because manufacturers can only charge patients the direct costs of providing such drugs, without profit, manufacturers may decline to make their investigational medicines available. Second, even if a manufacturer is willing to supply the drug, the cost of the drug and related clinical care is often not covered by insurance. Therefore, investigational drugs remain economically inaccessible to many patients. Finally, even with liability protection, some providers may be uncomfortable prescribing unapproved drugs.

    In *Abigail Alliance*, 495 F.3d 695 (en banc), the D.C. circuit court held that individuals do not have a constitutionally protected liberty interest in accessing drugs that are not yet approved by the FDA, in light of the longstanding tradition of government drug safety regulation.

206. **Answer**: Expanded Access, formerly known as Compassionate Use, requires FDA approval and involves FDA oversight. This should ensure enforcement of the conditions for access but may also slightly delay receipt of the investigational drug. By law, the FDA must grant or deny a request for Expanded Access within 30 days, and the agency often responds more quickly. Substantively, the requirements under the federal Right to Try Act and the FDA's Expanded Access program are similar.

Topic 24 **Answers**

Medical Aid in Dying & Other End-of-Life Issues

207. **Answer (C) is the best answer.** Most state statutes that authorize medically assisted dying require that a patient be a capable adult with a terminal disease. Such laws do not allow a health care provider or any other person to end the patient's life. So, the patient must also be physically able to self-administer the prescribed drugs. *See, e.g.*, N.J. Stat. Ann. § 26:16-4 (West 2023).

Answers (A) and (B) are not the best answer. Each answer is correct but incomplete.

Answer (D) is incorrect. A patient must be 18 years old but need not be older to seek medical aid in dying. In fact, some state laws expressly provide that age alone is not a basis to seek medical aid in dying. *See, e.g.*, Or. Rev. Stat. § 127.805(2) (2022).

208. **Answer (E) is the best answer.** Provider unwillingness, geographic inaccessibility, and lack of insurance coverage are all reported barriers to accessing medical aid in dying. For example, in Colorado, five years after legalization, only 8.5% of physicians likely to work with patients interested in medical aid in dying reported having acted as the attending physician prescribing drugs to hasten death. Eric G. Campbell et al., *Physicians' Attitudes and Experiences with Medical Aid in Dying in Colorado: A "Hidden Population" Survey*, 37 J. Gen. Internal Med. 3310, 3315 (2022). Moreover, patients report having to travel hours and to pay out-of-pocket costs to access medical aid in dying. *Id.* Most private insurance covers the medication costs, but Medicare does not.

Answers (A), (B), (C), and (D) are not the best answer. Each is correct but incomplete, as all answers describe reported barriers to accessing medical aid in dying.

209. **Answer (C) is correct.** It is factually untrue that historically undervalued racial minorities utilize medical aid in dying at higher rates. To the contrary, medical aid in dying is primarily utilized by white individuals. Overall, historically underserved populations are less likely to receive end-of-life planning, and some argue that this inequity in information and access to services must be remedied. *Healthcare Equity at the End of Life*, Compassion & Choices, https://www.compassionandchoices.org/our-issues/healthcare-equity-end-of-life (visited August 10, 2023).

Answers (A), (B), and (D) are incorrect. These answers reflect commonly expressed concerns regarding unethical efficiency, ableism, and inadequate oversight. Medical aid in dying laws are criticized by many in the disability rights community for undervaluing disabled life and encouraging "aid in dying" rather than providing the means for those with disabilities to live fully. *See, e.g.*, Press Release, Disability Rts. Educ. & Def. Fund, Disability, Patients' Rights Groups Issue Joint Statement Opposing the Expansion of Assisted Suicide in Observance of Suicide Prevention Month, (Sept. 2, 2021), https://dredf.org/2021/09/02/disability-patients-rights-groups-issue-joint-statement-opposing-the-expansion-of-assisted-suicide-in-observance-of-suicide-prevention-month/. Some also argue that individual and structural biases warp decision-making. Interestingly, others have expressed concern that people with disabilities may unfairly face barriers to accessing desired medical aid in dying. *See, e.g.*, Alicia Ouellette, *Barriers to Physician Aid in Dying for People with Disabilities*, 6 LAWS 23, 1–9 (2017). Others oppose medical aid in dying based on concerns that legal protections may not be enforced in practice. Still more oppose the practice on religious or moral grounds, and some argue such laws erode the physician's role as a healer.

210. **Answer (D) is correct.** In *Washington v. Glucksberg*, 521 U.S. 702, the Court held that Washington's blanket law prohibiting all forms of assisted suicide, including medical aid in dying, did not violate the 14th Amendment. Relying on history and tradition, the Court concluded that assistance in suicide is not a fundamental liberty interest. The Court also found that the State had a legitimate interest in preserving human life and preventing suicide, as well as other interests, and that its law was rationally related to these state interests.

Many people distinguish medical aid in dying from assisted suicide because medical aid in dying is limited to competent, terminally ill individuals. By definition, such individuals are already expected to die within six months. Often, these individuals do not want to die. In seeking aid in dying, they are merely acknowledging the reality that their death is imminent and trying to control the time and manner of their passing. Some, but not all, view this distinction as morally or legally significant. The Washington law at issue made no distinction between assisted suicide and medical aid in dying.

Answer (A) and (B) are incorrect because the Court upheld the state law prohibiting all forms of assisted suicide, finding no constitutional infirmity.

Answer (C) is incorrect because the Court applied rational basis scrutiny, not strict scrutiny.

211. **Answer**: Procedural due process requires a state to follow fair procedures before depriving a person of life, liberty, or property. Substantive due process requires a state to have sufficient reason to deprive a person of life, liberty, or property; it recognizes that procedural protections alone can be insufficient when a protected liberty interest is at stake. To justify curtailing a constitutionally protected liberty interest, strict scrutiny applies; a state must show a narrowly tailored, compelling state interest. Without a fundamental liberty interest at stake, a state law will be upheld if it is rationally related to a legitimate state interest.

212. **Answer (B) is correct.** According to Justice Rehnquist's majority opinion in *Washington v. Glucksberg*, 521 U.S. 702, substantive due process only protects unenumerated constitutional

rights that are deeply rooted in U.S. history and tradition. Because U.S. history has not traditionally treated assistance in suicide as a fundamental liberty, and, in fact, assisting suicide was often criminalized, the Court concludes that assistance in suicide is not a fundamental liberty interest protected by the Constitution. Justice Rehnquist rejects a plea to define the liberty interest at stake as determining the time and manner of one's own death. In 2022, the Court relied on Justice Rehnquist's "deeply rooted in history and tradition" approach to determine the scope of liberty interests protected by substantive due process in its abortion decision overturning *Roe v. Wade*, 410 U.S. 113. *Dobbs*, 142 S. Ct. 2228.

Answer (A) is incorrect because, by definition, the text of the Constitution itself does not speak to *unenumerated* liberty interests.

Answer (C) is incorrect because Justice Rehnquist's decision did not consider emerging norms in determining whether a constitutionally protected liberty interest exists. Justice Rehnquist's narrow view of unenumerated liberty interests contrasts with the more expansive view of substantive due process reflected in several U.S. Supreme Court decisions delivered by Justice Kennedy. *See, e.g.*, Lawrence v. Texas, 539 U.S. 558 (2003) (fundamental right to conduct a personal relationship in private invalidates anti-sodomy laws); Obergefell v. Hodges, 576 U.S. 644 (2015) (fundamental right to marry guaranteed to same sex couples).

Answer (D) is incorrect because Answer (B) is correct.

213. **Answer**: In *Washington v. Glucksberg*, 521 U.S. 702, the Court recognized a legitimate state interest in preserving human life; preventing suicide; protecting the integrity and ethics of the medical profession; protecting vulnerable groups (especially the poor, elderly, and disabled) from abuse, neglect, and mistakes; and avoiding the slide toward euthanasia.

214. **Answer (A) is correct.** *Vacco* upheld New York's assisted suicide law, finding no Equal Protection violation. The Court reasoned that the New York law did not infringe a fundamental right nor target a suspect class. The law permitted all competent adults to refuse unwanted medical treatment and did not allow any person to assist a suicide. It treated those similarly situated alike, even if the practical effect of the law was to allow those in need of life-sustaining medical care to hasten death while those without such need could not. Contrary to the Court of Appeals, the U.S. Supreme Court concluded that the legal distinction between assisting suicide and refusing medical treatment was rational, as it rests on differences in causation (death from disease vs. death from medication) and intent (intent to respect patient's wishes vs. intent to end life). The Court held, therefore, that the state's classification was rationally related to a legitimate government interest.

Philosophers often use the doctrine of double effect to contrast ethical dilemmas where a result is intended from those where the same result is expected but not intended. A pure consequentialist may regard intention as irrelevant, but deontologists and many others regard intent as ethically significant, even if the expected consequence is the same.

Answers (B) is incorrect because the Court, finding no constitutional infirmity, upheld the state law criminalizing assisted suicide.

Answer (C) is incorrect because the Court held that New York's distinction between terminating lifesaving medical treatment and assisting suicide is rational, given the differences in causation and intent.

Answer (D) is incorrect because the Court applied rational basis review, not strict scrutiny. The law criminalizing assisted suicide did not target a suspect class.

215. **Answer (D) is the best answer.** In Washington and Oregon, the overwhelming majority of patients who have utilized medical aid in dying are over 65 years old (72%) and have cancer (76%). A mentally competent adult with terminal cancer is typically able to self-administer medication and is therefore the most likely to able to utilize medical aid in dying.

Answer (A) is incorrect because a patient who cannot self-administer medication cannot utilize medical aid in dying, even if the patient is mentally capable. Some ethicists challenge this differential treatment based on physical limitation.

Answer (B) is incorrect because no state law currently allows pre-commitment, through an advance directive or otherwise, to satisfy the required informed consent for medical aid in dying. A patient who will not be mentally capable by the time the patient is terminal cannot legally use medical aid in dying. In pop culture, the book and later movie *Still Alice* poignantly captures the challenges inherent in seeking to live as long as possible without losing the window of mental capacity and self-administration.

Answer (C) is not the best answer because a patient cannot use medical aid in dying if depression or other psychiatric or psychological disorder is causing impaired judgment. While Answer (C) is vague regarding the extent to which the patient's depression is currently impairing judgment, at minimum, the patient's depression is likely to trigger a counseling referral and may make the attending and consulting physicians more reluctant to sign off on medical aid in dying.

216. **Answer (C) is correct.** *Cruzan v. Director, Missouri Department of Health*, 497 U.S. 261, is commonly cited for the premise that a competent adult has the right to refuse life-sustaining medical treatment (although the decision's actual language casts this conclusion as possible but not certain). The case also recognizes a state's interest in preservation of life. Without expressly addressing the proper standard of review, the Court concludes that Missouri permissively requires heightened evidentiary proof, clear and convincing evidence of the patient's prior desire, before allowing a surrogate to withdraw life-sustaining treatment. The Court describes Missouri's law as a "procedural safeguard" for a now-incompetent patient who is no longer able to make an informed and voluntary choice, and the Court concludes that this law does not violate the U.S. Constitution's Due Process Clause.

In dissent, Justice Brennan argues that a state's general interest in life should never outweigh a patient's particularized interest in self-determination.

Answers (A) and (B) are not the best answers. Both answers are correct but incomplete.

Answer (D) is incorrect because Answer (C) is correct.

217. **Answer (C) is correct.** In cases involving the refusal or withdrawal of life-sustaining treatment, including hydration and nutrition, courts have recognized a state's interest in preservation of life and prevention of suicide. However, a competent patient's right to refuse medical care trumps these state interests.

Many courts also recognize a state's interest in maintaining professional ethics and "protecting innocent third parties." *Cruzan*, 497 U.S. 261, 271. Generally, courts find these state interests outweighed as well. The oft-cited state interest in maintaining professional ethics is of questionable merit, as the AMA Code of Ethics and most other statements from relevant professional organizations provide that a competent patient's decision to refuse or terminate life-sustaining treatment should govern. AMA Code of Medical Ethics Op. 5.3. However, Topic 21 discusses maternal-fetal conflicts and the varied ways courts have responded when a competent adult carrying a fetus refuses Caesarian section or other purportedly life-saving care. Topic 25 discusses public health and the fines and confinement that the state may impose on a competent adult who refuses care or prevention for an infectious disease that may threaten the health of others.

Answer (A) is incorrect. As set forth above, courts have recognized a state's interest in preserving life, preventing suicide, and preserving professional ethics in cases involving withdrawal or refusal of life-sustaining care.

Answer (B) is incorrect. It is true that the state has an interest in preservation of life and prevention of suicide, but that interest does not outweigh the individual's right to refuse medical treatment.

Answer (D) is incorrect because the right of a competent adult to refuse unwanted medical care is generally considered a fundamental right protected by substantive due process, triggering strict scrutiny, not rational review.

218. **Answer (C) is the best answer.** Generally, courts defer to surrogate health care decision-makers, but futile care is an exception. Providers are not required to provide care that is medically unnecessary or inappropriate. It is not clear, however, that the requested care here is medically unnecessary or inappropriate. States vary regarding how they define and respond to "futile" care. Some state Health Care Decision Acts expressly authorize physicians to decline to provide futile care. Texas Advance Directives Act, Sec. 166.046, sets forth a procedure for declining to provide futile care that involves an ethics committee hearing. The result may vary by state.

Answer (A) is not the best answer. Generally, courts defer to surrogate health care decision-makers, but providers are not required to render care that is contrary to the standard of care and will not accomplish the result desired by the patient.

Answer (B) is not the best answer. Physicians may be experts on medical efficacy, but when "futility" refers to care that is contrary to the patient's best interests rather than medically ineffective, this determination appears to include subjective, value-laden judgments.

Answer (D) is not the best answer because it is incorrect in most states. While consulting a hospital ethics committee can provide additional information and possibly help the parties resolve an impasse, a committee decision does not have binding legal authority in most states. The Texas Advance Directives Act does authorize a procedure along these lines.

219. **Answer (C) is correct.** All states recognize brain death as well as traditional heart and lung cessation, under most circumstances. States vary in terms of their specific procedures, medical standards, and legal standards for determining death, however. Occasionally, this perversely results in a patient's being dead under the law of one state but not another. For example, Jahi McMath was declared dead under California law in 2013 but was not declared dead under New Jersey law until 2018. Some courts and commentators have also highlighted a potential disjunction between the legal standard, which requires irreversible cessation of all brain function, and medical guidelines for determining death, which may not in fact measure all function of the entire brain. *See, e.g., In re* Guardianship of Hailu, 361 P.3d 524 (Nev. 2015); Ariane Lewis, Richard J. Bonnie, & Thaddeus Pope, *It's Time to Revise the Uniform Determination of Death Act*, 172 Annals Internal Med. 143 (2020). The Uniform Determination of Death Act is currently being revised, and a new act is expected in 2024. The draft circulating as of July 2023 proposes two options for determining death: (1) retain the prior approach, or (2) redefine brain death as a permanent coma, cessation of spontaneous respiratory functions, and loss of brainstem reflexes. Draft Uniform Determination of Death Act § 3(a) (Unif. L. Comm'n 20__).

Answers (A) and (B) are not the best answers. Each answer is correct but incomplete.

Answer (D) is incorrect because either suffices, that is, both are not required.

Public Health

220. **Answer**: Public health strives to measure and improve the health and longevity of a population rather than any one individual. It involves organized measures, often but not necessarily taken by the state, to prevent disease, prolong life, and promote health in a population. *See* CDC, *Introduction to Public Health* (2022). During the 20th century, life expectancy increased by 62%, and many largely credit public health measures. Examples of successful public health initiatives include the decline in vaccine-preventable diseases, reduced motor vehicle deaths, reduction in tobacco use, implementation of folic acid in cereal occupational safety measures, and access to safe water and other sanitation.

221. **Answer**: States have the power to enact public health laws and orders pursuant to their police power. Jacobson v. Massachusetts, 197 U.S. 11 (1905); U.S. Const. amend. X.

222. **Answer**: Public health laws save lives, but to do so, they sometimes limit individual autonomy, privacy, and/or freedom of movement, as well as other rights like freedom of speech, freedom of religious exercise, or the right to bear arms.

223. **Answer (E) is the best answer**. While public health responds to infectious disease threats, its scope extends beyond disease to address a wide array of other challenges that threaten health, like motor vehicle safety, obesity, and substance abuse. This breadth acknowledges the reality that the social determinants of health often have a more significant impact on health outcomes than medical care. Moreover, while the most controversial public health measures are mandatory or coercive, much of public health focuses on education and voluntary behavioral changes.

    Answers (A), (B), (C) and (D) are not the best answers. Each correctly identifies a public health measure but is incomplete.

224. **Answer (D) is the best answer**. The language of Answer (D) is taken directly from *Jacobson*, 197 U.S. 11, and suggests a "non-arbitrary" standard of review. Scholars disagree regarding how to reconcile *Jacobson* with subsequent due process jurisprudence. Before *Roman Catholic Diocese of Brooklyn v. Cuomo*, 141 S. Ct. 63 (2020), some argued that *Jacobson* effectively suspended the Constitution during a public health emergency. After *Roman Catholic Diocese*, there can be no question that the suspension interpretation does not reflect current law.

Others contend that *Roman Catholic Diocese* abrogated *Jacobson*, but this seems unlikely since the court did not do so expressly. A better reading of both cases reconciles them and concludes that the Court will apply strict scrutiny to a public health order if it infringes a fundamental right.

This leaves the standard of review for a public health order alleged to impinge upon a liberty interest that is not a fundamental right unresolved. Some courts have reviewed these mandates under a rational review standard, reasoning that *Jacobson*'s deferential review is most akin to rational review. *See, e.g.*, Klaassen v. Trustees of Indiana Univ., 549 F. Supp. 3d 836 (N.D. Ind.), *aff'd*, 7 F.4th 592 (7th Cir. 2021), *vacated as moot* 24 F.4th 638 (7th Cir. 2022) (while vacating, the Court expresses "confidence in the correctness of our earlier decision"). Others have applied strict scrutiny or required the government to show "substantial risk." *See, e.g.*, City of Newark v. J.S., 652 A.2d 265 (N.J. Super. Ct. 1993). Still other courts have applied a "reasonableness" test. *See, e.g.*, Hickox v. Christie, 205 F. Supp. 3d 579 (D.N.J. 2016).

Answers (A), (B), and (C) are incorrect. When *Jacobson* was decided, the Court had not yet developed the three-levels of scrutiny utilized today.

225. **Answer (C) is the best answer**. In *Zucht v. King*, 260 U.S. 174 (1922), the U.S. Supreme Court upheld a vaccine mandate for public school attendance. Today, all states require proof of certain vaccinations for public school attendance, absent exemption, but the scope and ease of such exemptions vary widely. Because *Jacobson v. Massachusetts*, 197 U.S. 11 (1905) recognized the need for a vaccine exemption for individual medical contraindication, Answer (C) is the best answer. All fifty states grant exemptions for medical reasons.

The majority of states also recognize a religious exemption, although six states do not. Historically, most courts have held that vaccine mandates do *not* require a religious exemption. *See, e.g.*, Phillips v. City of N.Y., 775 F.3d 538 (2d. Cir. 2015); Brown v. Stone, 378 So. 2d 218 (Miss. 1980). However, this conclusion has been called into question by recent Supreme Court jurisprudence. Considering a different public health law, the Supreme Court held that the law was not a neutral law of general application and instead must satisfy strict scrutiny because the law treated certain other secular activities more favorably than a restricted religious practice. Tandon v. Newton, 141 S.Ct. 1294 (2021) (overturning a COVID-19 restriction on more than three families gathering in a private residence, including for religious worship, while hardware stores and hair salons were allowed to operate without such limitation). This suggests that if a vaccine mandate exempts medical contraindication, it *may* also be required to exempt religious exercise or to satisfy strict scrutiny. Given the legal uncertainty of whether (or when) religious exemptions may be required as compared to the well-established rule that individual medical contraindication is constitutionally required, Answer (C) is the best answer.

Answer (A) is not the best answer. *Jacobson* recognized the need for an exemption for individual medical contraindication; therefore, Answer (C) is the best answer. As discussed above, it is much less clear when or if a religious exemption is constitutionally required. Nonetheless, given the legal uncertainty, a religious exemption is often included in vaccine mandates. *See, e.g.*, CMS Omnibus COVID-19 Health Care Staff Vaccination Interim Final Rule.

Answer (B) is incorrect. In *Jacobson*, the Supreme Court rejected the argument that an individual is entitled to an exemption because the individual disagrees with the public health authority regarding the relative risk-benefit of the vaccine. Jacobson v. Massachusetts, 197 U.S. 11 (1905).

Answer (D) is incorrect. As discussed above, there is no constitutional right to a vaccine mandate exemption based on individual view that a vaccine poses more risk than benefit. Jacobson v. Massachusetts, 197 U.S. 11 (1905). Moreover, it is unclear whether a vaccine mandate must exempt religious exercise or be narrowly tailored to a compelling state interest in combatting the particular infectious disease.

226. **Answer (A) is correct.** Under similar facts, in *Roman Catholic Diocese*, 141 S. Ct. 63, the U.S. Supreme Court concluded that a public health order limiting the gathering size of religious services without regard to social distancing while allowing certain secular businesses like liquor stores to operate under more lenient terms was not a neutral law of general application. Accordingly, the Court treated the law as targeting religious practice, a fundamental right under the Free Exercise Clause, and applied strict scrutiny. The Court recognized a compelling state interest in controlling the infectious disease, but it held that the health order was unconstitutional because it failed to narrowly target that compelling interest.

Answer (B) is incorrect for the reasons set forth above. Courts apply intermediate scrutiny in equal protection cases involving gender classifications and some First Amendment cases.

Answer (C) is incorrect for the reasons set forth above. Some courts, however, have applied rational review to public health orders when there is not a fundamental right like free exercise at stake. *See, e.g.*, Klaassen v. Trustees of Indiana Univ., 549 F. Supp. 3d 836 (N.D. Ind. 2021), *affirmed*, 7 F.4th 592 (7th Cir. 2021) (finding no constitutional violation with public university's vaccine mandate that included a religious exemption).

Answer (D) is incorrect. The standard of review set forth in *Jacobson* was not used in *Roman Catholic Diocese*, which involved a free exercise question like this one. As a result, some argue that *Roman Catholic Diocese* abrogated *Jacobson*, but this seems unlikely since the Court did not do so expressly. A better reading of both cases reconciles them and concludes that the Court will apply strict scrutiny when a public health order infringes a fundamental right.

227. **Answer (B) is correct.** The non-delegation doctrine prohibits one branch of government from delegating its powers to another branch, largely because this would undermine the separation of powers upon which our system of democracy rests. The line between permissible and impermissible delegation is not always clear. Courts have generally recognized that the legislative branch may permissibly delegate authority to the executive branch if the delegation of power includes an intelligible principle and standards constraining the exercise of administrative discretion. Beshear v. Acree, 615 S.W.3d 780 (Ky. 2020). Typically, the legislature may rely on an administrative agency for interstitial rules or to develop regulations that involve specialized agency expertise but not to make political compromises or to solve problems the legislature has failed to solve. Boreali v. Axelrod, 517 N.E.2d 1350 (N.Y. 1987).

Answer (A) is incorrect because reasonable public health measures fall within the state's police power. So cases challenging public health measures pursuant to the non-delegation doctrine do not usually focus on limited government arguments.

Answer (C) is incorrect because non-delegation questions ask which *branch* of government, legislative or executive, has a particular power, not whether the state or federal government has that power.

Answer (D) is incorrect because non-delegation focuses primarily on checks and balances between branches of our government, not on individual liberty.

228. **Answer**: The Administrative Procedures Act (APA) or its state counterpart typically governs administrative agencies, including public health agencies. The APA generally, although not always, requires agencies to provide public notice and a comment period before issuing final rules. This can be a time-consuming process, and if the agency fails to comply, a court may declare an otherwise valid rule legally void. Often, emergency health power acts allow an administrative agency to act without complying with normal APA procedures.

229. **Answer (C) is correct.** A person injured by a recommended vaccine may submit a claim for compensation to the National Vaccine Injury Program. This no-fault system provides limited compensation to anyone injured by a recommended vaccine. However, individuals do not have the right to bring products liability, malpractice, or other state law claims for vaccine-related injury. 42 U.S.C. § 300aa-22(b)(1); Bruesewitz v. Wyeth LLC, 562 U.S. 223, 231–33 (2011).

Answers (A), (B), and (D) are incorrect. The National Vaccine Injury Program provides a potential remedy for an individual injured by a recommended vaccine. At the same time, the Vaccine Act preempts products liability and malpractice laws in connection with any vaccine-related injury. 42 U.S.C. § 300aa-22(b)(1); *Bruesewitz*, 562 U.S. 223, 231–33.

230. **Answer (C) is correct.** Answer (C) is correct. Forty states have adopted some form of the Model State Emergency Health Powers Act of 2001. Under the Model State Emergency Health Powers Act of 2001, a public health emergency is "an occurrence or imminent threat of an illness or health condition" caused by bioterrorism, novel or previously controlled infectious agent or biological toxin, natural disaster, or chemical or nuclear attack that poses a high probability of certain defined harms. THE MODEL STATE EMERGENCY HEALTH POWERS ACT § 104(m) (THE CTR. FOR L. & PUB.'S HEALTH AT GEORGETOWN & JOHNS HOPKINS UNIVERSITIES December 21, 2001). Here, it is not clear that youth e-cigarette use constitutes an "illness or health condition" per se. Even if it does, e-cigarette use is *not* caused by bioterrorism, infectious agent, or other cause listed in the Act, as required for a "public health emergency."

Interestingly, the explosion in youth e-cigarette use meets the new definition of a "public health emergency" under the Model Public-Health Emergency Authority Act of 2023 (PHE Act), which the Uniform Law Commission recently approved but as of publication, had not yet been adopted by any states. MODEL PUBLIC-HEALTH EMERGENCY AUTH. ACT (UNIF. L.

COMM'N 2023). The PHE Act defines a "public health emergency" to include widespread exposure to a "chemical agent or toxin," *regardless of cause*, that "poses a significant risk of substantial harm to a large number of individuals in the affected population." *Id.* at § 2(4). E-cigarettes contain chemical toxins that pose a significant risk of "substantial harm" to a large number of youth and such use spiked well above the prior baseline in a short period of time.

While the PHE Act was primarily designed to respond to issues raised by COVID-19, it is almost certainly not a coincidence that it broadens the definition of a public health emergency to cover problems like the 900% increase in youth vaping over 4 years. After the Surgeon General's advisory, several governors announced emergency bans on flavored nicotine vapor products. These emergency bans often did not survive court challenges. *See, e.g.*, Slis v. State of Michigan, 856 N.W.2d 569 (Mich. App. 2020). The PHE Act, if adopted by states, could give governors more tools to respond to similar problems in the future.

Answers (A) and (B) are incorrect. As discussed above, it is not enough for a health problem to be declared an epidemic, even if the epidemic is harmful and impacts millions. In order to justify the significant new government powers triggered by a public health emergency, the health problem must be so threatening as to risk near-term death or permanent or long-term disability.

Answer (D) is incorrect. A contagious disease is not the only trigger for a public health emergency. In fact, the CDC promulgated the Model State Emergency Health Powers Act in response to 9/11, largely over concerns that existing laws may not cover bioterrorism. Further, while the use of e-cigarettes is not a contagious disease under Section 104(c), it is worth noting that social factors influence behavior and increase the risk of spread, even for so called non-communicable diseases, like e-cigarette use.

Answers

Practice Exam

231. **Answer (C) is the best answer.** When a licensed individual brings an action in court to allege that a licensing board has taken an improper adverse action against them, a court will review that action to determine whether the licensing board had substantial evidence to support its decision. As such, Answer (C) is the best answer because it provides details about the Board's refusing to hear evidence that might otherwise show that Nurse Hernandez was not diagnosing patients but was using diagnostic equipment as part of a plan of care for treatment of a chronic condition.

    Answers (A) and (B) are incorrect. These answers might be effective if this were a malpractice case, but they do not address the standard that a court would apply. The fact that Nurse Hernandez has never harmed patients does not speak to the standard of review by a court and is not dispositive of the claims against Nurse Hernandez.

    Answer (D) is not the best answer. Although the decision of the Board was not the same as that of the hearing officer, there is nothing in Answer (D) indicating that Nurse Hernandez has facts that would prove that the decision of the Board was not supported by substantial evidence. The standard of review applied by the court would require the plaintiff to show that the Board's decision was not supported by substantial evidence. Absent additional information, this answer would not meet that burden.

232. **Answer (A) is correct.** It is not necessary to prove that protected health information has been accessed to prove that an unauthorized use or disclosure is a breach. In the context of ransomware attacks where it is not known whether data has been accessed, the breach analysis requires a covered entity or business associate to presume that the data has been accessed absent an ability to prove otherwise.

    Answer (B) is incorrect. While *most* ransomware attacks will be considered breaches, there are scenarios in which the hackers only access de-identified data or the attack is discovered quickly enough that it might not be a breach.

    Answer (C) is incorrect for the same reason that answer (A) is correct—the presumption dictates that it is not necessary to prove access.

    Answer (D) is incorrect. As stated in Answer (A), the standard breach analysis applies to ransomware attacks if such attacks involve the unauthorized disclosure of protected health information.

233. **Answer (D) is correct.** Answer (D) is correct because it is the only answer that describes a situation in which the nurses and other hospital staff had no knowledge of the negligent act. Under *Thompson v. Nason Hospital*, 591 A.2d 703, a hospital has five duties to its patients: (1) to maintain safe facilities and equipment; (2) to select and retain competent physicians; (3) to oversee all persons who practice medicine within its walls; (4) to formulate and adopt adequate policies and procedures; and (5) to uphold the proper standard of care owed to its patients, when the hospital has actual or constructive knowledge of the defect. In these facts, no one at the hospital had knowledge (actual or constructive) of the defect, and thus no obligation was triggered because they were unaware of the negligence.

    Answer (A) is incorrect. This answer represents a failure of the hospital's duty to maintain safe facilities and equipment.

    Answer (B) is incorrect. This answer represents a failure of the hospital's duty to formulate and adopt adequate policies and procedures.

    Answer (C) is incorrect. This answer represents a failure of the hospital's duty to select and retain competent physicians.

234. **Answer (B) is correct.** In *NFIB v. Sebelius*, 567 U.S. 519, the Court upheld the constitutionality of the individual mandate—the provision of the ACA requiring that all persons (subject to certain exceptions) purchase health insurance or pay a tax under Congress's power to tax and spend. Subsequently, Congress reduced the tax triggered by the failure to purchase health insurance to zero.

    Answer (A) is incorrect. In *NFIB v. Sebelius*, the Court struck down the provision of the ACA requiring states to adopt the expansion of Medicaid as coercive and therefore unconstitutional. Rather, states are now permitted to "opt-in" to expanding their Medicaid program to all individuals earning less than 135% of the FPL.

    Answers (C) and (D) are incorrect. These provisions under the ACA were not at issue in this case.

235. **Answer (D) is correct.** Under the ACA, an insurer can "rate" individuals based on age and tobacco use, as well as rating area. 42 U.S.C. § 300gg(a)(1)(A).

    Answers (A), (B), and (C) are incorrect. It is not permissible to rate based on sex, race, or disability.

236. **Answer (C) is correct.** Because non-profit organizations do not have shareholders to review and approve decisions of the Board of Directors, the state Attorney General often sits in the same position as shareholder for a non-profit organization and must review and approve transactions. When reviewing transactions for non-profit organizations, the Attorney General's office will determine whether the transaction will benefit the putative owners of the entity—the general public.

Answer (A) is incorrect. While a hospital must notify Centers for Medicare and Medicaid Services (CMS) regarding a transaction involving a change of ownership, it is not necessary for parties to seek approval in advance of a transaction.

Answer (B) is incorrect. A state licensing agency, such as the Department of Health, typically requires notice of a change of ownership, but parties are not required to seek permission in advance.

Answer (D) is incorrect for the same reason that Answer (C) is correct. The Attorney General is typically required to approve a transaction involving a sale of non-profit assets on behalf of the public.

237. **Answer (C) is the best answer.** Directors of a non-profit institution have a duty of obedience, which requires them to make decisions with the mission as the primary driver, otherwise known as mission primacy. In the facts, the directors do not discuss the mission, the charitable purpose of the entity, or how this decision will impact the beneficiaries of the entity's charitable purpose. Therefore, (C) correctly identifies this potential breach.

Answer (A) is incorrect. This answer correctly states that they forgot to consider the charitable purpose of the entity, but this failure falls under the duty of obedience, not the duty of loyalty.

Answer (B) is not the best answer. Although the meeting was short, there are not sufficient facts to definitively conclude that this was a breach of the duty of care.

Answer (D) is incorrect because Answer (C) is correct. Although the directors of a non-profit organization are generally afforded application of the business judgment rule, such a rule only applies if there was not a breach of fiduciary duty.

238. **Answer (B) is correct.** Under the Civil Monetary Penalties Law set forth in the Social Security Act, providers will be mandatorily excluded from participation in federal health care programs for a period of at least five years if they are convicted of a felony for the unlawful manufacture, distribution, prescription, or dispensing of a controlled substance. *Id.* §§ 1320a7-(a)(1)–(4). Additionally, if the government's financial loss results from an overpayment of more than $5,000 — as here, since the total amount improperly paid was over $100,000 — then such information can be used as an aggravating factor in determining the exclusion period.

Answer (A) is incorrect. If the distribution offense had been a misdemeanor as opposed to a felony, then the exclusion would have been permissive rather than mandatory. The fact that this is a Class E felony, however, triggers mandatory exclusion.

Answer (C) is incorrect. Dr. Jones's substance abuse may be a mitigating rather than aggravating factor here because it could be evidence that he had a mental, emotional, or physical condition during the commission of the offense that reduced his culpability.

Answer (D) is incorrect. While permissive exclusion is typically a term of three years, mandatory exclusion requires a minimum of a five-year exclusionary period in most instances.

239. **Answer (D) is the best answer.** The scenario described in this question has been a common False Claims Act issue in various academic medical centers across the country. This type of violation has been identified by courts as an implied false certification. Under *Universal Health Services v. United States ex rel. Escobar*, 136 S. Ct. 1989 (2016), an implied false certification claim can be a valid basis for liability if (1) a defendant's claim makes specific representations about the goods or services provided and (2) the defendant fails to disclose noncompliance with *material* statutory, regulatory, or contractual requirements that make those representations misleading half-truths. The Court stressed that the *qui tam* relator/government must show that the government would find the information material to payment of the claim and that such materiality standard should be demanding. In this instance, it seems likely that Sally will be able to prevail as long as she can show that the government would find the information regarding overlapping surgeries and the potential for over-billing indicative of a violation of the False Claims Act.

    Answer (A) is incorrect. As mentioned above, the Supreme Court in *Escobar* specifically recognized the viability of a claim for an implied false certification, which is noncompliance with an underlying regulation that results in payment for services by the federal government, under the False Claims Act.

    Answer (B) is incorrect. As set forth above, the U.S. Supreme Court has specifically recognized the viability of an implied false certification claim. The distinction between Answers (A) and (B) is that Answer (A) is describing what an implied false certification theory of liability is and Answer (B) is using the recognized term.

    Answer (C) is not the best answer because it is incomplete. While the Supreme Court has recognized the viability of an implied false certification claim, the Court has limited its application to claims that meet the two-part test outlined in Answer (D) above. The plaintiff (either the *qui tam* relator or federal government) must show that the implied false certification would be material to the government in its payment of the claim.

240. **Answer (C) is correct.** The scenario posed in this question describes a merger between two entities. Under Clayton Act Section 7, mergers are prohibited if the effect is to substantially lessen competition or to create a monopoly. To assess what kind of transaction might be prohibited, the Federal Trade Commission examines the product market and the geographic market to assess whether the merger would substantially lessen competition within those markets. Based on the limited facts, the providers appear to be in the same market of "hospitals" (although levels of care could be distinguished), and they appear to be operating within the same geographic region. Unlike violation of Sections 1 or 2 of the Sherman Act, it is not necessary under Section 7 of the Clayton Act to show intent of the parties to create a monopoly or unreasonably restrain trade. Rather, it is only necessary to show that the *effect* of the merger is likely to substantially lessen competition. Therefore, absent additional information regarding the intent of the parties in the facts, a Clayton Act Section 7 claim would be the easiest to prove.

Answer (A) is incorrect. To prove a claim under Section 2 of the Sherman Act, it is necessary to show that one party has both (1) the power to control market prices or exclude competition and (2) undertakes the willful acquisition or maintenance of that power as distinguished from growth. Under the facts as provided, it is not clear that St. Michael's Hospital has sufficient market power to be able to control market prices or exclude competition. While St. Michael's Hospital is the largest system, there are other providers in the area with some market power. Additionally, there are no facts given indicating that St. Michael's Hospital's intention with respect to the merger with MGH is for willful acquisition or maintenance of power. Thus, absent additional facts, a Sherman Act Section 2 claim may be difficult to prove.

Answer (B) is incorrect. Sustaining a Sherman Act Section 1 claim would require additional facts not stated in the question. To prove a claim under Section 1 of the Sherman Act requires a meeting of the minds of two parties to unreasonably restrain trade. Although there appears to be a meeting of the minds regarding the desire to merge, there are no additional facts indicating that the parties are colluding to unreasonably restrain trade. Whether this merger would be in violation of Section 1 of the Sherman Act based on these facts would be determined based on a Rule of Reason analysis, weighing the pro-competitive effects against the anti-competitive effects. More facts regarding the intent of the parties and the efficiencies would be necessary to establish this claim.

Answer (D) is incorrect. Pursuant to the Noerr-Pennington doctrine, the FTC has recognized that under the First Amendment, citizens have the right to request government action even if it supplants competition. There is nothing in this question regarding exercising First Amendment rights, and therefore this answer is inapplicable.

241. **Answer (A) is the best answer.** The information contained in this answer describes efficiencies that could be created through the merger. Although not all courts have accepted an efficiencies defense to a Clayton Act Section 7 claim, *see* St. Alphonsus Med. Ctr.-Nampa, Inc. v. St. Luke's Health Sys., Ltd., 778 F.3d 775 (9th Cir. 2015), some courts will consider evidence of efficiencies created by the merger to rebut the presumption that a merger substantially lessens competition. *See id.* (citing ProMedica Health Sys. v. FTC, 749 F.3d 559, 571 (6th Cir. 2014); FTC v. H.J. Heinz, 246 F.3d 708, 720–22 (D.C. Cir. 2001); FTC v. Tenet Health Care Corp., 186 F.3d 1045, 1054–55 (8th Cir. 1999); FTC v. Univ. Health, Inc., 938 F.2d 1206, 1222–24 (11th Cir. 1991)). The information in this answer would show efficiencies created as part of the merger and may rebut any presumption of substantially lessening competition.

Answer (B) is incorrect. Although the ability to transfer patients to St. Michael's Hospital for specialty services may be helpful for patients arriving at MGH, this could lead to antitrust concerns such as carving up the market for certain services. It could also increase prices overall because patients would be transferred to the hospital with greater market power and thus likely greater bargaining power with payors. This will likely result in higher prices for consumers.

Answer (C) is not the best answer. While increased pricing may be beneficial for MGH, this will decrease price competition and increase pricing overall for consumers. Increased pricing to bolster financial stability alone would not rebut the presumption that the merger would not substantially lessen competition. If St. Michael's Hospital could show that MGH's financial position was so dire that MGH would otherwise have to close the hospital unless it entered into the merger with St. Michael's, this may be sufficient to rebut the presumption. Answer (C) does not indicate that MGH would have to shut down, however — only that its financial position would be improved with better rates. Thus, Answer (A) is a better answer because more facts would be needed for Answer (C) to be correct.

Answer (D) is incorrect. Again, while the superior services may be beneficial for consumers, the superior services will likely come at an increased cost to them because St. Michael's Hospital will attempt to demand increased prices for these superior services. This will increase consumer prices overall by making MGH's patients seek services from the higher-priced St. Michael's Hospital. Generally, courts have not accepted improved quality as a defense to anti-competitive mergers.

242. **Answer (C) is correct.** A Certificate of Need law is a state law designed to manage the growth of health care facilities to control costs. Only a minority of states currently have Certificate of Need laws, and the laws vary greatly from state to state regarding coverage. For example, in Tennessee, before any provider can open a new hospital, the provider must file an application with the Health Services and Development Agency, establishing a need for new acute care beds in the desired area based on a specific formula. Thus, if a Certificate of Need law is in place, it could hinder the ability of investors to open a hospital unless they were able to prove a particular need.

Answer (A) is incorrect. The Corporate Practice of Medicine doctrine is a state law doctrine applicable in some states that would prevent corporations or other non-physician-owned entities such as a hospital from employing physicians. The rationale behind this doctrine is that a physician cannot be beholden to a corporation with corporate purposes which may be contrary to the physician's medical judgment and the best interest of the patient. While a hospital provider new to an area would want to know if a Corporate Practice of Medicine doctrine exists, it would not prevent a provider from opening a hospital; rather, it would impact the way in which the hospital interacts with its physicians.

Answer (B) is incorrect. This answer is not relevant to the facts. The State Action doctrine is an antitrust doctrine providing antitrust immunity for government actors and those acting pursuant to a clearly articulated and affirmatively expressed state policy while actively supervised by the state.

Answer (D) is incorrect. Although the Stark Law, otherwise known as the Physician Self-Referral Law, will be important for purposes of hospital operations, it does not prevent private investors from owning or establishing a hospital. The Stark Law could have an impact if the hospital owners were physicians, but the proposed owners in this question are private, non-physician investors.

243. **Answer (B) is the best answer.** In this question, Sally Jones is a hospital employee. As a hospital employee, Sally is the hospital's actual agent, and thus the hospital is vicariously liable for Sally's acts done within the scope of Sally's employment.

Answer (A) is not the best answer. *Thompson v. Nason Hospital*, 591 A.2d 703, establishes a five-prong test for direct liability for corporate negligence applicable against the hospital as an entity. This test targets negligence of the entity for patient injury caused by, for example, inadequate application of policies and procedures. While this claim may be possible, Answer (B) provides an easier basis to establish liability under the facts.

Answer (C) is incorrect. The facts as described show vicarious liability on the part of the hospital, but not necessarily direct liability. Sally appears to be responsible for the negligence and injury. It should be noted that while the facts here point to Sally's negligence, over time hospitals have developed systems for detection of foreign objects to avoid the inevitable pitfalls of human error.

Answer (D) is not the best answer. Although the hospital may try to use this as a defense to argue that the real claimant should be Dr. Hernandez as "captain of the ship," this does not change the fact that the hospital is vicariously liable for Sally's actions because Sally is the hospital's agent. Therefore, Answer (B) is a better answer because Jane will be able to at least file her claim against the hospital by proving that Sally is an actual agent.

244. **Answer (C) is the best answer.** Under the facts provided, the hospital only faces liability if Dr. Rossi is an agent of the hospital. If Dr. Rossi is an independent contractor, then she is not an actual agent of the hospital, though she may still be an apparent agent. To prove that Dr. Rossi is an apparent agent of the hospital, plaintiff must show that the hospital held out Dr. Rossi to the public as its agent, regardless of whether Dr. Rossi is in fact an agent, and that Mario reasonably relied on such holding out. The facts in the question show that the hospital has a billboard that advertises for Dr. Rossi's services and that Dr. Rossi has an office at the hospital during the week. This is likely enough to show that the hospital was holding out Dr. Rossi as an agent, if Mario can show that he reasonably relied on this holding out.

Answer (A) is not the best answer. For the same reason that Answer (C) is the best answer, Answer (A) is not the best answer. If Mario can prove that the hospital was holding out Dr. Rossi as its agent through the billboards and that Mario relied on the billboards in making his decision to seek services at the hospital, then the hospital will be liable for Dr. Rossi's acts if Dr. Rossi is found to be negligent.

Answer (B) is incorrect. It is not necessary to prove that Dr. Rossi is an actual agent to sustain a claim against the hospital. Also, the facts in the question do not support a finding that Dr. Rossi is an actual agent but rather that she is an independent contractor.

Answer (D) is incorrect. The fact that Dr. Rossi has privileges at two other hospitals is likely more indicative that Dr. Rossi is an independent contractor of the hospital than that she is an agent. This would not support Mario's claim against Dr. Rossi.

245. **Answer (B) is correct.** Section 504 of the Rehabilitation Act prohibits programs and activities that receive federal financial assistance from denying individuals treatment or services because of their disability. Under this law, it is necessary to show that the individual with the disability was discriminated against solely on the basis of such disability; that is, the disability was the sole basis for the refusal or denial of treatment.

Answer (A) is incorrect. Section 504 of the Rehabilitation Act requires that the individual's disability be the *sole* motivation behind the discrimination, not just one factor. This answer indicates that the claim could be sustained by showing that the plaintiff's disability was at least one factor, which is not accurate under Section 504.

Answer (C) is incorrect. Substance use disorder can qualify as a disability under Section 504 of the Federal Rehabilitation Act.

Answer (D) is incorrect. This answer is factually incorrect and is also not responsive to the call of the question. The fact that the screening was not appropriate is central in the context of an EMTALA claim, but a Rehabilitation Act claim is dependent on the reason for the discrimination, if any, and not whether the care was provided negligently.

246. **Answer (D) is the best answer.** Most states consider clinical practice guidelines relevant but not dispositive of the standard of care. Even the strongest and best supported guidelines only recommend care deemed optimal for most patients; they do not define the limits of "minimally competent" care. Likewise, guidelines may fail to reflect the view of a respectable minority or of recent clinical innovation. Moreover, even if generally accepted by the particular provider, departure from guidelines may be warranted in some cases based upon resource availability, patient preference, patient comorbidity, or other factors.

Answer (A) is not the best answer. States often vary the standard of care based upon the expertise the particular provider holds themselves out as having. *See, e.g.*, WY. STAT. ANN. § 1-12-601(a)(i) (the standard of care for providers certified by a national certifying board or association is set by that board or association, although it may be modified by available resources). As a result, the Endocrine Society's clinical practice guidelines likely have more relevance to a physician who holds themselves out as an endocrinologist, but the guidelines still likely have at least some relevance even for a non-specialist.

Answer (B) is not the best answer. The fact that another leading professional medical organization has issued a contrary guideline may impact the *weight* that should be accorded to the Endocrine Society guidelines, especially for a non-endocrinologist, but it does not render the guidelines inadmissable.

Answer (C) is not the best answer. While some courts have excluded evidence of clinical practice guidelines, most courts generally admit guidelines as some evidence of the standard of care, although not dispositive thereof.

247. **Answer (B) is correct.** Generally, a valid advance directive should govern the care provided to a patient when the advance directive answers the particular question at issue. Here, Kat's

advance directive provides that she wants life-sustaining treatment, which includes ventilation and artificial hydration. While the Uniform Health Care Decisions Act allows oral instructions, Kat's oral statement was made years *prior* to execution of her written advance directive which therefore supersedes the oral statement.

Answer (A) is incorrect. While the result (ventilation and hydration) is correct, it is not true that a physician has authority to make treatment decisions or that life should be preserved as long as possible if such is contrary to the patient's wishes (as expressed or as determined by agent or surrogate). Providers must generally follow the instructions given by agents or surrogates. If the provider believes that such instructions deviate from the standard of care, request futile care, or request care for which the provider has a conscience objection, the provider should make a reasonable effort to transfer the patient to a willing provider.

Answer (C) is incorrect. First, if married and not separated, a patient's spouse has the right to make health care decisions over the patient's brother. Second, a surrogate should generally adhere to the patient's specific instructions if not revoked.

Answer (D) is incorrect. Specific instructions set forth in a patient's advance directive should generally govern care. When no specific instructions exist, the patient's health care surrogate should decide based on the patient's values and subjective best interest.

248. **Answer (D) is correct.** Jacob does not qualify for Medicare. He is not age 65 or older, nor does he have a permanent disability or other basis for eligibility. Similarly, Jacob does not qualify for Medicaid. Because he lives in a non-expansion state, he must be both financially and categorically eligible. Although Jacob's income is below the poverty level, he is not categorically eligible. To be categorically eligible, he must be age 65 or older, blind, permanently disabled, pregnant, a minor, or a caretaker relative to a minor. Jacob does not fall within any of these categories. Unfortunately, because Jacob makes less than 100% of the FPL, he also is not eligible for a premium tax subsidy to purchase individual insurance on a state or federal health insurance exchange. Jacob will likely be uninsured.

Answer (A) is incorrect. Jacob is not eligible for Medicare. He is not age 65 or older, nor does he have a permanent disability, end stage renal disease, or amyotrophic lateral sclerosis (ALS).

Answer (B) is incorrect. While Jacob would qualify for Medicaid in the majority of states because his income is below 100% of the FPL, he will not qualify for Medicaid in a non-expansion state. Non-expansion states still require categoric eligibility for Medicaid, and Jacob is not categorically eligible for the reasons set forth above.

Answer (C) is incorrect. As a U.S. citizen living in a non-expansion state and earning less than 100% of the FPL, Jacob is not eligible for a premium tax subsidy, for the reasons discussed above.

249. **Answer (C) is correct.** Palliative sedation is the monitored use of medication to decrease awareness or even cause unconsciousness to address otherwise intractable pain. Because the intent of such sedation is pain management, it is not considered assisted suicide. It is not in-

tended to cause death. Nonetheless, palliative sedation, if continued, generally results in death within a week. Patricia Claessens et al., *Palliative Sedation: A Review of the Research Literature*, 36 J. Pain & Symptom Mgmt. 310, 326 (2008). When medically indicated and properly performed, palliative sedation is legal in all states.

Answer (A) is incorrect. In the majority of U.S. states, medical aid in dying remains illegal. Even in states that allow medical aid in dying, the procedural requirements for obtaining a prescription greatly exceed those of most other prescription medicines. Common requirements include having a terminal condition, providing written informed consent, satisfying a waiting period, and obtaining the signature of two different physicians or advance practice providers. Historically, states also commonly required residency, but recently, some states have eliminated this requirement. *See, e.g.*, Vt. Stat. Ann. tit. 18, § 5283 (2023) (effective May 2, 2023) (no longer requiring state residency).

Answer (B) is incorrect. In the majority of U.S. states, medical aid in dying remains illegal. While there is a gradual trend toward states' adopting so-called Death with Dignity Acts that allow medical aid in dying, this trend still reflects far fewer than the majority of states. In most states, medical aid in dying is not legally differentiated from assisted suicide and can be criminally prosecuted. In *Washington v. Glucksberg*, 521 U.S. 702, the U.S. Supreme Court rejected a constitutional challenge to such laws, finding no 14th Amendment substantive due process right to aid in dying. As a result, states remain free to allow or to criminalize medical aid in dying.

Answer (D) is incorrect. As discussed above, with consent, providers may prescribe the type, amount, and duration of sedation necessary to control pain, even if the use of such medication may hasten death.

250. **Answer (C) is the best answer.** Once a physician-patient relationship is formed, the physician owes the patient certain duties, including confidentiality and continuing attention. Before any invasive procedure, the physician must obtain informed consent, and in the performance of all professional tasks, the physician must apply the knowledge and skill of at least a minimally competent physician. Physicians are also sometimes said to owe a duty of loyalty to the patient.

Answer (A) is not the best answer. Formation of a physician-patient relationship triggers certain fiduciary obligations, even without discussion or agreement. Moreover, to the extent the parties seek to alter or limit these duties, courts will only enforce agreements deemed to be in accordance with public policy. So, for example, the parties may be able to contractually agree to limit the scope of services provided by a physician, but a blanket release for any malpractice liability is not generally enforceable.

Answer (B) is incorrect. A physician owes a duty to obtain informed consent when appropriate, to maintain patient confidentiality, and to avoid abandoning a patient. However, a physician does not ordinarily owe a duty to act primarily for charitable purpose. Pursuant to Section 501(c)(3) of the Internal Revenue Code, a tax-exempt hospital must operate exclusively for charitable purpose, but a physician has no such fiduciary duty under common law, and physicians in private practice typically operate on a for-profit basis.

Answer (D) is incorrect. As set forth above, formation of a physician-patient relationship results in imposition of several common law duties.

251. **Answer (C) is correct.** While individuals whom physicians have diagnosed with a terminal illness may be vulnerable to taking unjustified risk in research as a result of desperation, they do not enjoy specific additional protections under current human subject research regulations. 45 C.F.R. § 46. Federal regulations provide specific heightened protections for prisoners, minors, pregnant women, and fetuses, but there are other types of subjects who may be prone to being more vulnerable to coercion, undue influence, or unjustified risk who do not trigger specific additional safeguards. Examples include those in the military, refugees, and those facing significant economic disadvantage. Even without specific additional protections, researchers have a duty to ensure that consent is voluntary.

Answer (A) is incorrect. Regulations provide additional protection to individuals who are incarcerated due to concerns that consent obtained from prisoners may not be truly voluntary and uncoerced, given their environment. 45 C.F.R. § 46, Part C.

Answer (B) is incorrect. Regulations provide additional protection to children, neonates, and fetuses because they cannot consent for themselves. 45 C.F.R. § 46, Parts B & D. The regulations also recognize the importance of including minors in appropriate research, as manifestations of disease and pharmacokinetics of medicine in children can differ from adults.

Answer (D) is incorrect. Federal regulations provide additional hurdles to including pregnant women in research. 45 C.F.R. § 46, Part B. Since 2018, the regulations recognize that pregnant women are not in fact "more vulnerable" than other subjects to coercion or undue influence. Nonetheless, specific additional safeguards exist, largely to protect the woman's developing embryo or fetus. The regulations do caution that excluding pregnant women from appropriate research exacerbates existing disparities in knowledge and understanding.

252. **Answer (A) is the best answer.** While selling her kidney would have the highest market value, the National Organ Transplant Act of 1984 prohibits an individual from selling organs and tissues, including a kidney. Most, but not all, countries prohibit selling organs, primarily due to concern over exploitation of economically disadvantaged individuals. Some advocate for the sale of organs, but this is a minority view. Interestingly, the U.S. prohibition covers bone marrow but not eggs, even though a woman has a finite (albeit usually quite high) number of eggs, and the egg retrieval process requires surgery. Because selling one's eggs is legal and has the highest market value of the legal options, this is the best answer, although some women may oppose helping to produce a genetic offspring raised by another or undergoing the ovarian stimulation and egg retrieval process.

Answer (B) is not the best answer. It is legal to sell blood plasma in the U.S. The Food and Drug Administration limits such sales to twice within seven days, with at least one day in between, although the Red Cross will only accept plasma once every 28 days. Blood plasma is used primarily to make pharmaceuticals, and in most people, it regenerates naturally every 24 to 48 hours. Selling plasma is a legal option for Tina, but it is not likely to produce as much income as selling her eggs, although it may be preferable for other reasons.

Answer (C) is incorrect. As discussed above, it is illegal in the U.S. to sell a kidney. An individual may donate one. Arguably, the market value of a kidney would be even higher than $73,000, as the cost associated with a kidney in U.S. transplant procedures averages $262,000. The lower estimate arises from averaging the market rate of a kidney in India ($20,000), China ($40,000), and Israel ($160,000).

Answer (D) is incorrect. As discussed above, U.S. law prohibits the sale of organs and tissue. Yet it allows other body parts to be sold, arguably without entirely coherent ethical differentiation. Some low-income individuals report feeling compelled to sell their plasma to make ends meet, and the disparity in donation of plasma by socio-economic level is stark, with lower income individuals donating at substantially higher rates.

253. **Answer (A) is correct.** Informed consent does not require the disclosure of clinical practice guidelines and the recommendations therein, as such opinions are not material risks, benefits, or alternatives. The physician appears to have disclosed the material risks of a mammogram, as well as the material benefit and alternative. It is also worth noting that the doctor's recommendation is consistent with American Cancer Society guidelines, which recommend mammograms starting at age 45. It may sometimes be best practice for a physician to discuss guideline recommendations to help a patient contextualize other information, but informed consent does not require specific guideline disclosure.

It is worth noting that in 2023, the USPSTF guideline on breast cancer screening was updated to recommend biannual mammograms for women of average risk starting at age 40, although this change is not relevant to the physician's informed consent disclosure obligation in 2022.

Answer (B) is incorrect. If the USPSTF guideline were a required disclosure (it is not), then Anna may be able to show that omitting the disclosure led her to incur unnecessary medical expense and to experience unnecessary anxiety.

Answer (C) is incorrect. While many patients might consider the USPSTF recommendation material to their decision-making, courts have generally been reluctant to force disclosure of recommendations, positions, or legal status (in the context of off-label prescribing) as part of informed consent. Guidelines are not required disclosures.

Answer (D) is incorrect. As discussed above, guidelines are not generally considered required informed consent disclosures. So it will not matter whether Anna lives in one of the minority of states that accepts subjective causation.

254. **Answer (D) is correct.** Most states have a general expert testimony rule similar to Rule 702 of the Federal Rules of Civil Procedure, allowing an expert to be qualified based on knowledge, skill, training, or education. Two-thirds of states further limit permissible experts in medi-

cal malpractice cases, however, by specifying minimum qualifications like licensure or recent practice. Despite such requirements, most states will not disqualify an otherwise qualified medical malpractice expert based on alleged bias. Instead, bias is typically considered a matter for cross-examination and goes to the weight to accord the expert's testimony. Answer (D) is the only answer that reflects disqualification for perceived bias rather than for the expert's knowledge, skill, training, education, or a proxy therefore. It should be noted, however, that some states will exclude an expert who is paid on a contingency fee, and paying an expert based on the outcome of the case violates the ABA Model Rules of Professional Conduct.

Answer (A) is incorrect. When the physician being sued is a board-certified specialist, some but not all states require that any medical malpractice expert also hold that specialty.

Answer (B) is incorrect. Some but not all states require any medical malpractice expert to hold the same licensure as the defending physician. So, for example, only a physician may testify against another physician regarding the standard of care and any breach thereof, even if an advance practice nurse, podiatrist, or other individual arguably has sufficient expertise based on knowledge, skill, or training.

Answer (C) is incorrect. Some but not all states require active or recent practice in the same subject matter area as the alleged malpractice in order to testify regarding the standard of care or its breach in a medical malpractice case.

255. **Answer (D) is the best answer.** In *Alabama Association of Realtors v. Department of Health and Human Services*, 141 S. Ct. 2485 (2021), the Supreme Court vacated a stay of the district court's injunction prohibiting enforcement of the CDC's second nationwide eviction moratorium. The Court reasoned that an eviction moratorium exceeds the CDC's authority pursuant to Section 361 of the Public Health Services Act. 42 U.S.C. § 264(a); 42 C.F.R. § 70.2 (2020). While the Court found that the CDC lacked authority to issue the eviction moratorium, it recognized that Congress could enact a nationwide moratorium with proper legislation or clearly authorize the CDC to do so. Previously, in March 2020, Congress had enacted a 120-day eviction moratorium on properties participating in federal assistance programs or secured by federally backed mortgages, as part of the Coronavirus Aid, Relief, and Economic Security Act (CARES Act) § 4024. The CDC issued its second moratorium after Congress declined to renew or extend its moratorium.

Answer (A) is incorrect. Despite broad language in the Public Health Service Act granting authority "to make and enforce such regulations as in [its] judgment [is] necessary to prevent the introduction, transmission, or spread of communicable disease," the Court construed Congress's grant of authority to the CDC narrowly. Specifically, the Court determined that the second sentence of the Act should be read to limit the CDC's authority to regulations that *directly* combat the spread of the disease itself, such as inspection, fumigation, and sanitation measures. With this construction, the Court held that the CDC exceeded its authority by issuing the eviction moratorium. The Court reasoned that landlord-tenant relationships are a particular domain of state law and too indirectly related to preventing the spread of communicable disease.

Answer (B) is not the best answer. The Fifth Amendment Takings Clause prohibits the government from taking private property for public use without just compensation. Some have argued that an eviction moratorium without just compensation constitutes a taking if the property owner otherwise would have had the right to remove the tenant. In discussing the balance of the equities in *Alabama Association of Realtors*, the Supreme Court described the eviction moratorium as an intrusion on the right to exclude, suggesting that the Court may agree. However, given the posture of the review, the Court did not expressly find a violation of the Takings Clause. Moreover, the traditional remedy for a taking would be monetary relief, not an injunction.

Answer (C) is incorrect. The Court did state that the landlord-tenant relationship is a particular domain of the state, but it also recognized that Congress has authority to enact an eviction moratorium with proper legislation, justification, and limits.

256. **Answer (B) is correct.** In *Buck v. Bell*, 274 U.S. 200, 207 (1927), Justice Holmes infamously concluded that "[t]hree generations of imbeciles are enough," in rejecting a 14th Amendment due process challenge to a state law allowing compulsory sterilization of the "unfit," including those deemed to have an intellectual disability. *Buck v. Bell* has been widely criticized for its eugenic approach, factual inaccuracy, and misconception of heritable traits, but it has not been expressly overruled.

Answer (A) is incorrect. In *Skinner v. Oklahoma ex rel. Williamson*, 316 U.S. 535, the Court struck down a state law providing for the penal sterilization of certain "habitual" criminals on 14th Amendment equal protection grounds. *Skinner* described procreation as a fundamental right, but it distinguished rather than overruled *Buck v. Bell.*

Answer (C) is incorrect. In *Stump v. Sparkman*, 435 U.S. 349 (1978), the Court considered available legal remedies for the wrongful sterilization of a minor pursuant to a court order obtained by the minor's parents. The Court held that the parents were not state actors and judicial immunity shields the judge who issued the order from potential liability for actions taken in his official capacity. Aside from the judge who enjoyed immunity, there was no state action found in *Stump*.

Answer (D) is incorrect. *Burwell v. Hobby Lobby Stores, Inc.*, 573 U.S. 682, involved a free exercise challenge to the contraceptive mandate contained in the ACA.

Table of Cases

G

H

I

J

K

L

M

N

O

P

Index